IMAGES
of America

THE LITTLE BIGHORN

TIOSPAYE

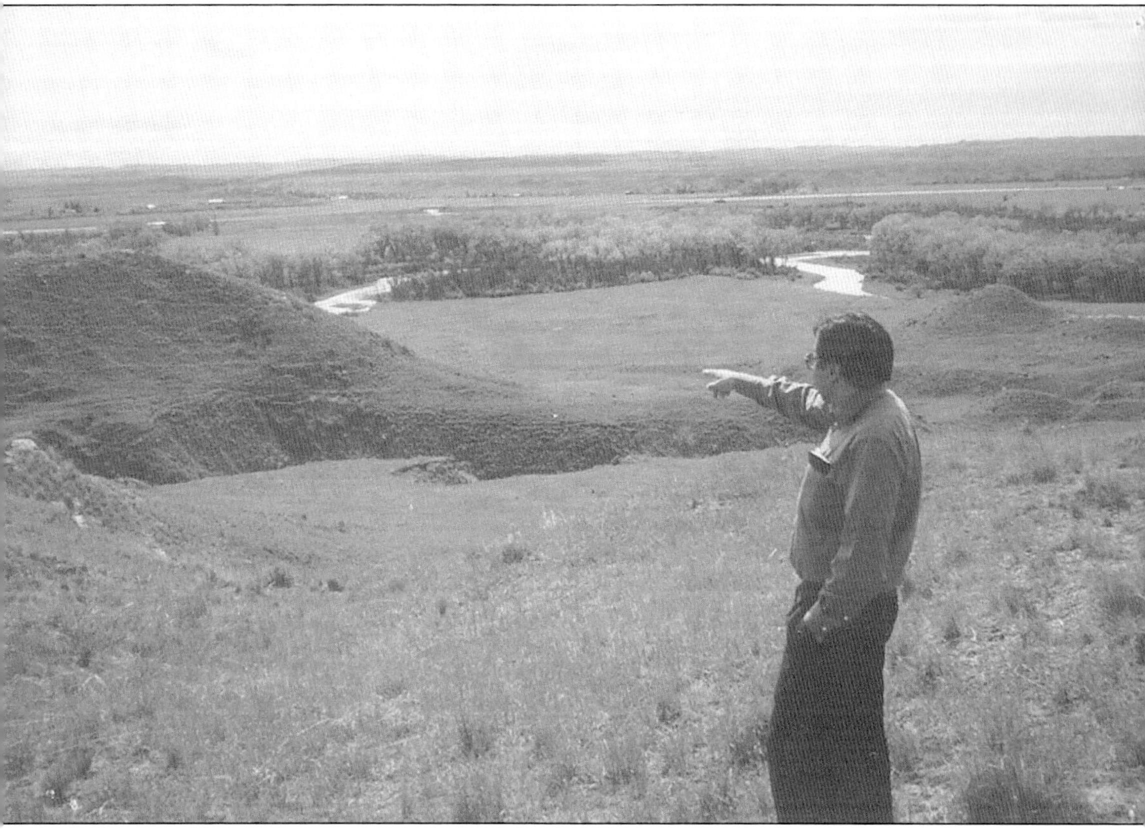

Author Kenneth D. Shields Jr., indicates the location of *Tiospaye,* the Golden Encampment, which made history during the month of June in 1876. Mr. Shields is a Dakota Sioux from the Bad Temper Bear Band. (Photograph from the author's private collection.)

Following their victory at the Battle of the Little Bighorn, Indian bands left in different directions. Elders told children not to mention their participation for fear of retribution. Therefore, the names of those who celebrated during the days of Tiospaye went "underground." The author and the Tiospaye Foundation are attempting to recover their names and place them on a virtual memorial on the Internet. For more Arcadia books by Mr. Shields, and information about the Tiospaye Foundation, visit www.Tribe-Net.com.

IMAGES
of America

The Little Bighorn *Tiospaye*

Kenneth Shields Jr.

ARCADIA
PUBLISHING

ISBN 978-0-7385-0828-3

Published by Arcadia Publishing
Charleston, South Carolina

Printed in the United States of America

Library of Congress Catalog Card Number: 00108398

For all general information contact Arcadia Publishing at:
Telephone 843-853-2070
Fax 843-853-0044
E-mail sales@arcadiapublishing.com
For customer service and orders:
Toll-Free 1-888-313-2665

Visit us on the Internet at www.arcadiapublishing.com

Contents

ACKNOWLEDGEMENTS

To my wife Judy and our children for their love and support. Togetherness is forever.

For this work we gratefully acknowledge the following people for their cooperation and contribution of knowledge, support, historic resource material, and cultural enrichment: Neil Mangum, Little Bighorn National Battlefield superintendent, Ms. Kitty Deernose, Museum Curator, and Mr. Ken Woody; to Ms. Desi Lambert for her understanding and patience and providing me the time and opportunity to travel to Little Bighorn; to Elder Hugh W. Pinnock in Salt Lake for his great and eternal friendship; to Mrs. Lenora Red Elk for her prayers of faith and inspiration; to Mr. Ernie Bighorn for his understanding and prompting me to success; to Mr. Billy Mills, Olympic champion for telling me to "Follow Your Dreams;" to Mr. Earl Bullhead for his cultural expertise; to Mr. Tom Christian for his examples to young people; to Margaret Campbell for her confidence and belief in me; to Gilbert "Ed" Broadus for sharing photos and historic accounts; to Floyd Waters, Gilbert Little Wolf, Douglas, Josephine, Ronnie, Rhoda, and "Bucky" Glenmore at Northern Cheyenne for helping me through my school years and being my family away from home; to Nick Selage and their family for their hospitality when I pull in hungry and want something to eat; to Marilyn Breeze in New York for her thoughtfulness and friendship; to Bonnie Red Elk for the opportunity to enhance my writing skills in the Wotanin Wowapi; to Robert McAnnally for his work in education; to Robert Fourstar for his work in culture and language; to Cousin Dolly and Wayne Boyd and their children for their kindness and love for me; to Jerry, Jean, Mike, Clete, and Mark Leinen for affording me transportation to Little Bighorn; to my friends forever in the Youth Council and their supporters; LeAndra Follet, Faye Hotomanie, Robin Perry, Pauline Smoker, Michael Red Stone, Jonathan Cantrell, Mabel Clark, Terra Pronto, Billy McDonald, Tim Red Eagle, Noble Drags Wolf; Carrie Christian, Mary Bighorn (for taking me bungee jumping), Pearl McDonald, Michelle Cantrell, Timothea Red Eagle, Ashley Moran, June Daniels, Dayton Rush, and Andrea Sansaver; to my co-workers Debbie Boyd, Theresa Knoble, Joyce Martell, Shannon Loans Arrow, Nelson Crowe, Maynard Black Dog, Wayne Martell, George Ricker and all the others too numerous to name; to my friends "Down Under" in New Zealand, Boyd and Karen Turner; to my good friend James Snell for his showing me the historic areas of Fort Peck; to Shep Ferguson for sharing events that happened long ago; to Steve Grey Hawk for his contributions of example; to our good friends in Sedona, Arizona: Carol Hay-Greene and Joann Garay; to Georgene Scott and family in Cleveland for the warm hospitality afforded us on our visit; to our friend in Oldenburg, Germany, Manfred Kappesser; to very special powwow Koda's Larry Youngman, Willard and Walter Loves Him, James Boyd, Cody Eagleman, Mike Kashube, Harry Three Stars, Jerome First, Charles Eagleman, Robert "Boy" Murray, James Grambois; Don Laroque, Little Crow, Jerry Alfrey, Patrick Baker, Otis Runs Through, Harold "Buddy" Adams, Troy and Jerry Shepard, Viola Spotted Bird Drum,

Shoots The Arrow, and a very special salute to my home at Fort Peck Tribes! All these people are going to make great change! Remember—Don't Let the Light Go Out!

My sincere appreciation is given to Ms. Lori Swingle, Western History Department of the Denver Public Library, for her prompt and excellent service, and to Sharon A. Silengo of the State Historical Society of North Dakota for helping me obtain a photograph of my great-great-grandfather Feather Earring.

My thanks go to Keith Ulrich, Midwest Editor of Arcadia Publishing, for his encouragement and patience during the *Little Bighorn* project. He shared in the understanding of the importance of this work.

I would like to thank Scott L. Zanger for his review and word processing assistance. His editing comments helped make writing the book an enjoyable experience. Thanks too, to Evan Stampoulos for his contribution to this work. I am grateful to Jay M. Arancio of Media Works. His assistance during the scanning of the photographs was outstanding. Very special thanks go to Mr. Peter Yarrow for his permission to use the lyrics from his song "Light One Candle," the words of which serve as an inspiration to us all.

DEDICATION

FROM LINDA STAMPOULOS AND KENNY SHIELDS JR.

In thanksgiving for our loving guardian angels in the spirit world for inspiring us to lay the foundation for this work we inscribe: Margaret and Edward Aschoff, Patrick and Stella Necklace, Lucy Emma Feather Earring Shields Elk, Charles Shields, Reuben and Cora Feather Earring, Thomas and Lucy Firemoon, James Turning Bear, Gerald Red Elk, and Robert Dumont. These wonderful people were matriarchs and patriarchs for posterity that shared historical accounts in witnessing and revealing the fabric of a beautiful people. Impressive in spirit and rich with knowledge, they were ancient in wisdom. From what we learn, we need sound discovery and exploration to unfold these mysteries. For an understanding of even a portion of these people and their lives, the following photographic composition is presented here for you and dedicated to them. And for the children of our day: these people believed in good things for all people- but the greater things were reserved for the future—posterity.

Let us put our minds together to see what we can do for our children.

Tatanka Iyotanka
Sitting Bull, Dakota-Hunkpapa Holyman

INTRODUCTION

In June of 1876, a few days before America would mark its centennial celebration, a gathering of Indian people made history in a rich valley on the Little Bighorn River. Their legacy consists not of a victory in battle, but in the events that happened in the weeks prior to the arrival of Custer and his troops.

It was spring, a time to celebrate new life and freedom, to follow the buffalo and other game. Men, women, and children came to thank the Creator, *Wakan Tanka*, for safely bringing them through the harsh winter. They camped in the place where from ages past, they called the "Greasy Grass," a place of solitude and worship. There were a few lodges at first, but over a period of weeks, the gathering—often referred to as Tiospaye, or the Golden Encampment—would grow to become the largest in recorded American history. Eyewitnesses reported there being over 1,000 lodges, with up to 7,000 people, almost 1,500 of them warriors. Among the many tribes represented were the Dakota, Yanktonais, Cheyenne, Arapaho, and of the Lakota Sioux: the Oglala, Hunkpapa, Miniconjous, Sans Arc, Brule, Two Kettle, Blackfeet, and Santee Sioux.

Tatanka Iyotanka, Sitting Bull of the Hunkpapa, served as the people's spiritual leader. Earlier that month, he had ordered a Sun Dance to be held in the nearby hills. The Sun Dance would purify the people and give them endurance. It was here that he had his vision of dead soldiers and horses falling into the Indian camp. Sitting Bull was a warrior and a visionary. He dedicated his life to preserve the beautiful culture of his people.

There was a powerful majesty surrounding the people in attendance, strong leaders who protected the tribes: Crazy Horse, Gall, American Horse, He Dog, and their camps were joined as one statement of Freedom. Black Elk, an Oglala holy man, was 13 years old at that time, and has offered accounts of the gathering. Four years earlier, Black Elk had camped here with his family and also experienced a vision—one that he would spend his life trying to fulfill.

During the day, the elders would sit in Counsel, women would dig turnips and prepare meals, the children swam in the river and rode their ponies. After dark, the drums would echo the heartbeat of the dancers and tales would be of told victories and the old ways. The evening fires of Tiopsaye would burn late into the night. The full moon made it seem like daylight and the dancing could go on forever. Never before was there such a feeling of confidence and freedom. From Sitting Bull's vision, they knew they were invincible.

This book is an attempt to convey the wonder and the power of Tiospaye. The author's great-great-grandfather, Feather Earring, was there and has handed down in the oral tradition many stories of the event. Although there were no photographs taken during Tiospaye, the author has collected images representing these stories and the people who shared this moment in time. Actual photos of those who were in attendance are also included among these pages.

It is the author's prayer that the songs of independence and courage of those who rejoiced at the fires of Tiospaye will still be sung 125 years later by our people today. The flames can still burn as an inner Freedom and a cry: "Don't let the Light go out, let it shine through our love and our tears."

One

IN THE MOON WHEN THE PONIES SHED

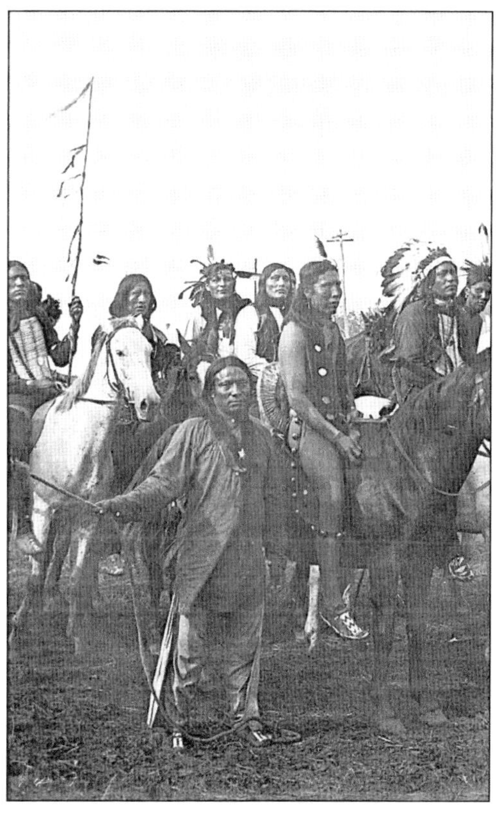

It has been said that if one is to truly appreciate a sunset, you must view it from the corners of your eye; to look straight on would be harmful. Over the generations, the events of Little Bighorn came to be viewed in just a skewed manner. The actual details surrounding the event remain a mystery. Objectivity is not always easy. Myth, bias, and the very passage to time all serve to erode what is fact. The Indian people were striving to preserve a way of life. This story is about them.

After a long, harsh winter, as was their custom, families of the various bands followed the buffalo herds. It was in 1876, in the Moon When the Ponies Shed (May) that they camped in Powder River Country, territories of Wyoming and Montana.

They traveled to this sacred area to come together and celebrate a thanksgiving to the Creator, Wakan Tanka, for all his gifts. In this photograph, a group of Sioux men are mounted on horseback. Their faces shine with excitement and anticipation as if they know they are about to become part of history. (Photograph courtesy of the Denver Public Library.)

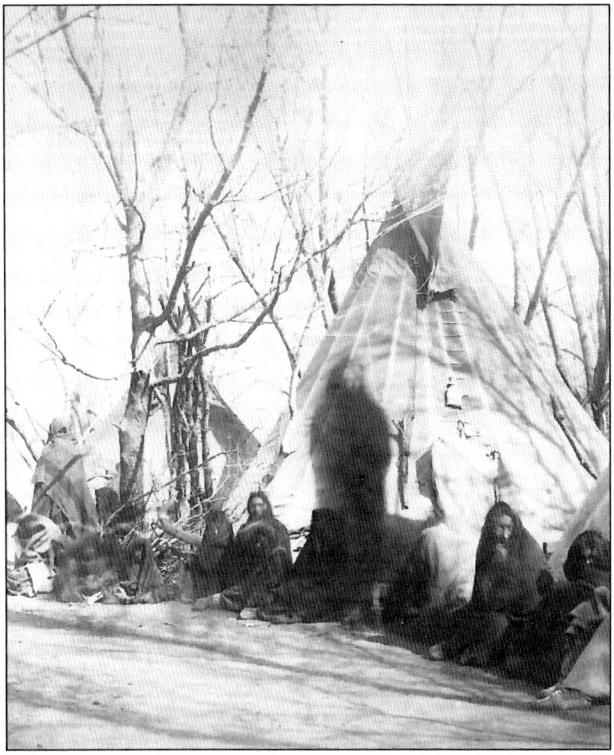

Hunting bands followed the game throughout the year. Here a group of men gather near their lodges as they prepare to leave a winter camp. (Photograph courtesy of the Denver Public Library.)

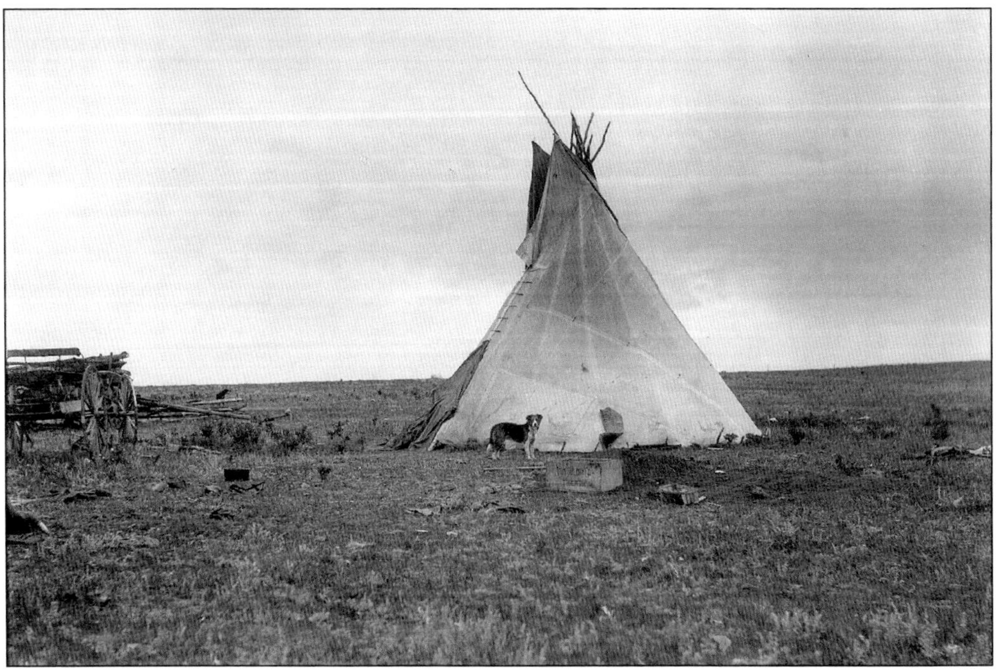

Living in freedom, following the buffalo herds, the life of the Indian people was close to nature. They believed that everything had a life spirit: the rocks, the water, the plants, the clouds, and the animals. Most of all they respected the two-legged kind, man. (Photograph courtesy of Fort Peck Tribal Archives.)

Sitting Bull was a warrior and a holy man. He was sincerely dedicated to his people, determined to remain free and preserve their way of life. Here is a photograph of his camp, with six lodges visible. (Photograph courtesy of the Denver Public Library.)

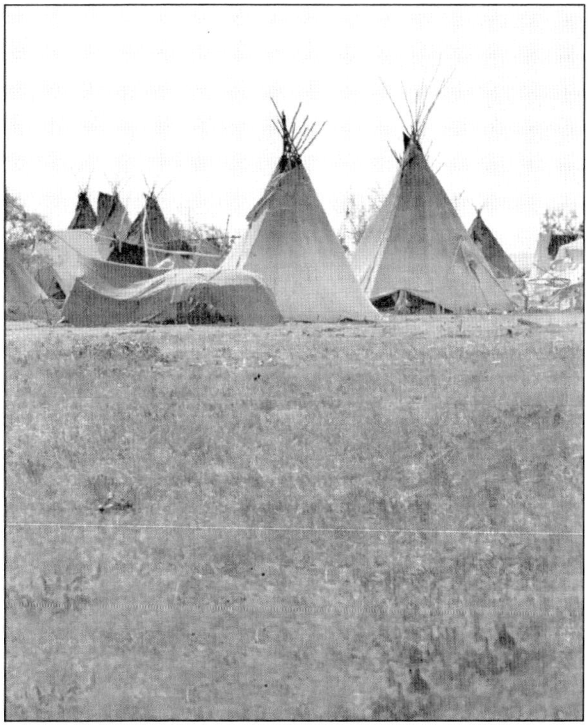

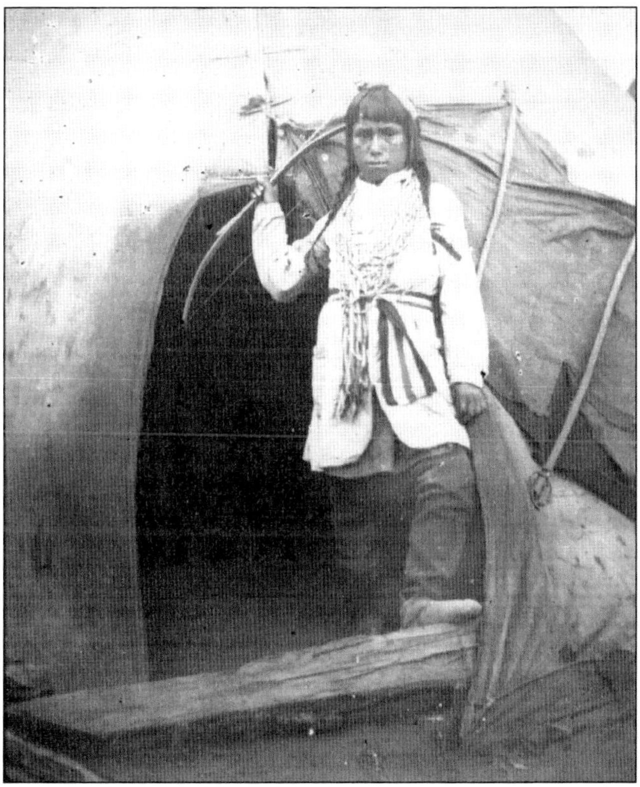

A Dakota boy stands in the opening of a tipi holding a bow and arrows. He wears a knee-length jacket with a striped sash belt, necklaces, leggings, and moccasins. (Photograph courtesy of the Denver Public Library.)

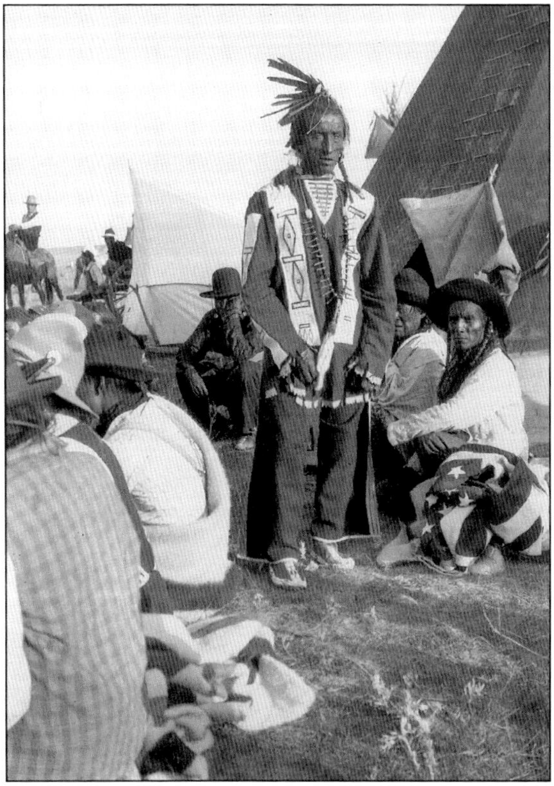

The beauty and majesty of the dancer's beaded clothing added to the beauty of this place. (Photograph courtesy of Fort Peck Tribal Archives.)

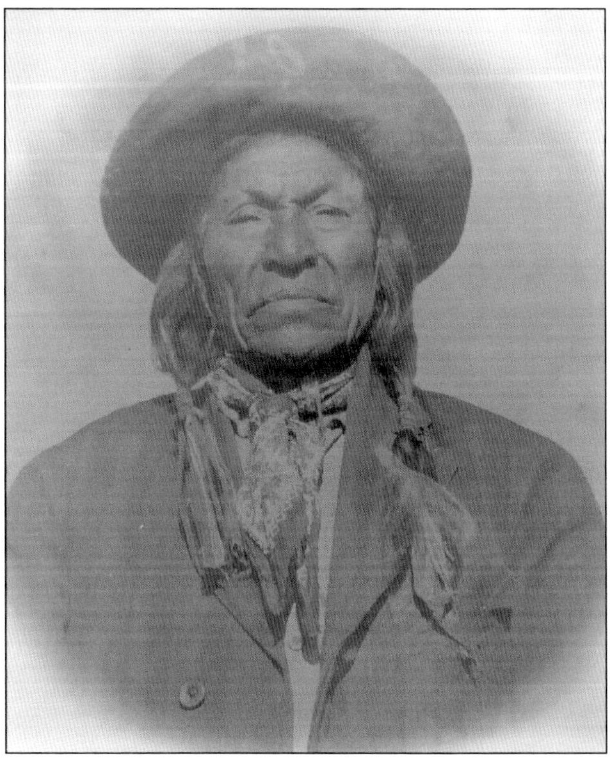

Chief Redstone is pictured in this rare photograph. His character and integrity are etched in the lines of his face. (Photograph courtesy of Fort Peck Tribal Archives.)

Red Cloud was a strong Oglala leader during this time. He did not travel with the tribes to the Little Bighorn, yet remained an important part of history. (Photograph courtesy of Fort Peck Tribal Archives.)

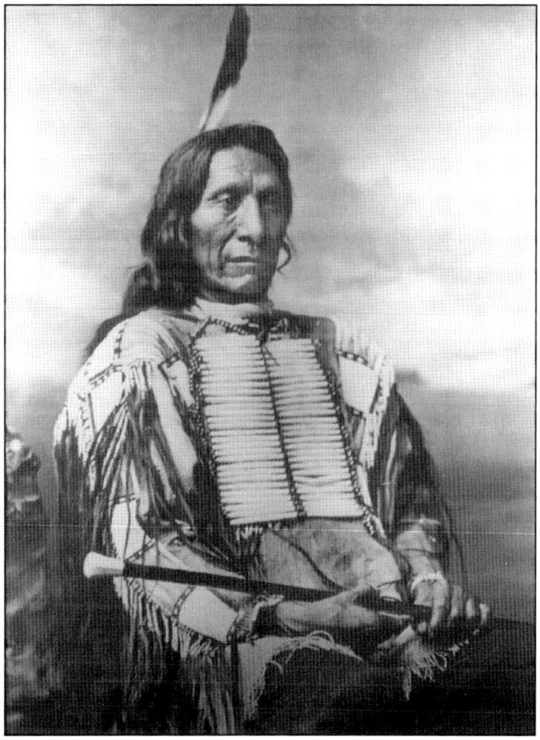

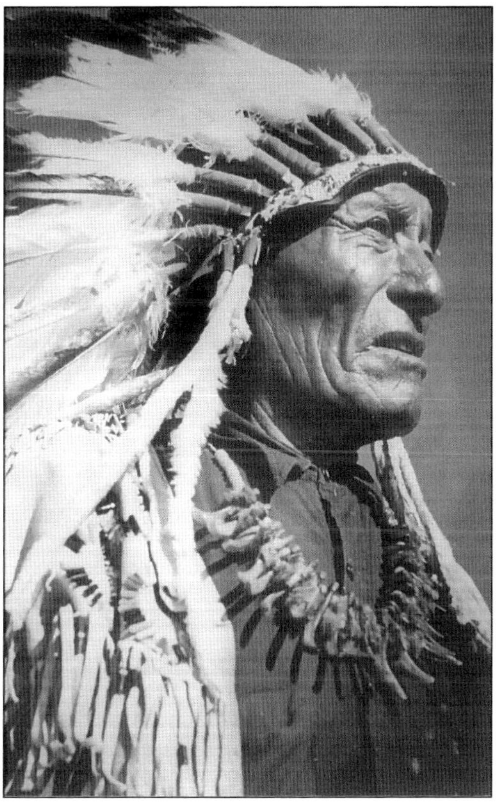

The legends told around the campfires were the passing of history from one generation to the next. This noble chief would inspire children with his stories of war and the hunt. (Photograph courtesy of the National Park Service, Little Bighorn Battlefield National Monument.)

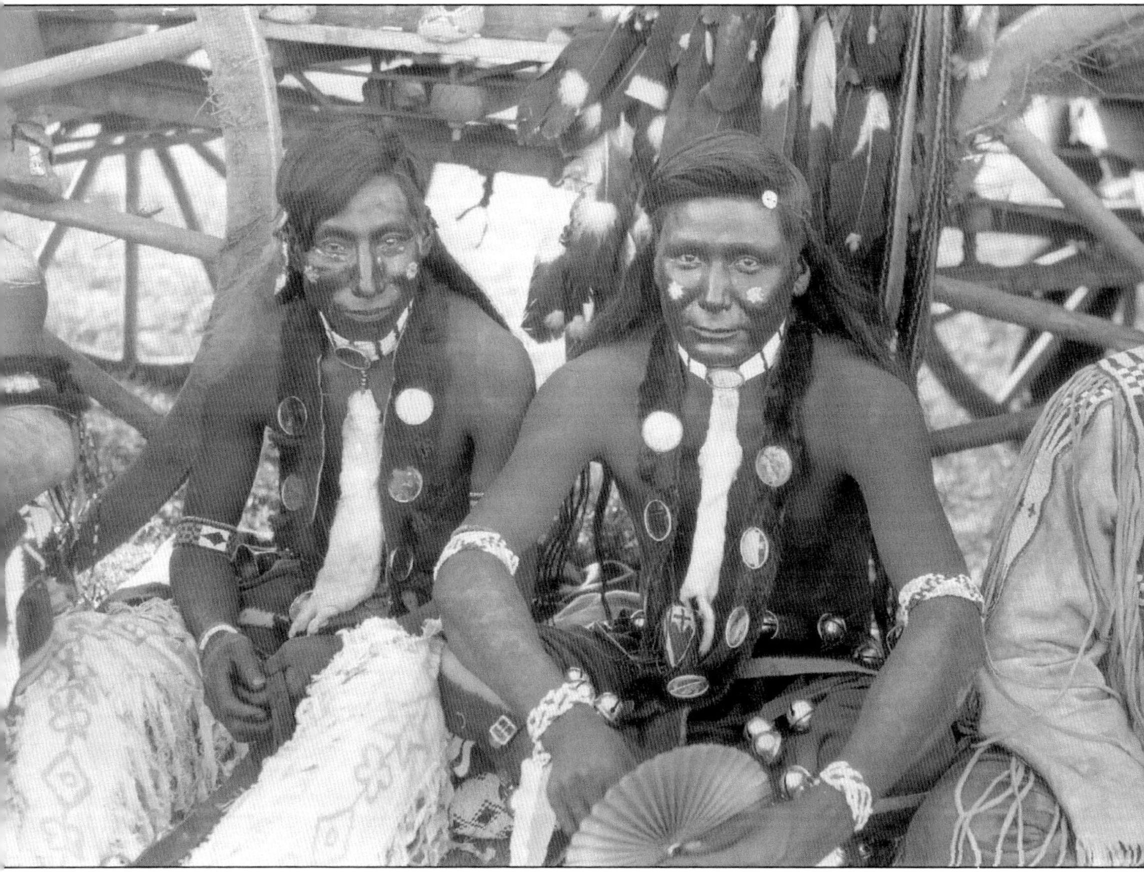

As their faces reveal, the Indian people celebrated the gifts from the Great Creator. He blessed them with a successful hunt and loving families. (Photograph courtesy of Fort Peck Tribal Archives.)

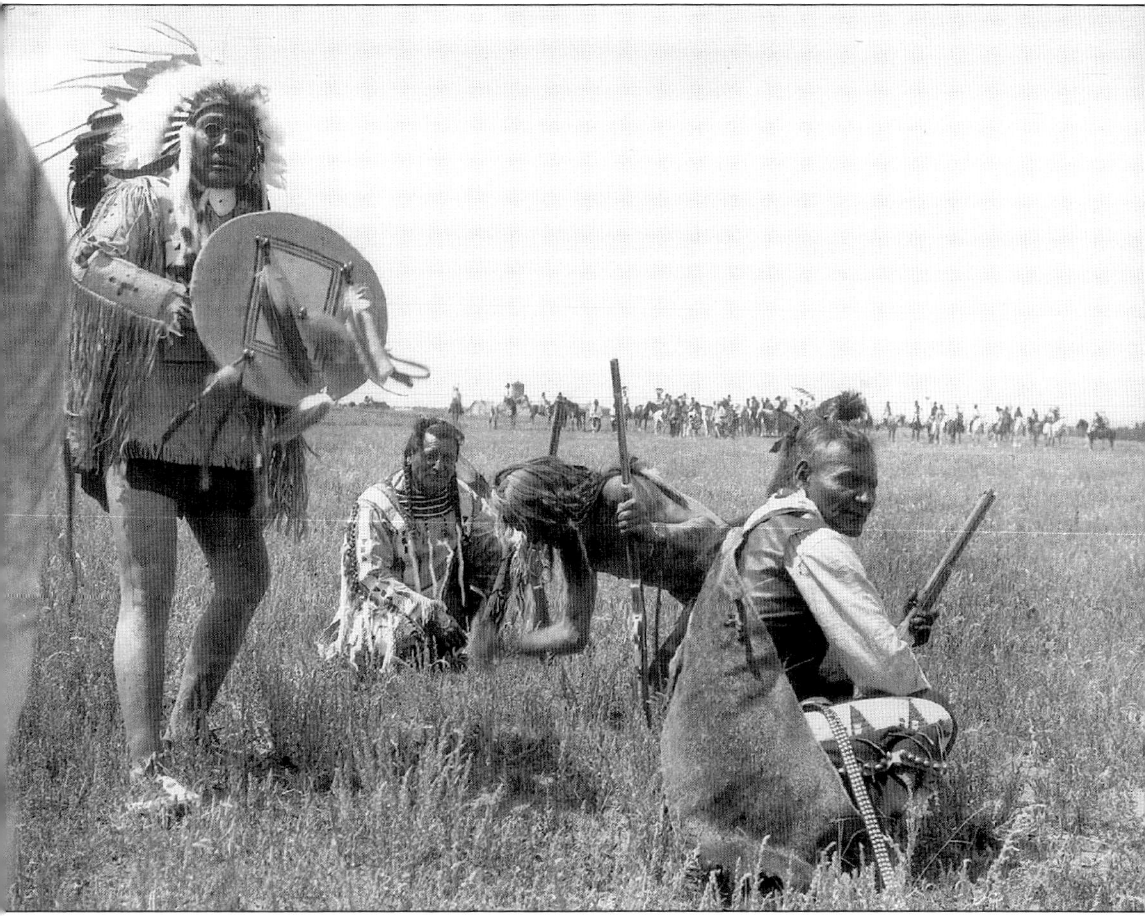

Hunting bands such as the one in this photograph were responsible to provide the tribe with food. The stronger men had the responsibility to feed and care for the elderly and the widowed. (Photograph courtesy of Fort Peck Tribal Archives.)

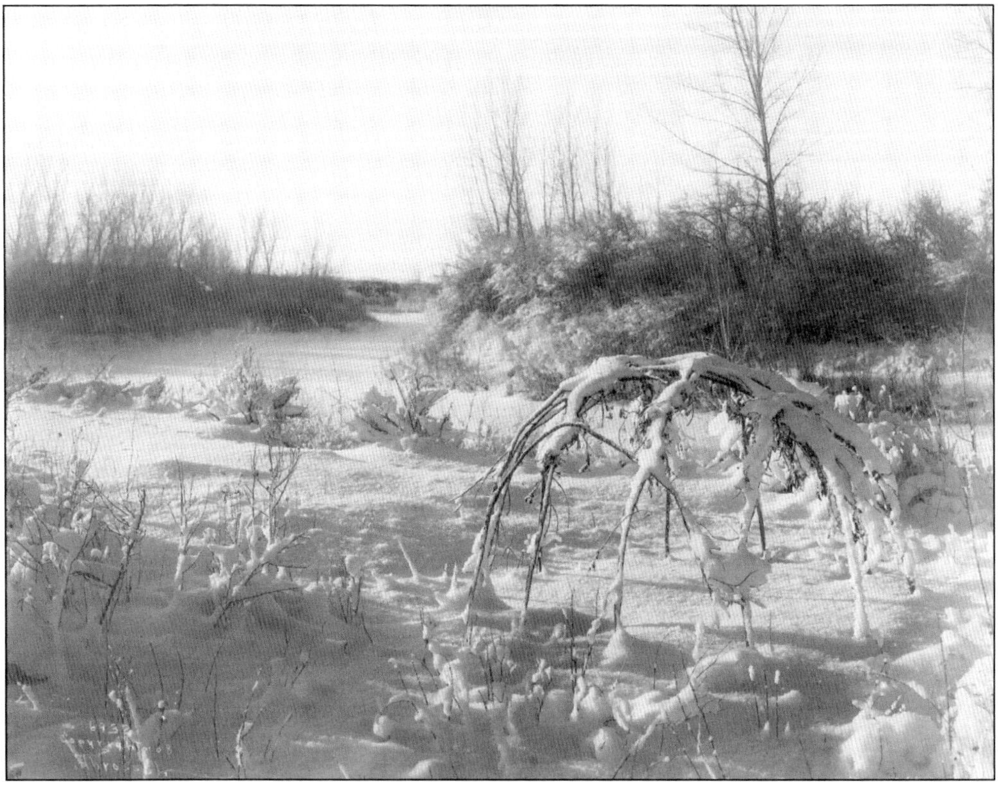

The wooden frame of a dome shaped lodge stands abandoned in snow on the bank of an iced-over river. (Photograph courtesy of the Denver Public Library.)

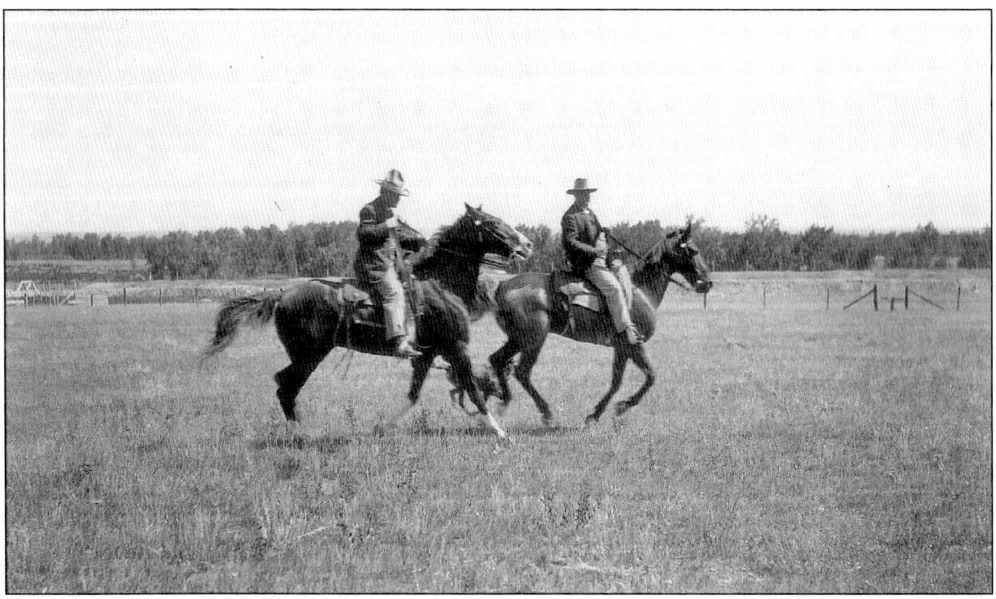

For generations, Indian ponies were trained as skillful partners in the buffalo hunt. A good pony could mean the difference between a feast and going hungry. (Photograph courtesy of Fort Peck Tribal Archives.)

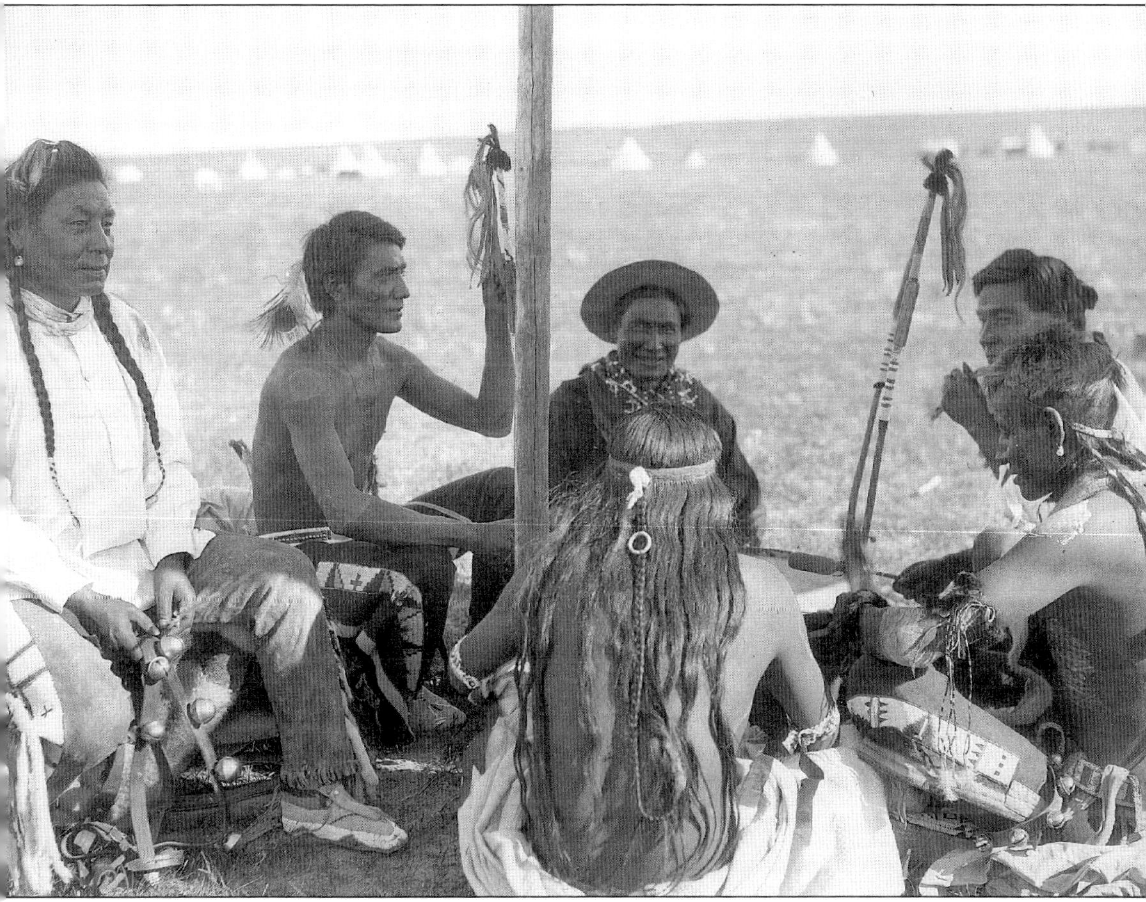

Braves sat in council to discuss the events of the day, as well as the needs of the tribe. There was a strong social structure in place, one that needed complete cooperation to survive in these extreme times. (Photograph courtesy of Fort Peck Tribal Archives.)

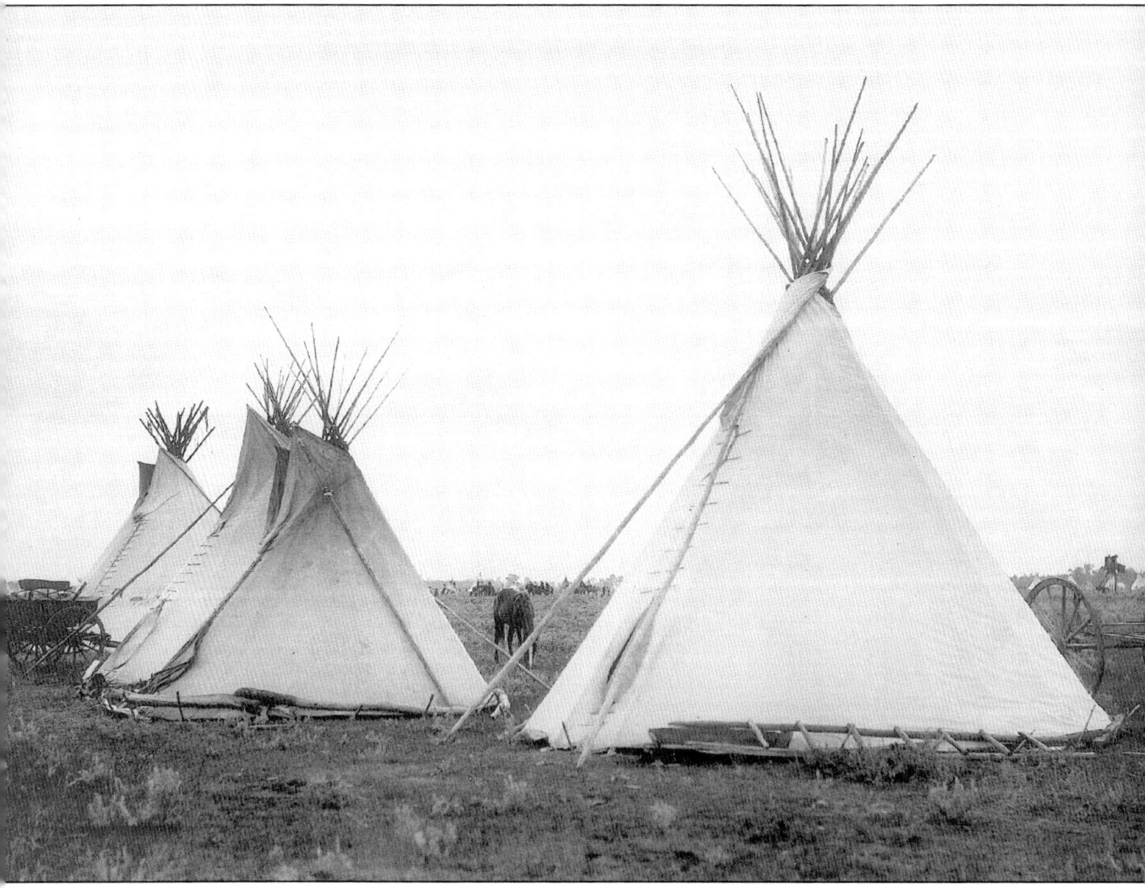

The lifestyle of a tribe included moving from place to place, following migrating animals and the buffalo. This required housing structures that were easily and quickly taken down and put up again. (Photograph courtesy of Fort Peck Tribal Archives.)

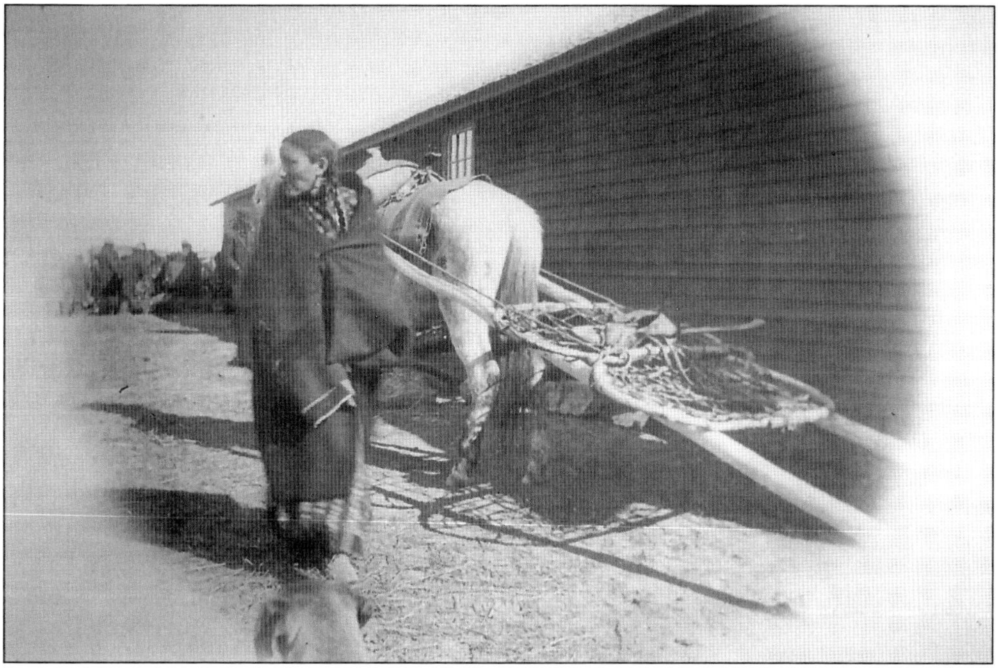

Moving the encampment was the responsibility of the women. They would use a carrier, or travois, that would hold the long lodge poles and heavy hides. (Photograph courtesy of the National Park Service, Little Bighorn Battlefield National Monument.)

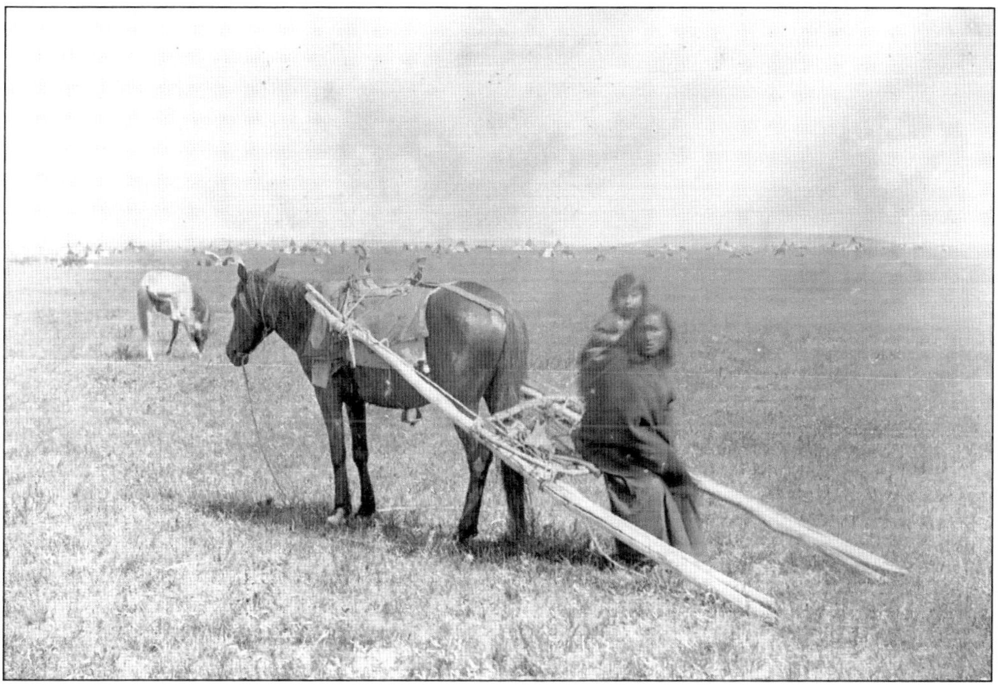

A woman and child lean on a travois attached to a horse. Lodges are shown in the background. Indian women designed the tipis and crafted them from buffalo hides. (Photograph courtesy of the Denver Public Library.)

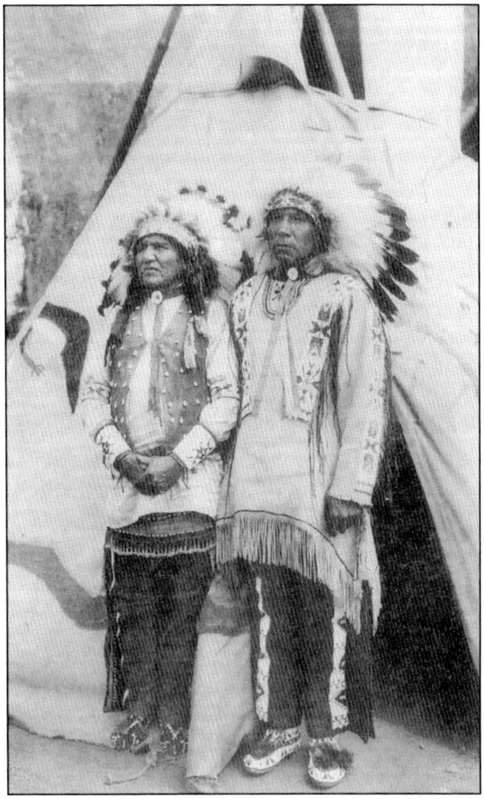

Dakota men stand outside a tipi. They wear feather headdresses, buckskin shirts and cotton shirts, leggings, and moccasins. (Photograph courtesy of the Denver Public Library.)

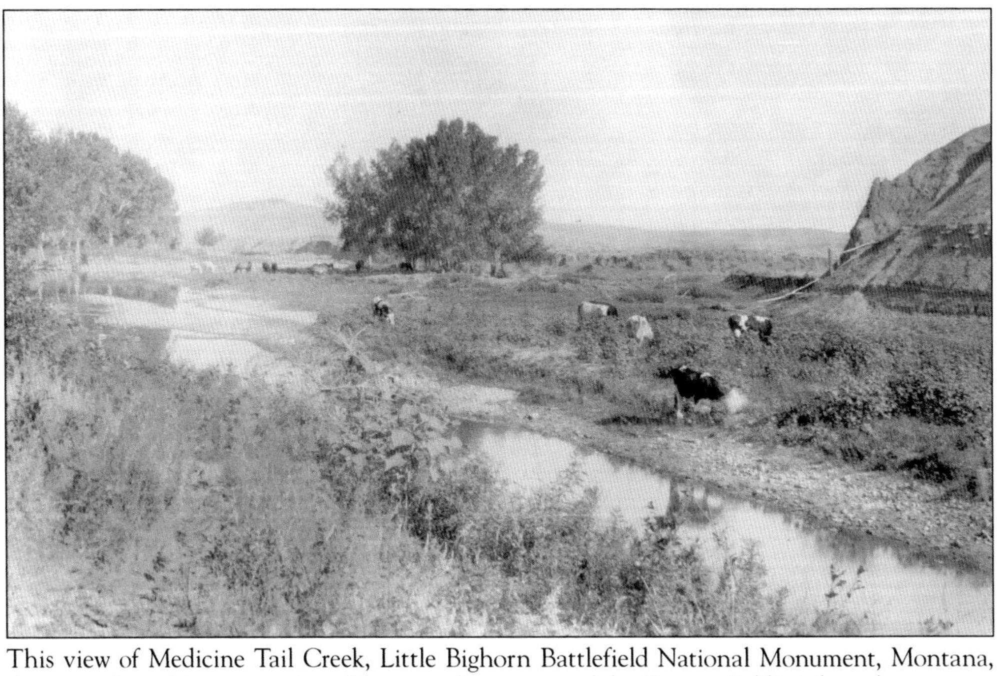

This view of Medicine Tail Creek, Little Bighorn Battlefield National Monument, Montana, shows cattle and horses grazing. (Photograph courtesy of the Denver Public Library.)

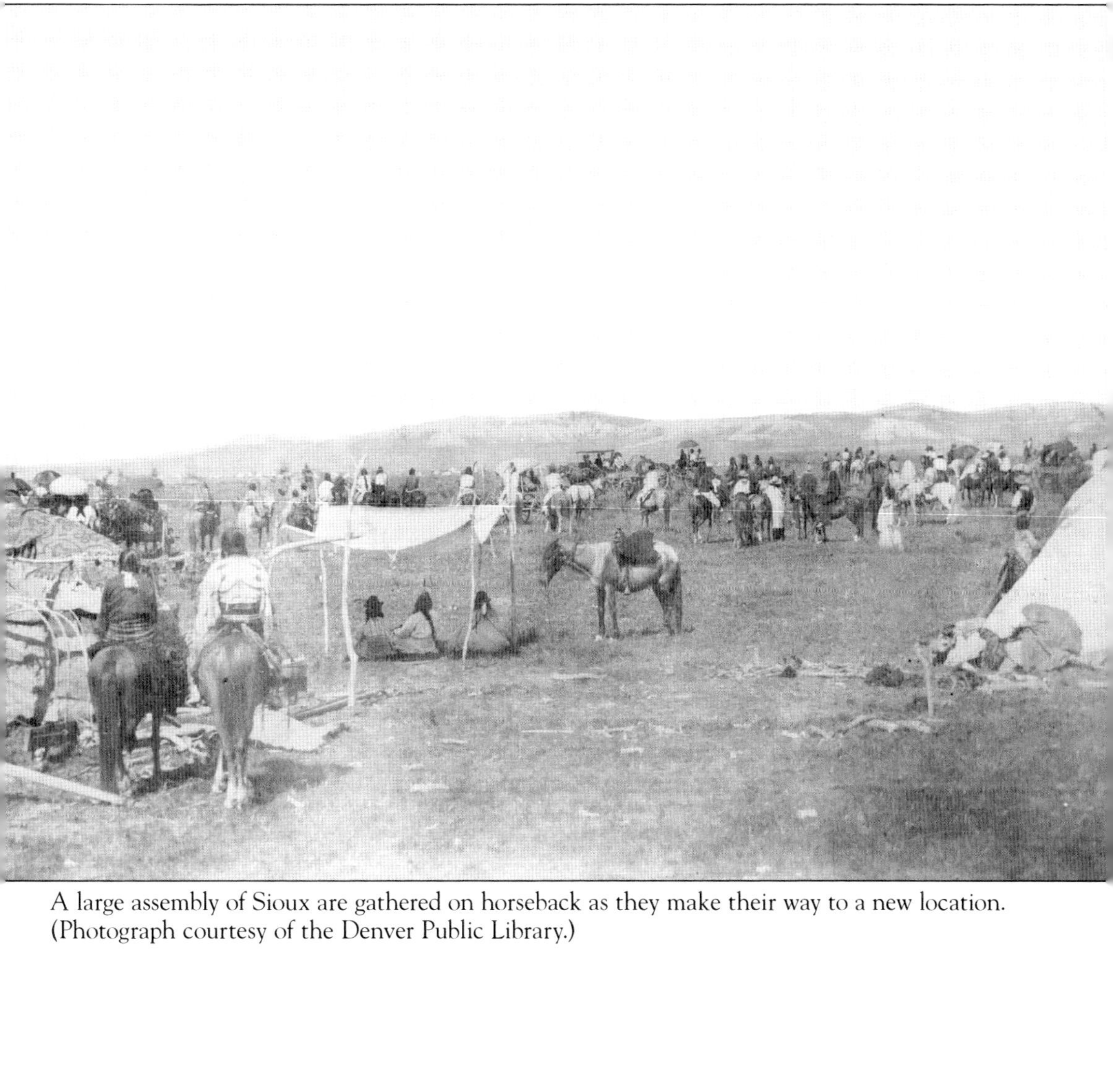

A large assembly of Sioux are gathered on horseback as they make their way to a new location. (Photograph courtesy of the Denver Public Library.)

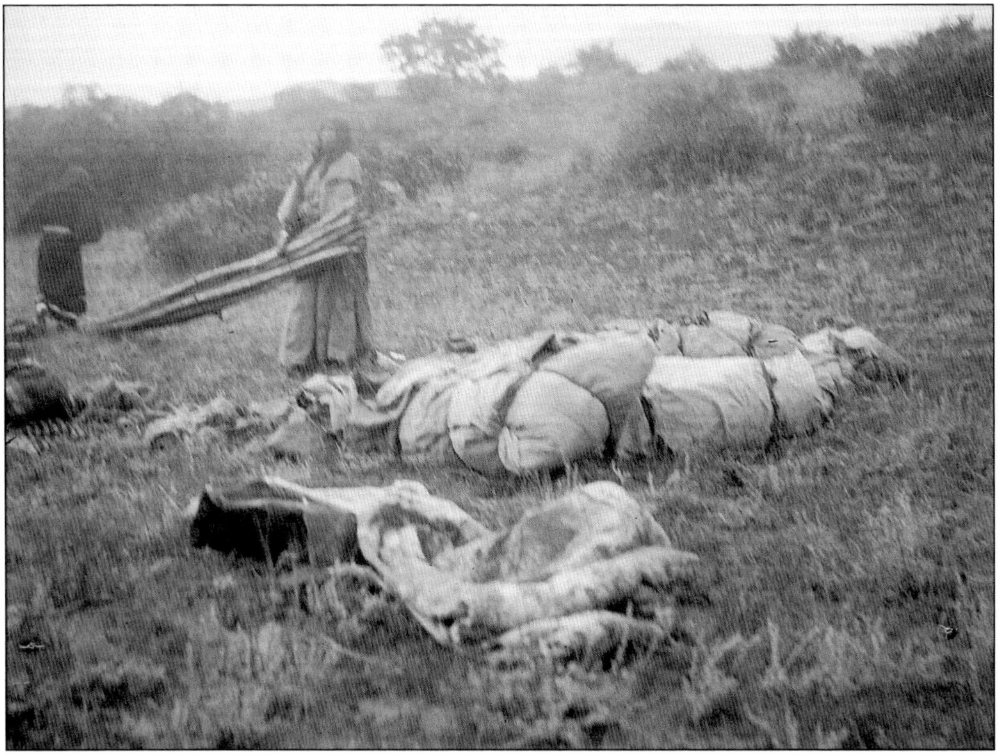

Trees and bushes dot the grassy landscape where women drag wooden lodge poles toward a pile of rolled canvas. (Photograph courtesy of the Denver Public Library.)

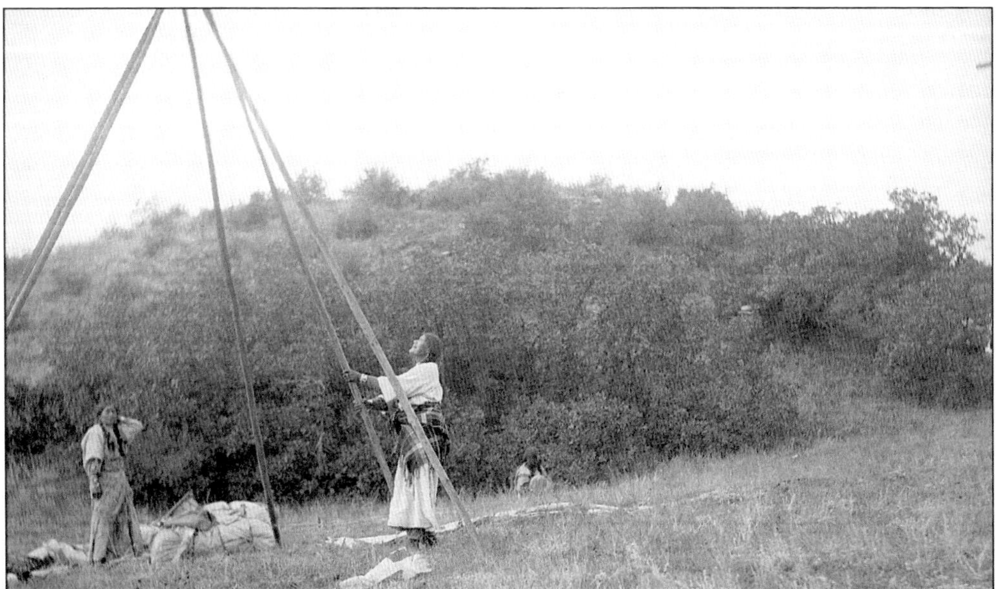

In this photograph, Indian women construct a tipi. One woman pulls an erect wooden pole away from the center of the tipi frame. Another woman stands near the rolled tipi canvas and looks on. (Photograph courtesy of the Denver Public Library.)

A woman sits near the entrance to her lodge. She wears a dress and a belt. (Photograph courtesy of the Denver Public Library.)

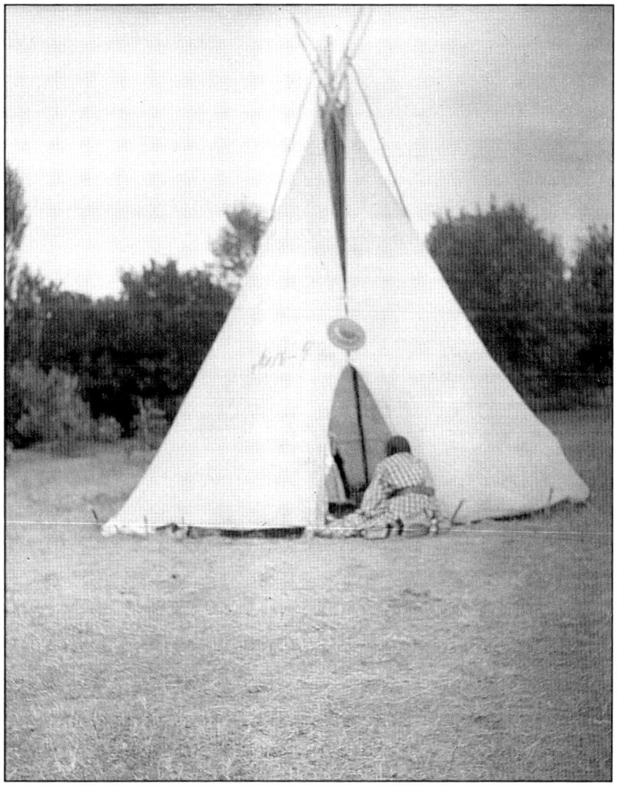

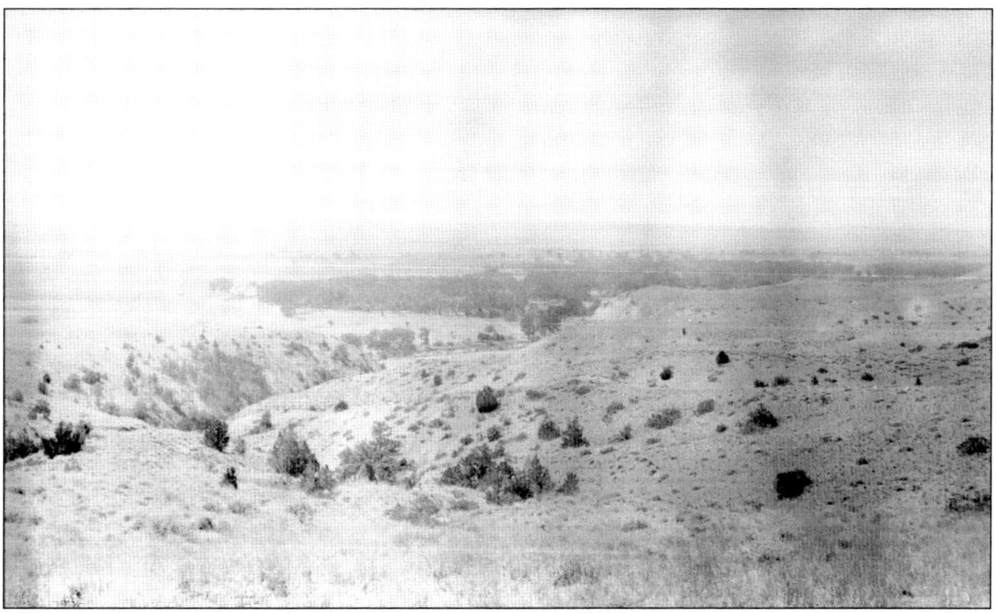

Another view of Little Bighorn Battlefield National Monument, Montana. (Photograph courtesy of the Denver Public Library.)

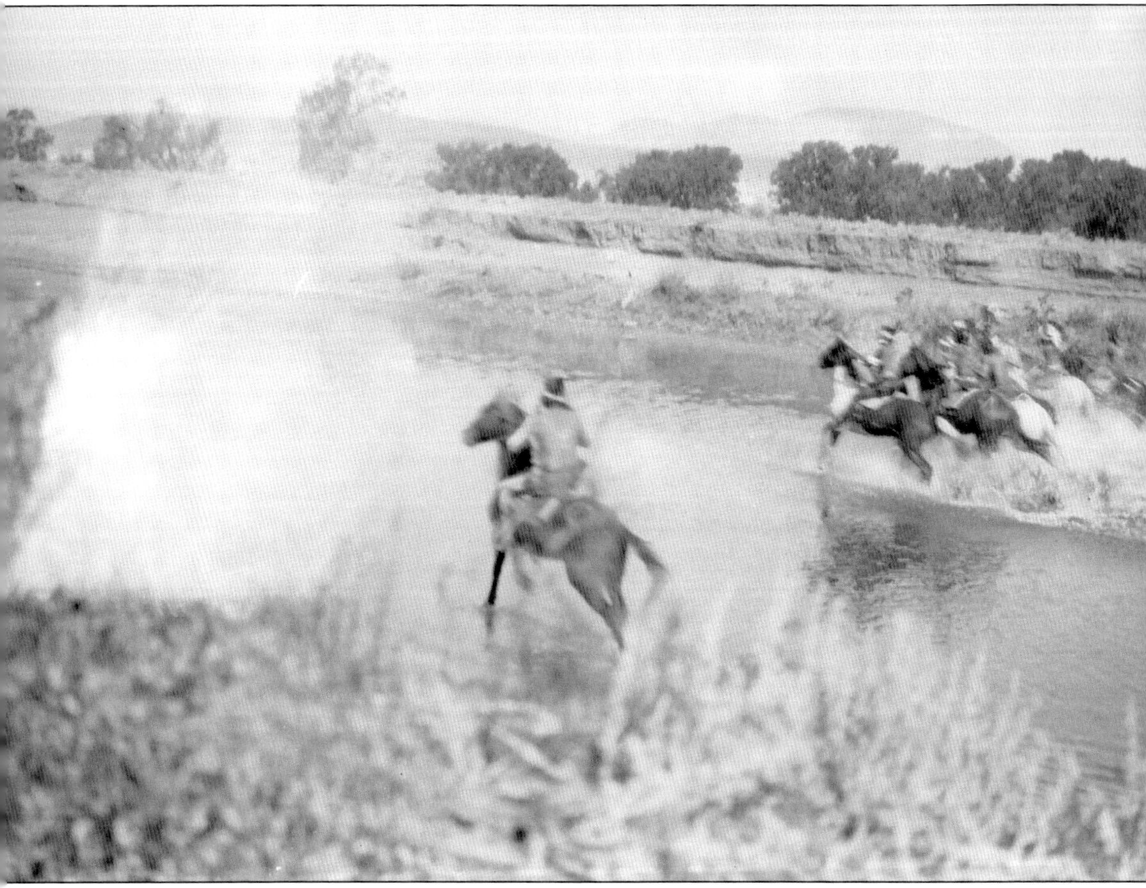

Fast riding Northern Cheyenne show their skills as horsemen. Indian ponies were swift and could easily maneuver quick turns and sudden stops. This made them valuable in the hunt. (Photograph courtesy of the Denver Public Library.)

Two

TIOSPAYE
THE GOLDEN ENCAMPMENT

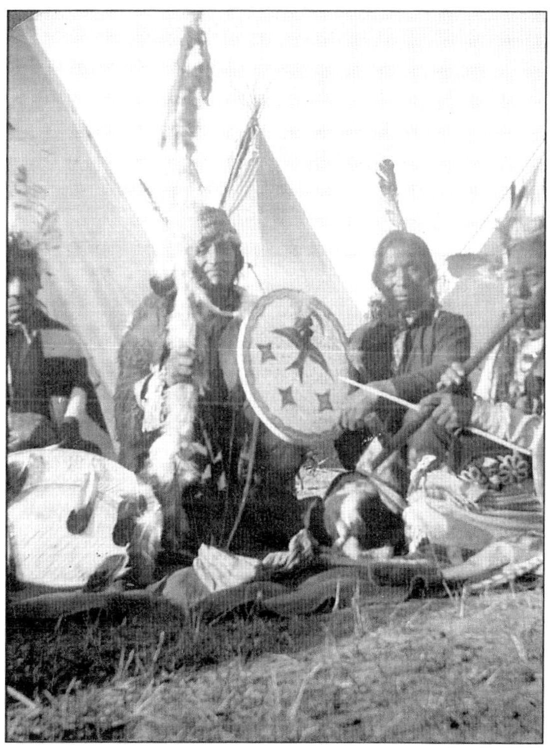

The chiefs from the various bands would meet in council to plan the movement of the camp. Fighting was avoided unless the enemy threatened their women and children. The chiefs decided to continue to move the encampment, tracking the buffalo herds. They finally arrived in the valley of the Greasy Grass and the Little Bighorn River. The Indians called it "Greasy Grass" because the plant had oils on one side. If it fell down it would be very slippery, especially on the slope of a hill.

Their first lodges to camp consisted of year-round hunting bands. The village would grow to become the largest in recorded American history, estimated of there being over 1,000 lodges, with up to 7,000 people, almost 1,500 of them warriors. This photograph shows a council of Sioux chiefs. Two of the men hold shields, a third smokes a pipe. Other items include a fur covered staff and headdresses. (Photograph courtesy of the Denver Public Library.)

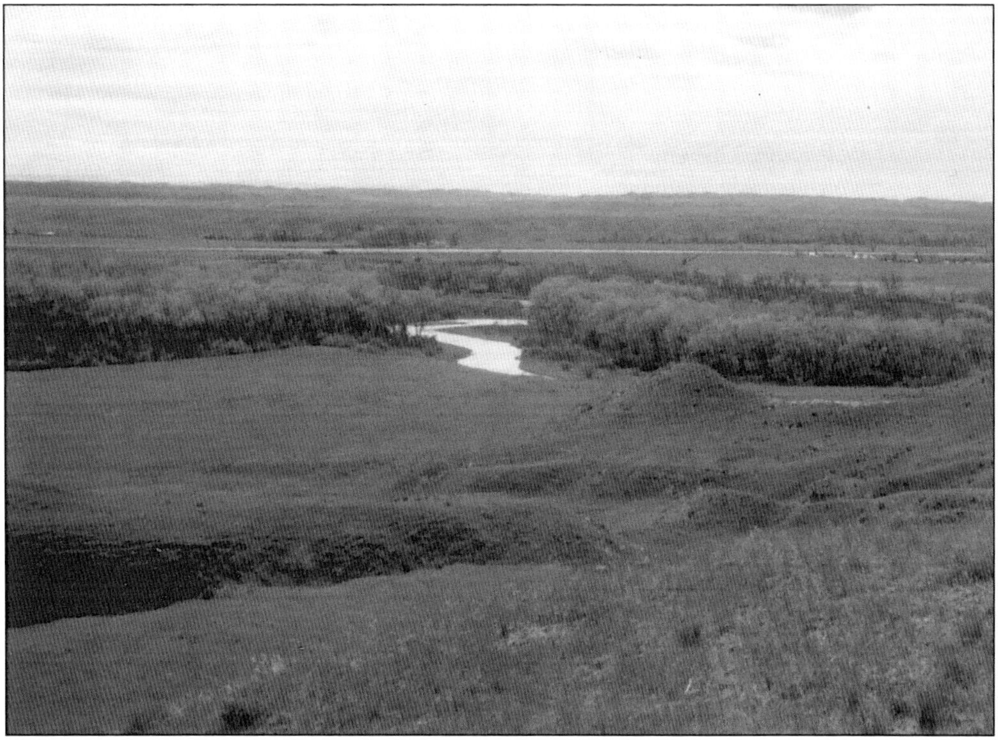

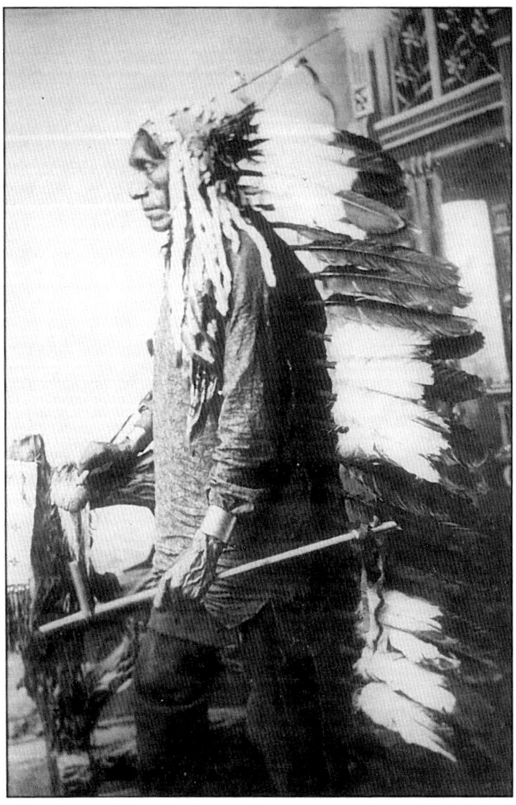

The site of the great encampment with the Little Bighorn River off in the distance, as it appears today. Standing quietly where the photographer is located, one can almost envision the tremendous gathering, and hear on the gentle breezes the voices of a people long ago. (Photograph from the author's private collection.)

An 1881 photograph captures not only Circling Bear and his magnificent headdress, but the equally magnificent features of his strong yet aging face and body. (Photograph courtesy of the National Park Service, Little Bighorn Battlefield National Monument.)

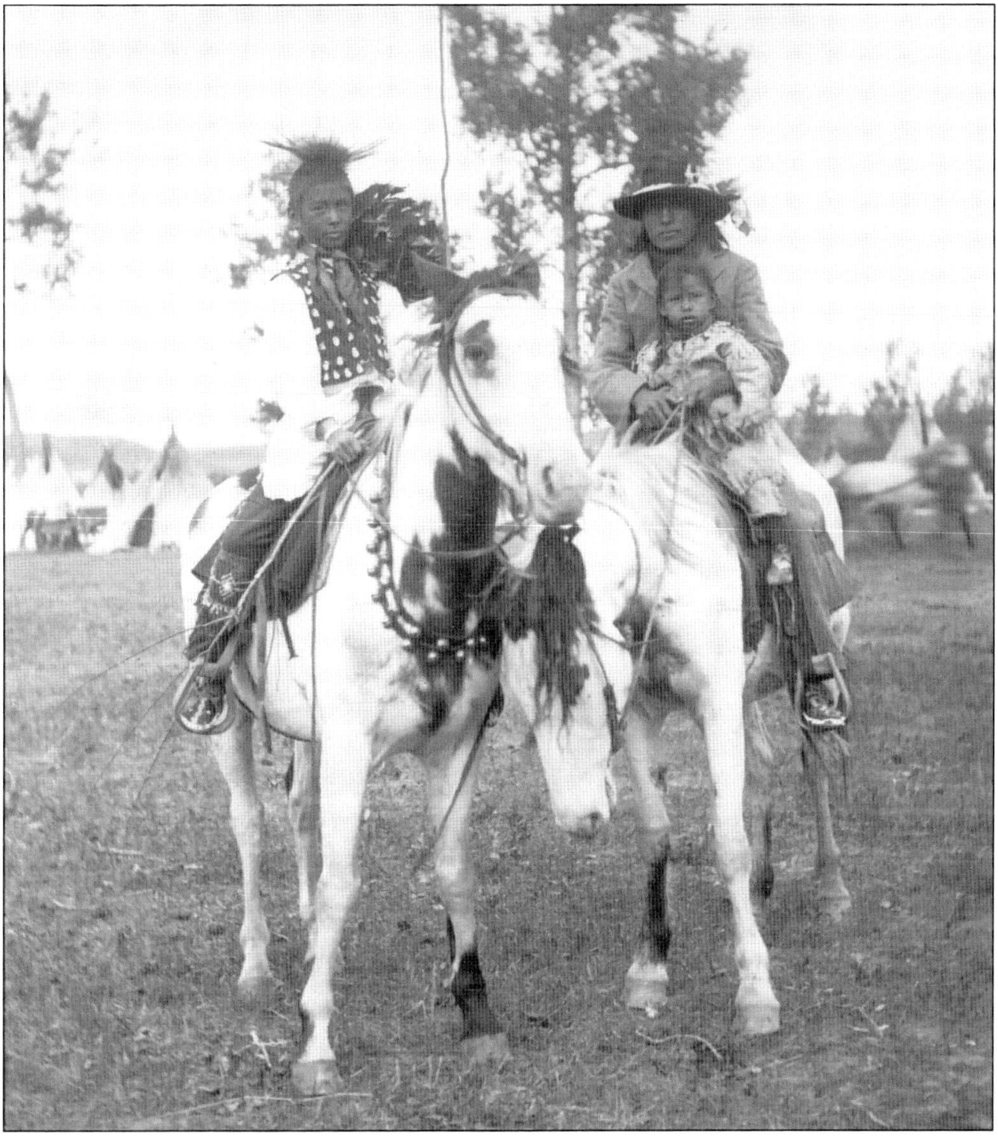

A Dakota Sioux man and boy are shown mounted on horses outside their camp. The man wears a jacket and hat, and holds a child wearing buckskin. The boy wears a roach, cotton tunic, vest, leggings, and moccasins. (Photograph courtesy of the Denver Public Library.)

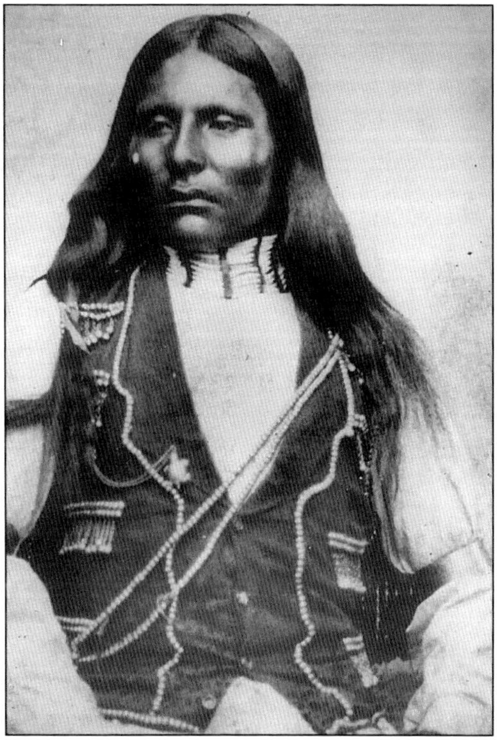

This man is named Big Belly, a proud warrior. (Photograph courtesy of the National Park Service, Little Bighorn Battlefield National Monument.)

Pictured is Man Afraid of Horses, an Oglala Chief. He was a warrior who rode with Red Cloud. (Photograph courtesy of the Denver Public Library.)

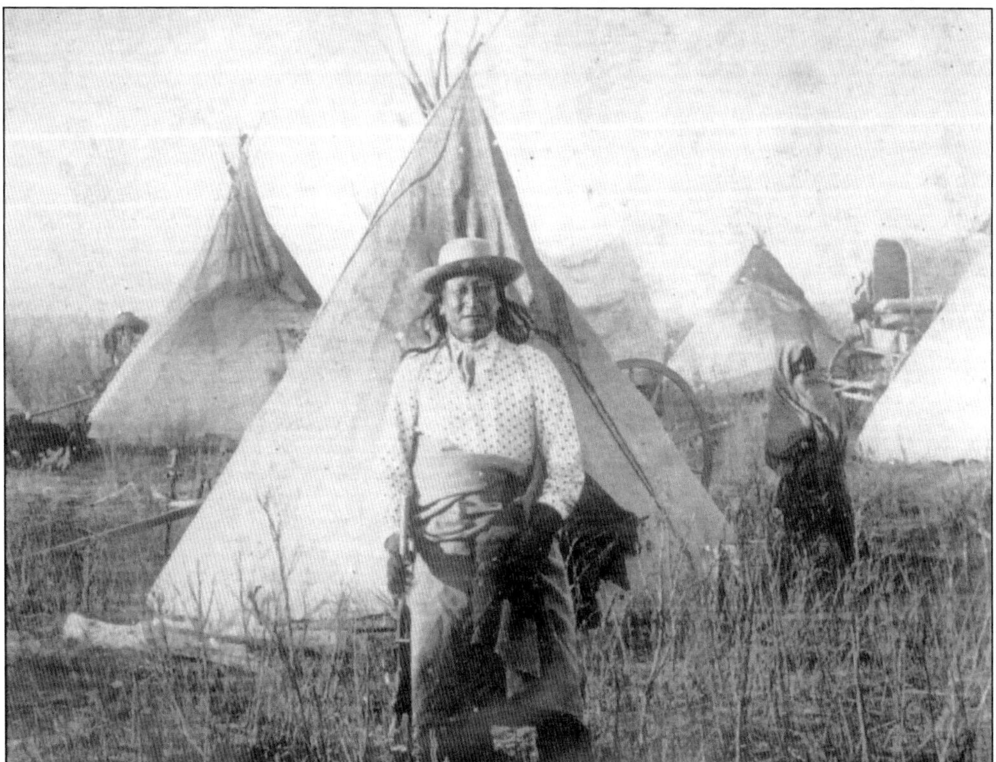

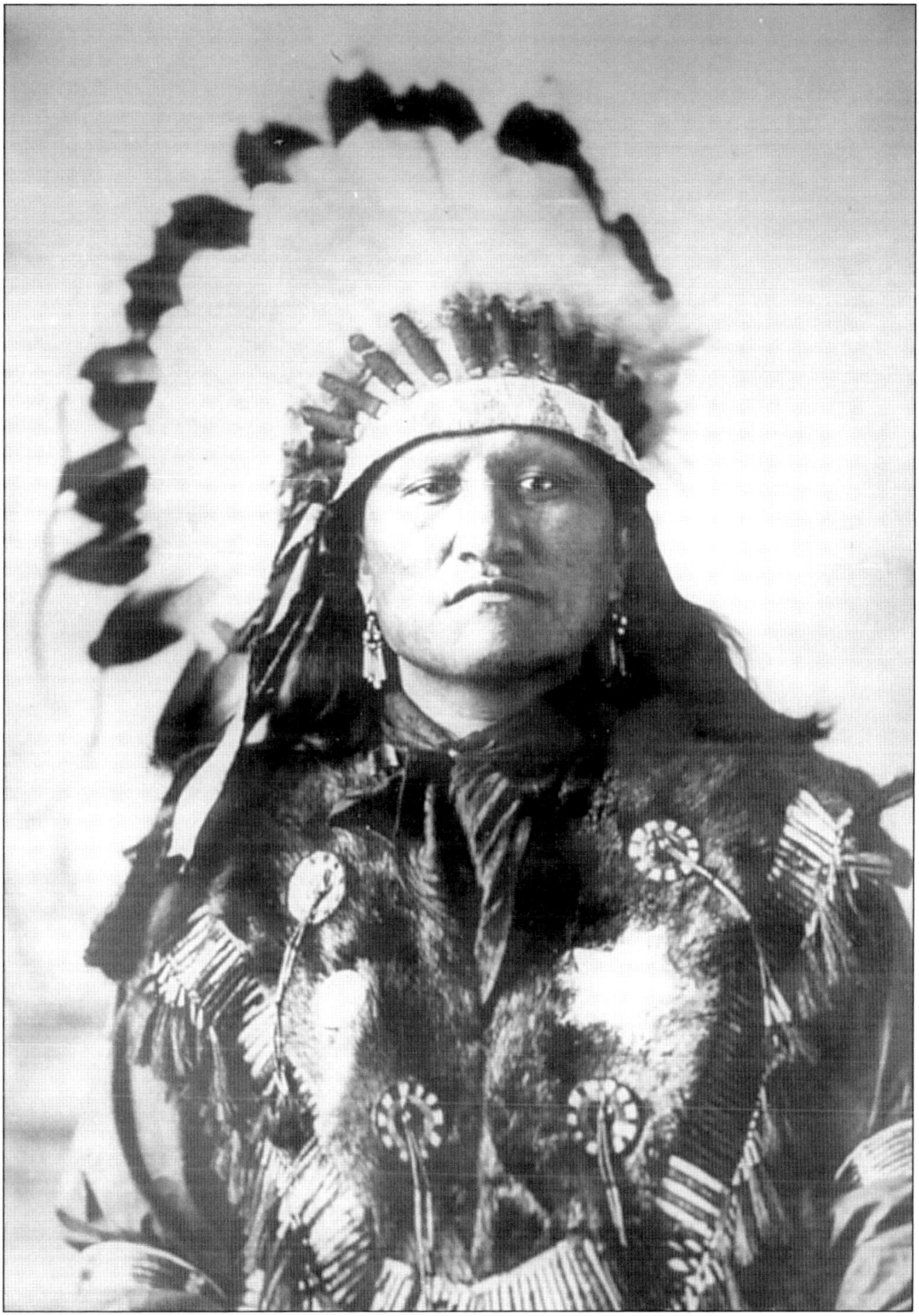

Most warriors were as Chief Good Horse, shown here, deeply spiritual, caring, and compassionate. Beneath his colorful headdress and tribal garb, one can perhaps sense the heart of a brave, courageous leader and man of high character. (Photograph courtesy of the National Park Service, Little Bighorn Battlefield National Monument.)

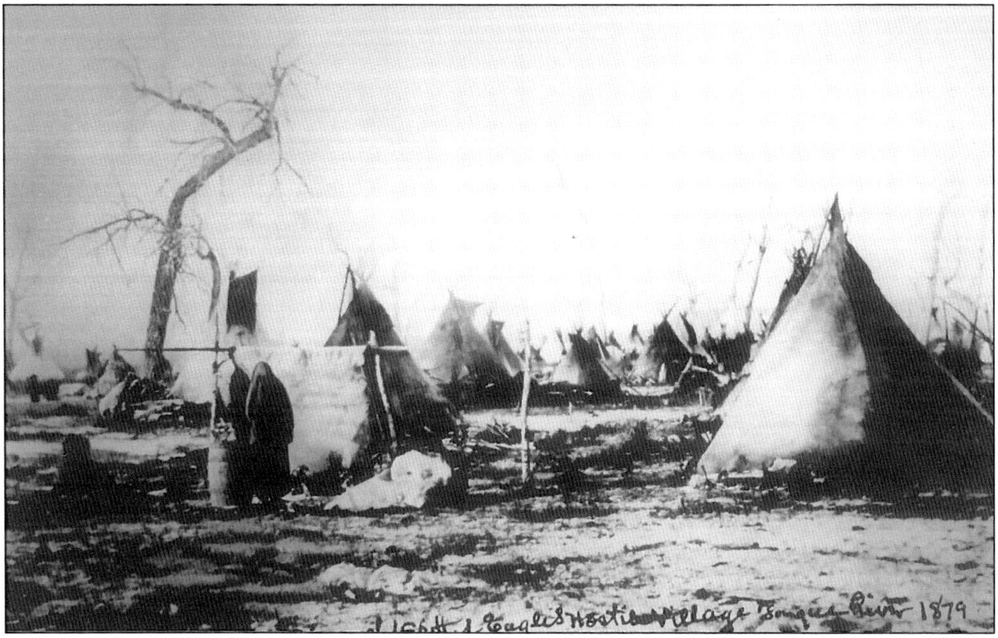

This is a view of Spotted Eagle's village. Many of the hunting bands had heard of the encampment on the Little Bighorn and joined the village. (Photograph courtesy of the National Park Service, Little Bighorn Battlefield National Monument.)

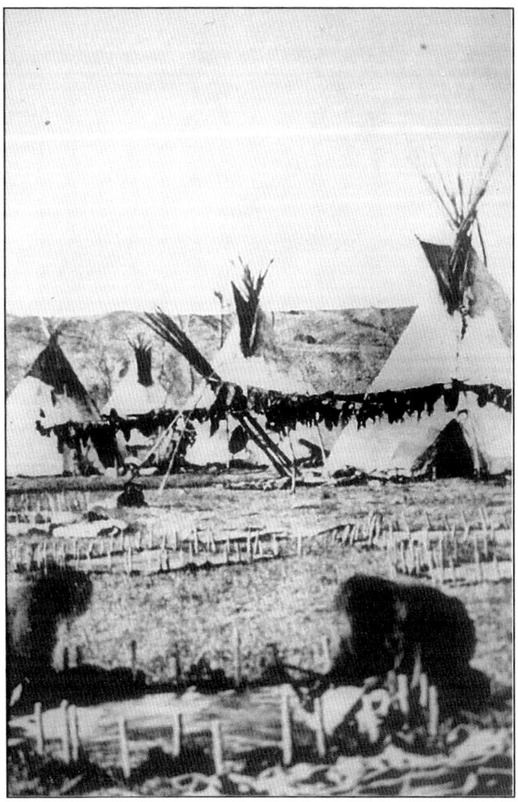

The buffalo was considered a sacred animal, giving its life so the tribe could live. The women would use every part of its body. Here women stretch buffalo hides. (Photograph courtesy of the National Park Service, Little Bighorn Battlefield National Monument.)

A man sits on a blanket in front of a large tipi. He has a striped tail tied to one braid and wears a beaded necklace and bracelets. A blanket covers his lap and he wears moccasins. A large drum is on its side next to him on the blanket. A portion of the tipi is folded up revealing a log pole supporting it. (Photograph courtesy of the Denver Public Library.)

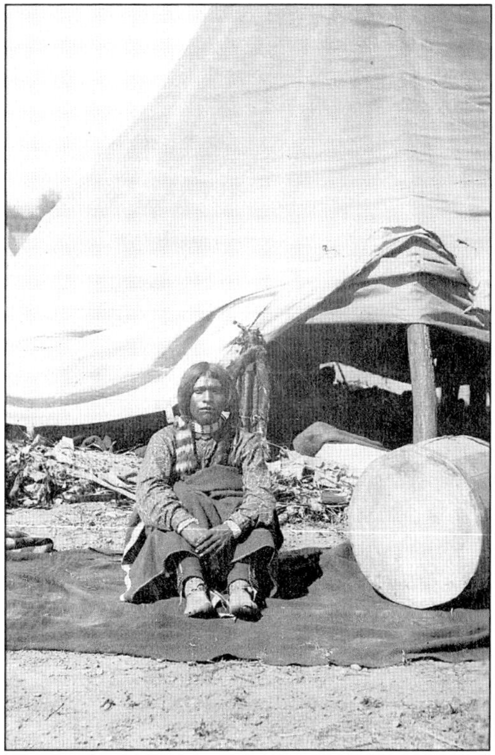

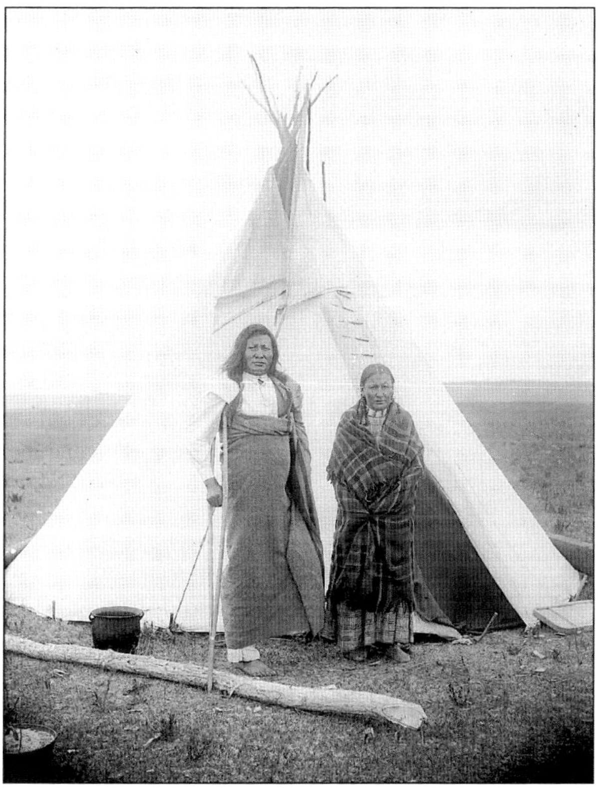

Full length photograph of Rain-in-the-Face, Dakota Chief, and his wife, Sati, both wrapped in blankets, standing in front of a tipi. (Photograph courtesy of the Denver Public Library.)

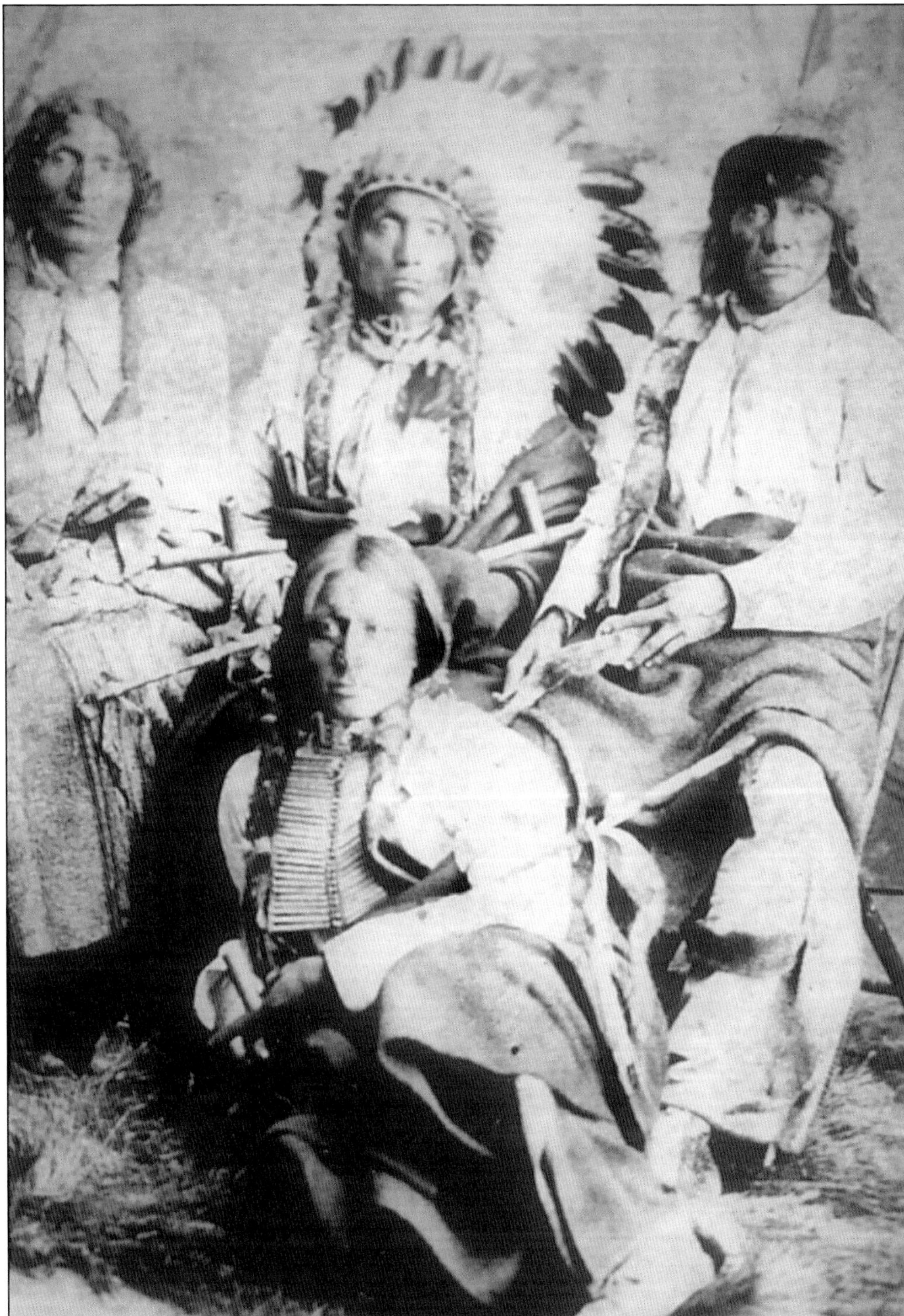

Pictured are four proud warriors, representative of those who joined the Tiospaye encampment to be with Sitting Bull and Crazy Horse. (Photograph courtesy of the National Park Service, Little Bighorn Battlefield National Monument.)

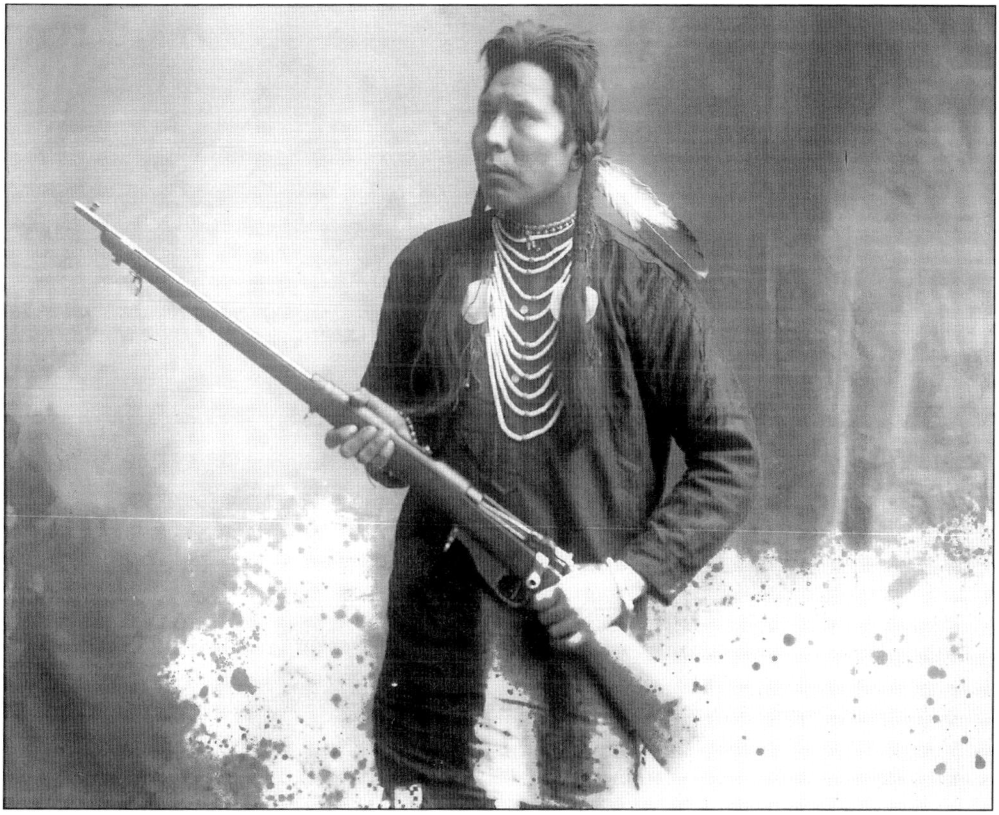

A young warrior brandishing his rifle looks ready for the hunt. (Photograph courtesy of Fort Peck Tribal Archives.)

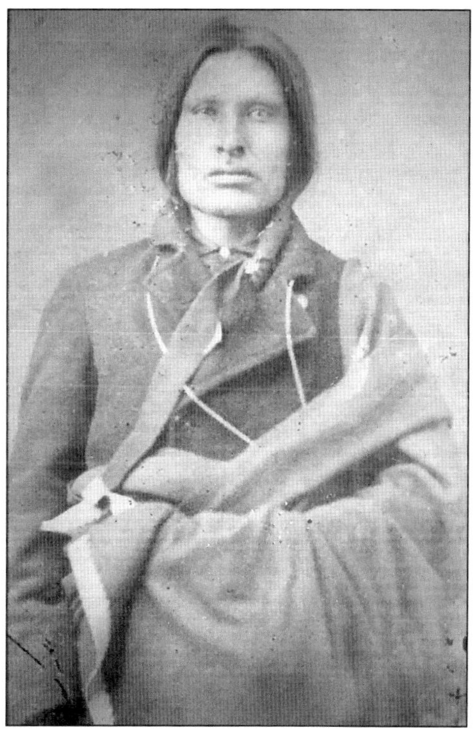

Three Stores is pictured holding a blanket. (Photograph courtesy of the National Park Service, Little Bighorn Battlefield National Monument.)

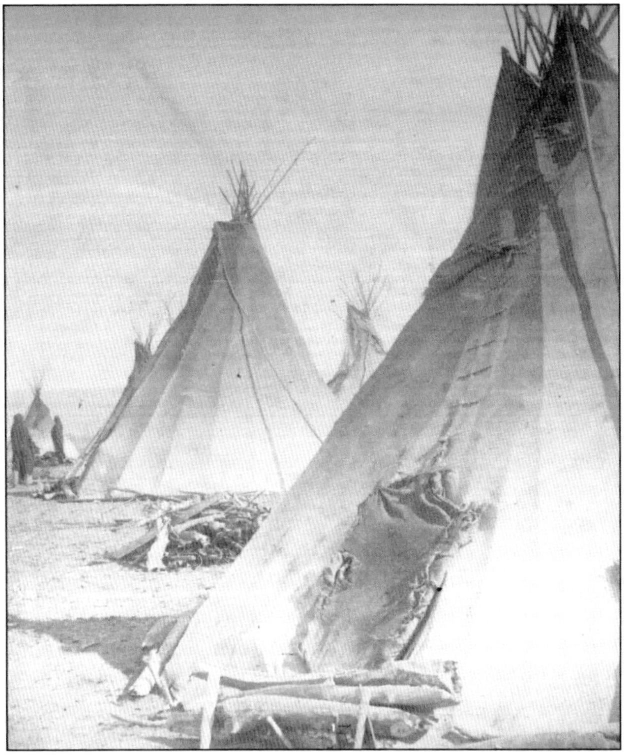

This view of a Sioux camp, on the open prairie, is similar to the village that began to take shape on the Little Bighorn. (Photograph courtesy of the Denver Public Library.)

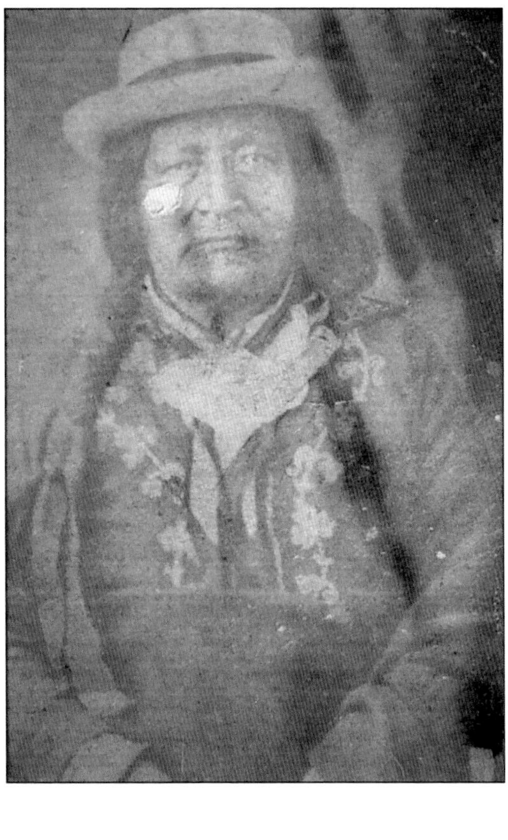

In a rare and very old photograph, Black Bear is pictured. (Photograph courtesy of the National Park Service, Little Bighorn Battlefield National Monument.)

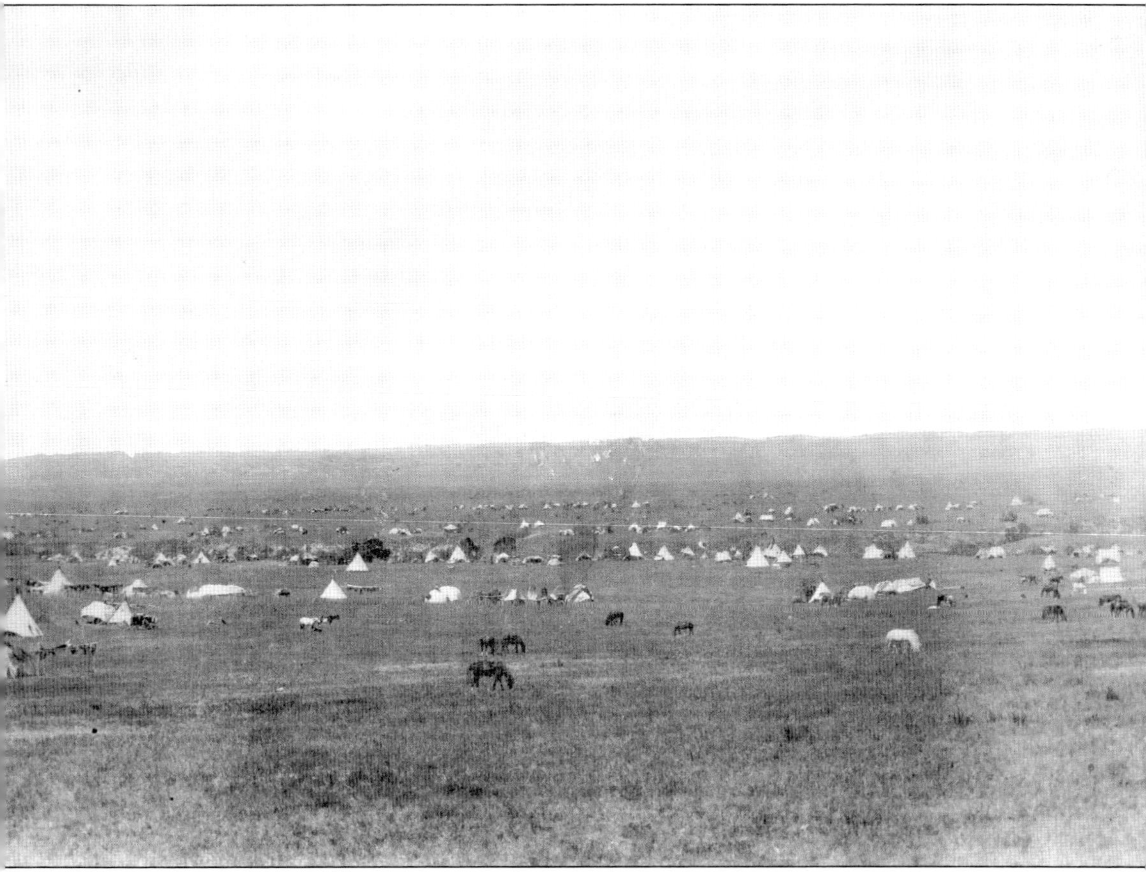

A view over plains of a Sioux camp with scattered tipis. (Photograph courtesy of the Denver Public Library.)

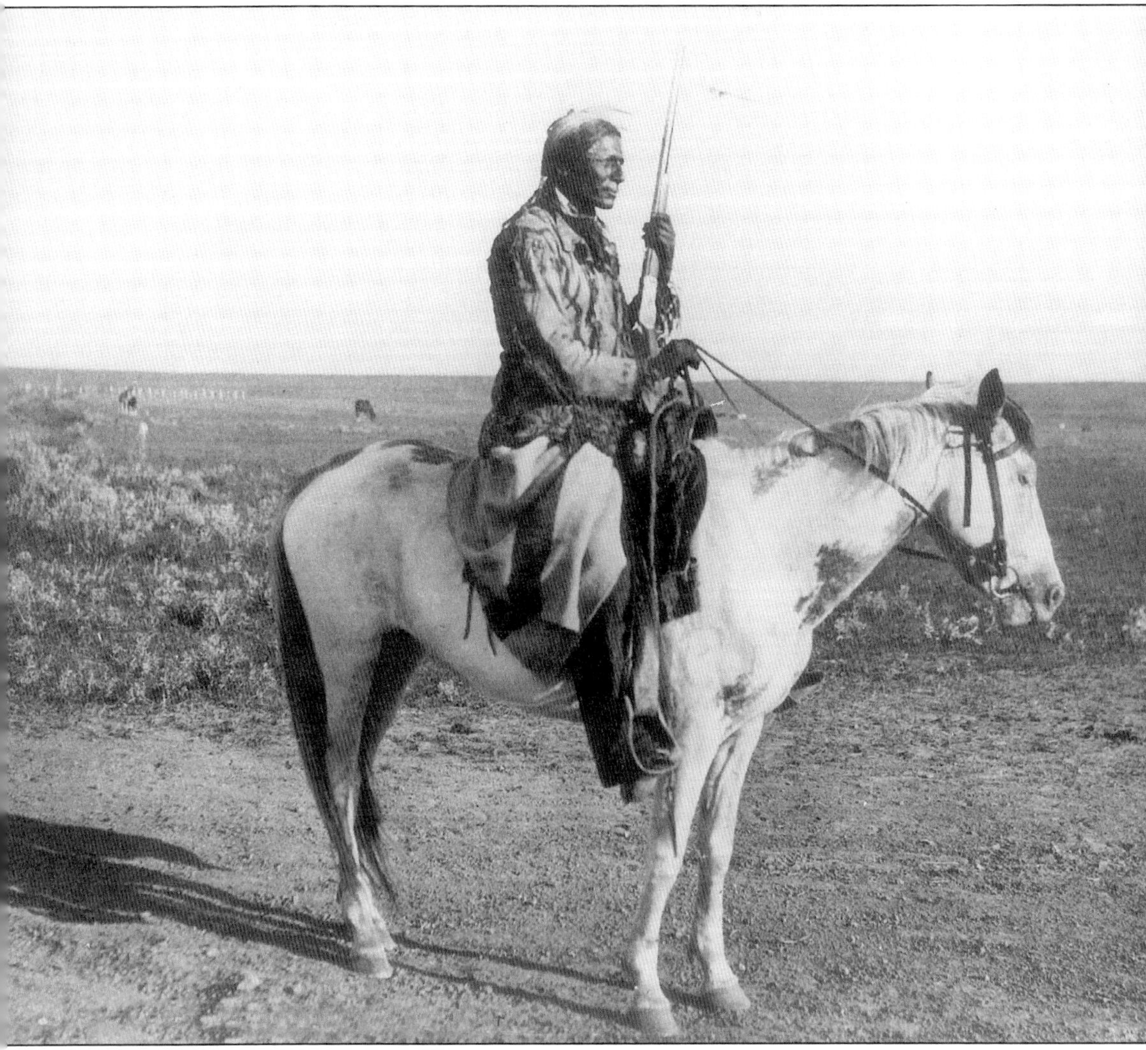

A scout sits astride his horse, keeping watch on the outskirts of camp. (Photograph courtesy of Fort Peck Tribal Archives.)

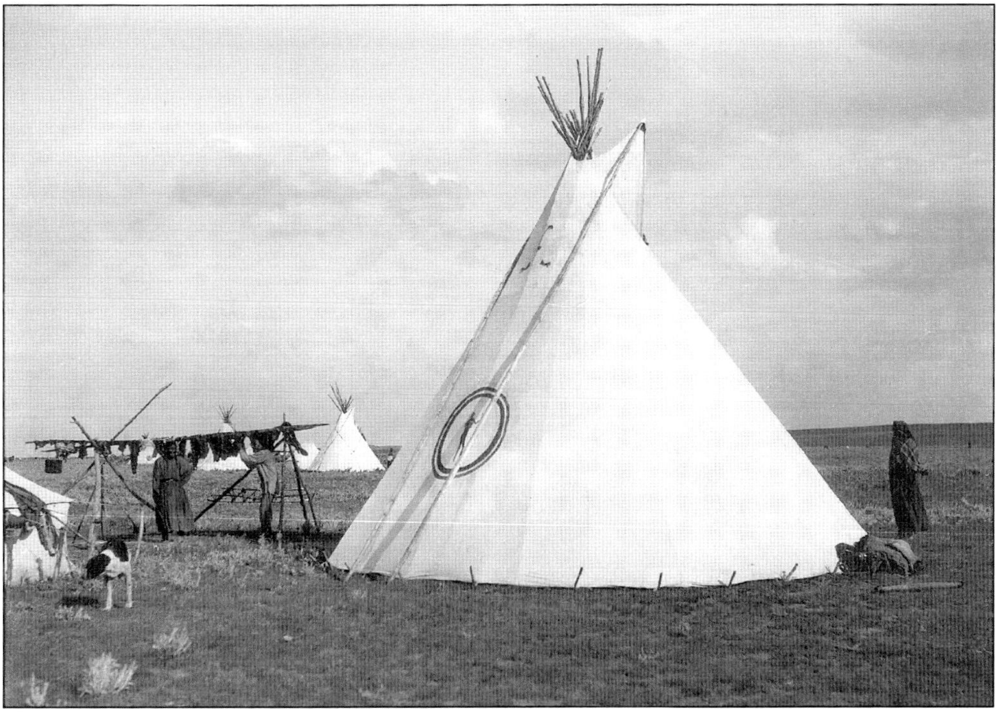

Pictured are several lodges; the Tiospaye encampment numbered over 1,000 of these. (Photograph courtesy of Fort Peck Tribal Archives.)

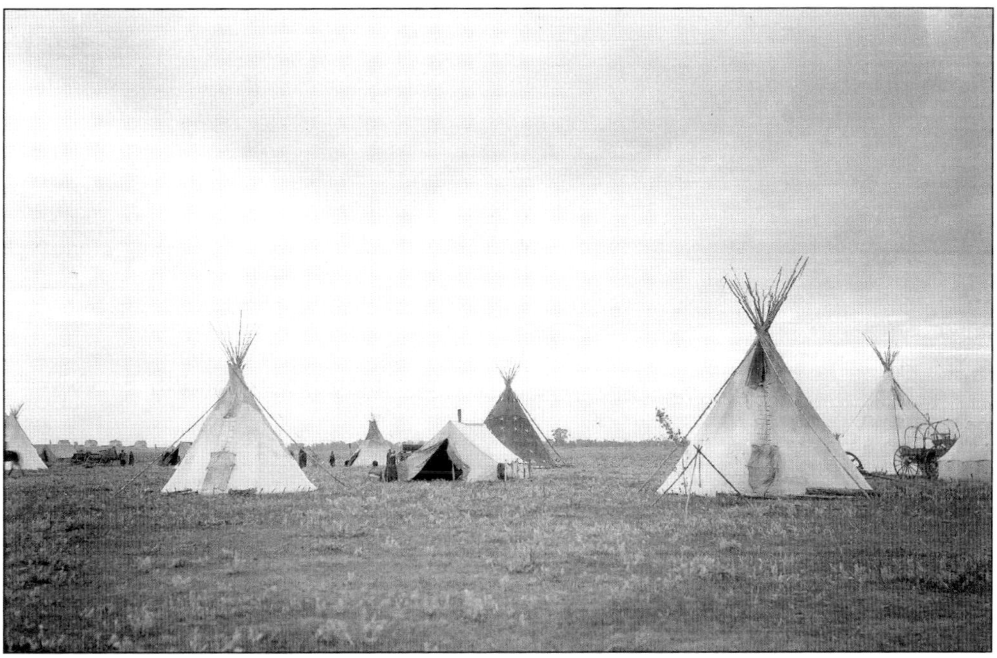

Lodges dot the horizon. Unfortunately, the area could not support so many for longer than a week. Fuel and game would soon run out, and the people would have to follow new food sources. (Photograph courtesy of Fort Peck Tribal Archives.)

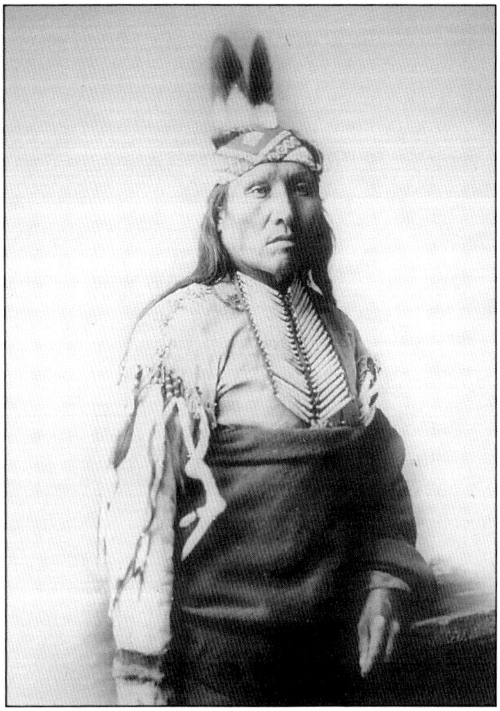

Here Thunder Hawk stands noble and brave. (Photograph courtesy of the National Park Service, Little Bighorn Battlefield National Monument.)

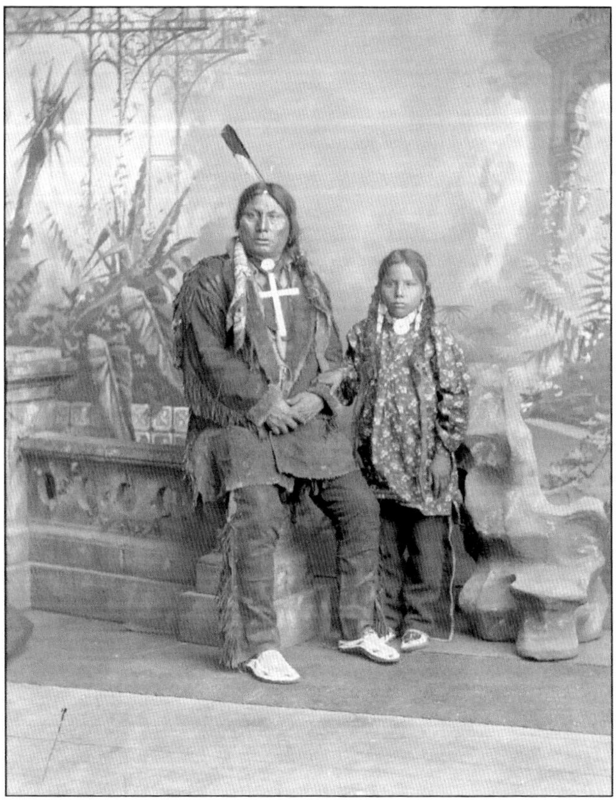

Full length photograph of Gall, a Hunkpapa Chief, and his nephew, William Hawk. Gall, wearing large crucifix and leather jacket, is resting against a stone wall. William Hawk is wearing a flowered shirt and necklace. (Photograph courtesy of the Denver Public Library.)

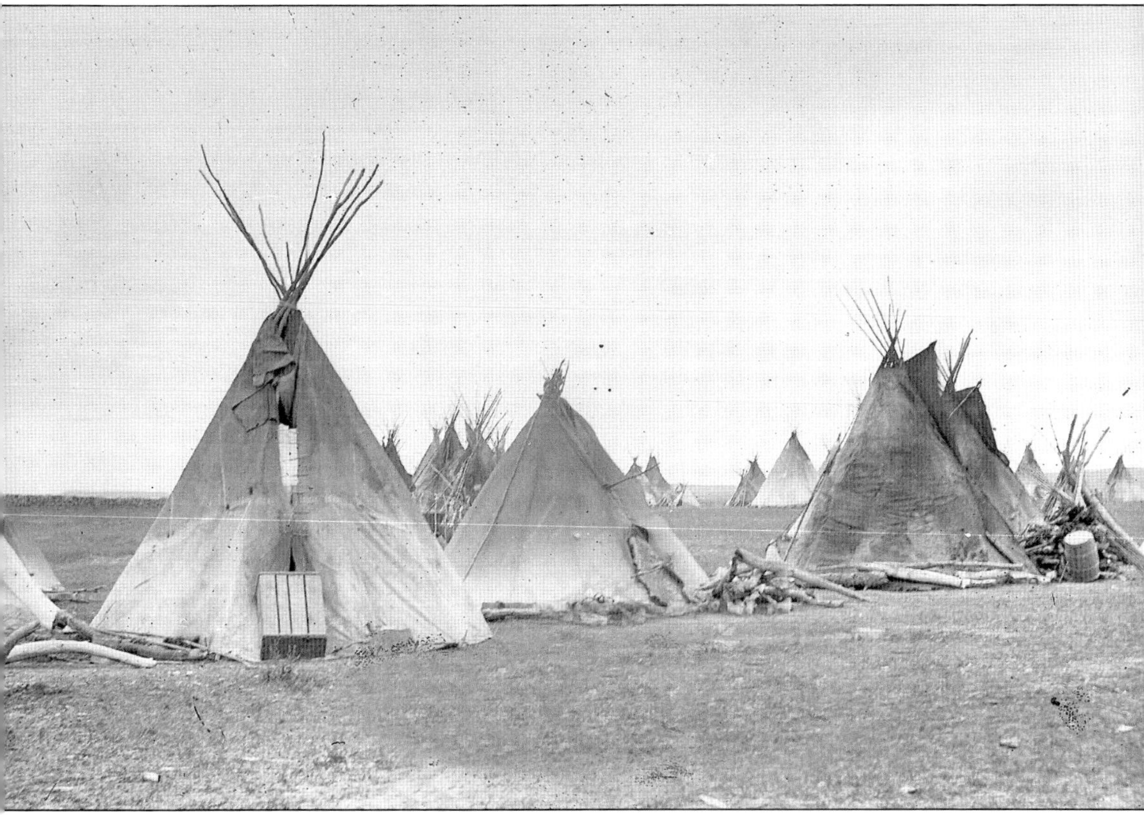

At the camp of Hunkpapa, Chief Gall joined those of Sitting Bull and Crazy Horse at Tiospaye. There were 20 tepees grouped together with firewood, kindling, wooden barrel, and crates stacked outside. (Photograph courtesy of the Denver Public Library.)

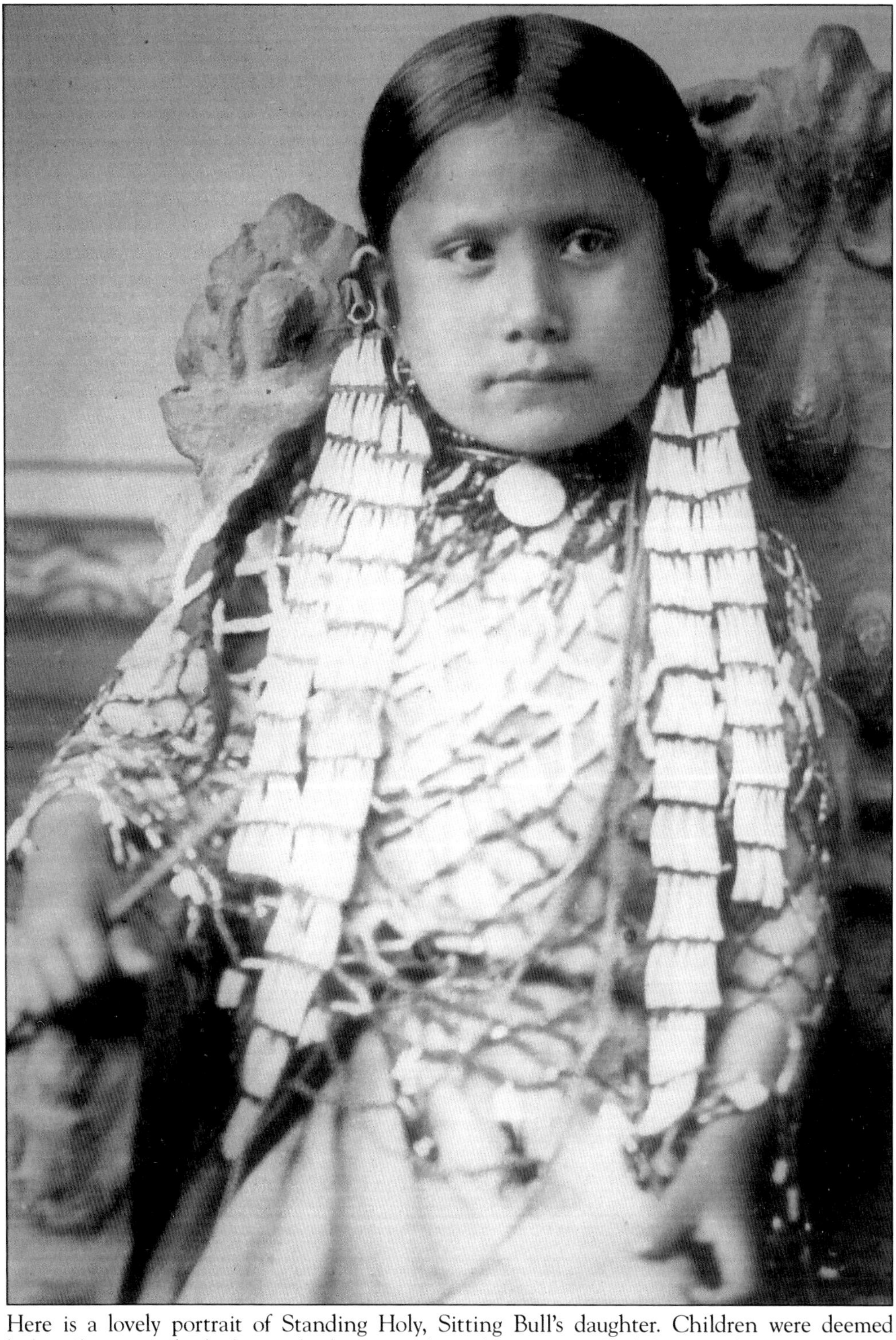

Here is a lovely portrait of Standing Holy, Sitting Bull's daughter. Children were deemed holy. They were the little people that came from the spirit world. (Photograph courtesy of the National Park Service, Little Bighorn Battlefield National Monument.)

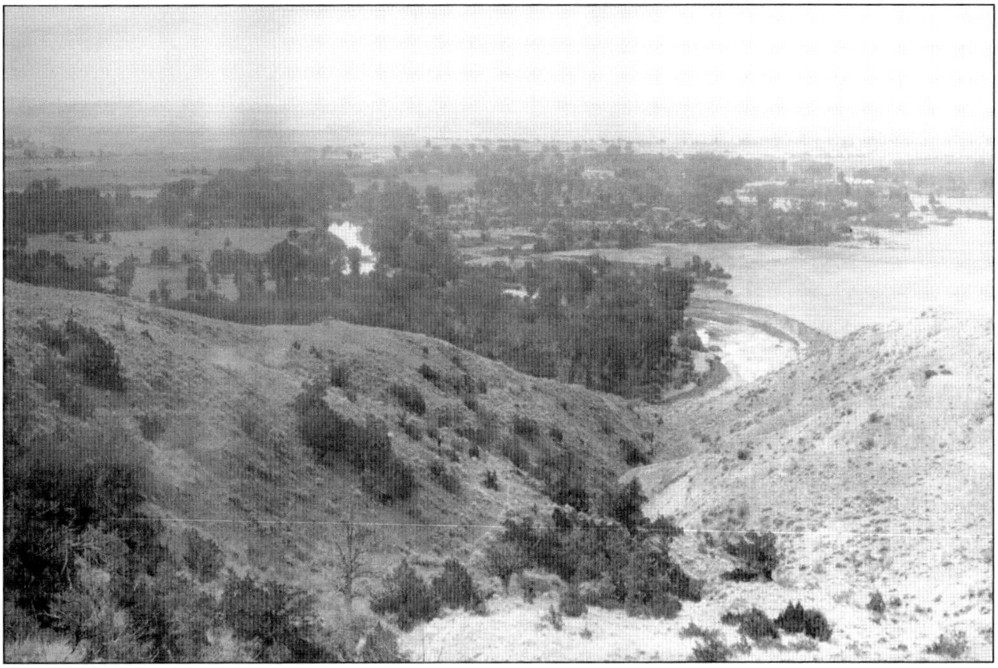

This is a scene looking west from bluffs over Little Bighorn River. (Photograph courtesy of the Denver Public Library.)

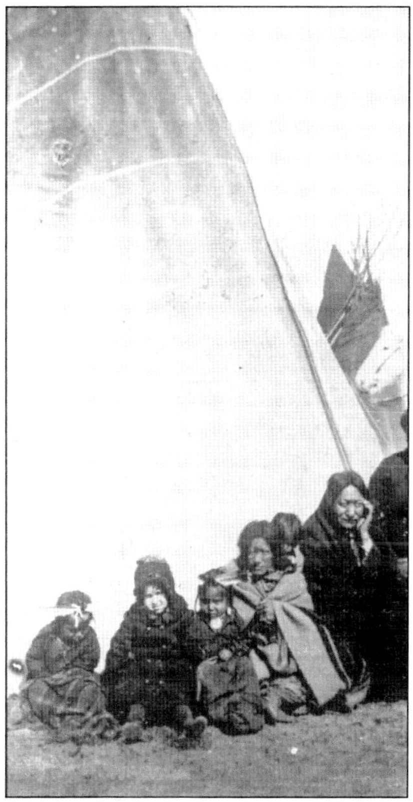

Sitting Bull and his family sit near their tipi. He was the spiritual leader to all at Tiospaye. (Photograph courtesy of the Denver Public Library.)

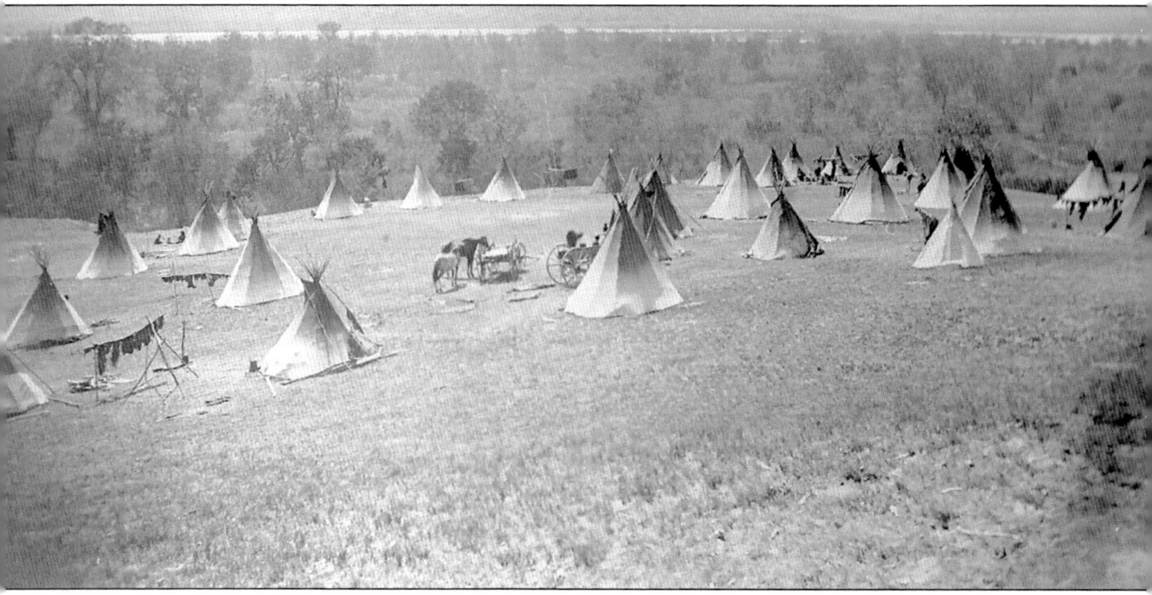

There were six circles at the Tiospaye village. Pictured here are Sitting Bulls' Hunkpapa lodges. There was dancing, feasting, and celebrating for many days. Among the many tribes represented were the Dakota, Yanktonais, Cheyenne, Arapaho, and of the Lakota Sioux: the Oglala, Hunkpapa, Miniconjous, Sans Arc, Brule, Two Kettle, Blackfeet, and Santee Sioux. (Photograph courtesy of the Denver Public Library.)

Three

The Place of Prayers and Promises

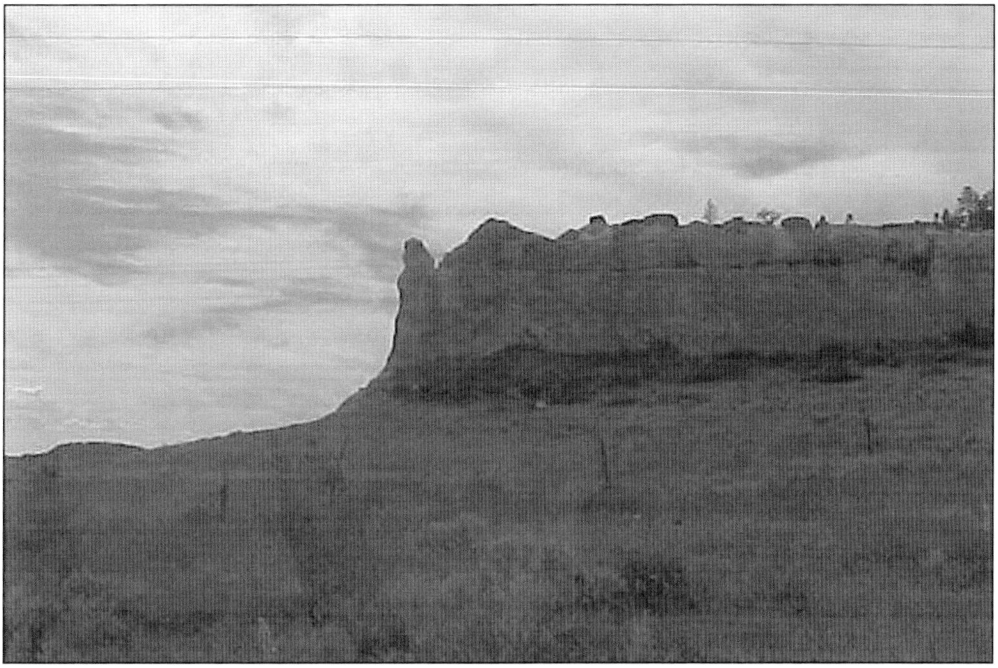

In the Moon When the Ponies Shed, Tatanka Iyotanka, or Sitting Bull, had a vision. He was called by Wakan Tanka to a nearby butte, a sacred place He fell asleep after praying and meditating, and there he had a dream. He saw a dust storm with high winds approaching from the east. Sailing in the opposite direction was a white cloud resembling an Indian village at the foot of snow-capped mountains. Fiercely the gale charged toward the cloud, and behind the storm, Sitting Bull could see soldiers, horses, and weapons in the sun. This was accompanied by thunder, lightning, and rain. Sitting Bull called a council of the chiefs and told them his dream and its interpretation.

A few weeks later, in the Moon of Making Fat, Sitting Bull organized *Wiwanyag Wachipi*—the Sun Dance. During the ceremony, 50 pieces of flesh were removed from each of his arms as a measure of endurance and a sacrifice to *Wakan Tanka*. He experienced another vision, dead soldiers and horses fell head first into the Indian camp. The Indian people would experience a great victory. This is a photograph of a butte on the Northern Cheyenne Reservation near the site of the Sun Dance. These rocks, called Prayer Rocks or Deer Medicine Rocks, are sacred to the Northern Cheyenne. (Photograph from the author's private collection.)

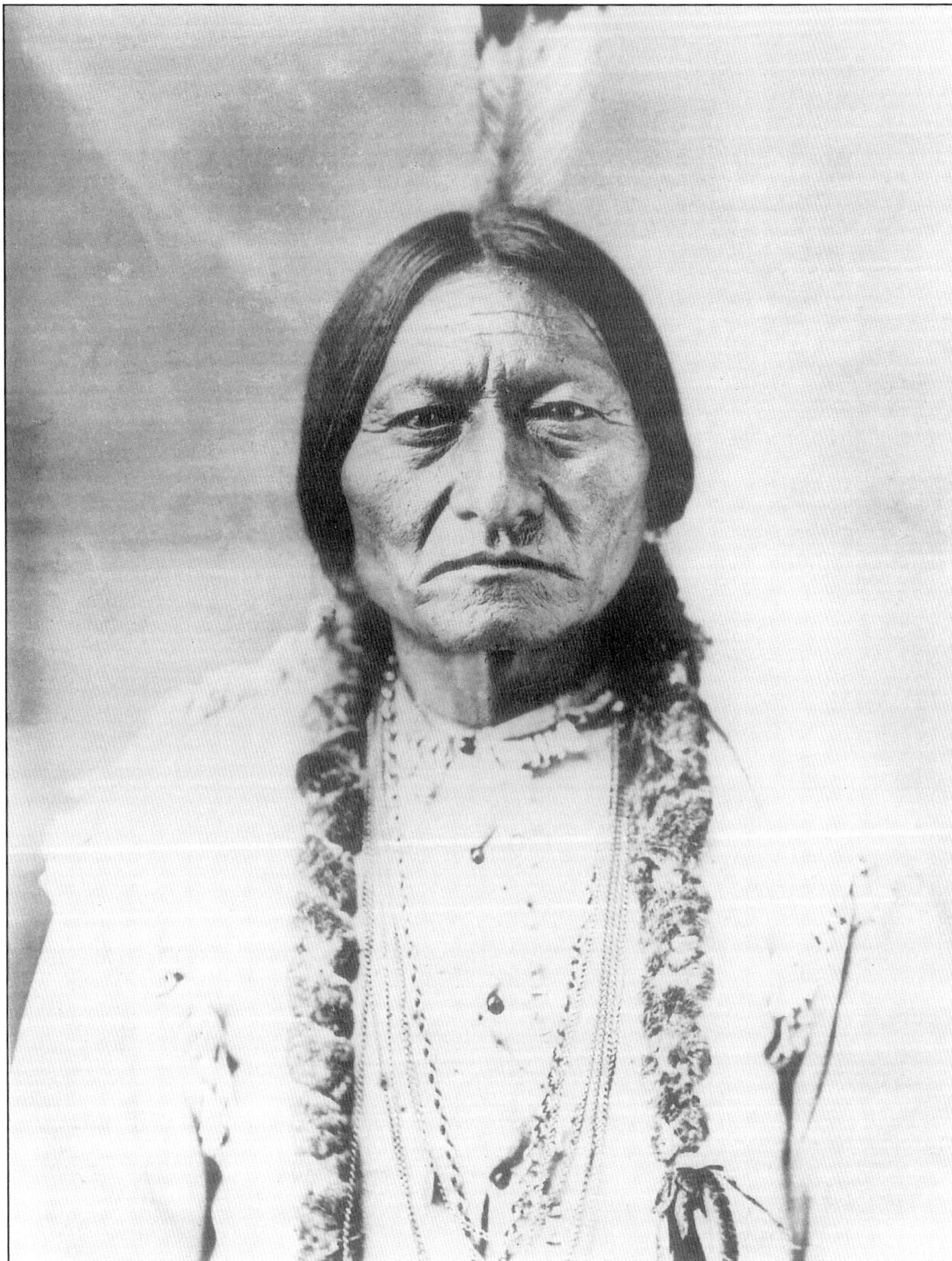

Tatanka Iyotanka, Sitting Bull of the Hunkpapa, served as the people's spiritual leader. Sitting Bull was a warrior and a visionary. He dedicated his life to preserve the beautiful culture of his people. He organized the Sun Dance. Sun Dances are the spiritual dances for fulfillment of the ways the ancients taught and lived. For the Hunkpapa, Oglala, Teton, Sans Arc, Brule, Cheyenne, and Arapaho it was a gathering to worship the Great Spirit *Wakan Tanka*. (Photograph courtesy of Fort Peck Tribal Archives.)

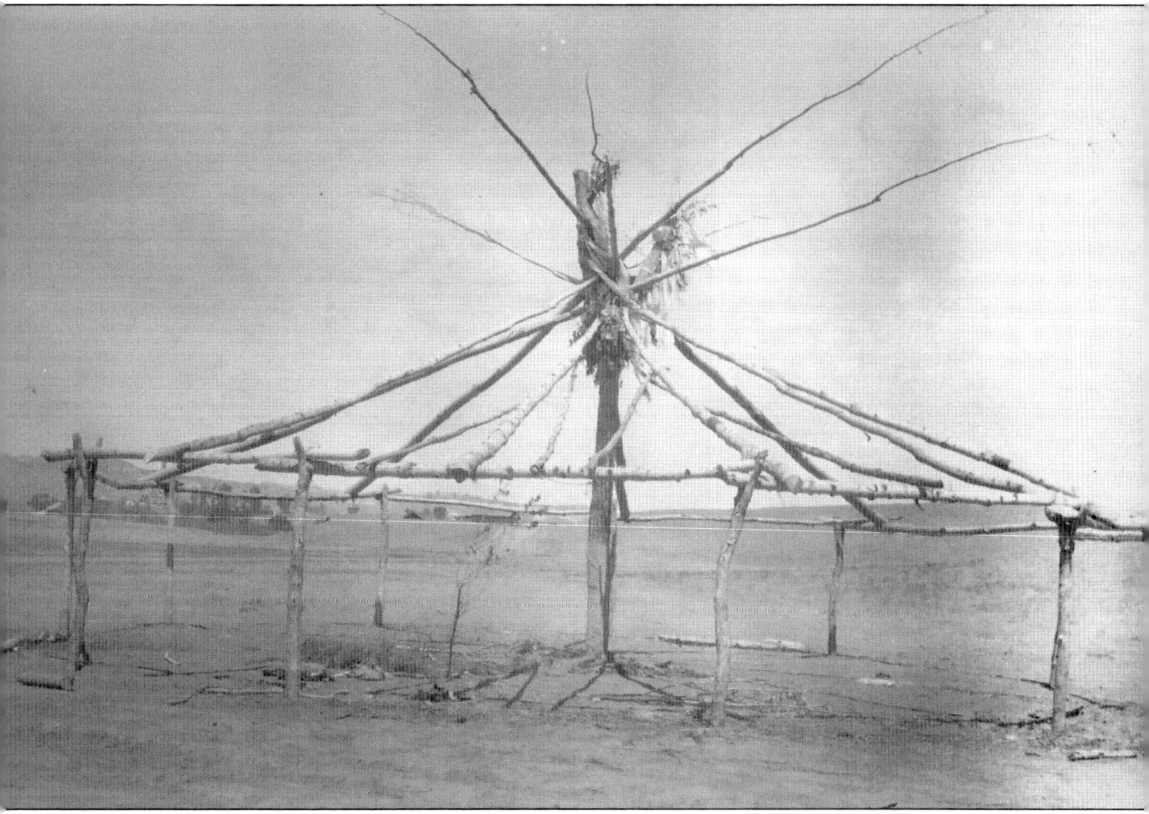

This is a photograph of the framework of a Sun Dance lodge. For the ceremony a choice cottonwood tree was blessed and taken out of the ground. Then a medicine man trimmed the limbs and left it for curing. Days later it was erected for the ceremony, which was held when the moon was full. Centered in a circle, it was the spiritual giving force for the people. From the early days they were taught of the "Tree of Life," through which life would improve to perfection. Prosperity and posterity would be sweet and happen because it. (Photograph courtesy of the Denver Public Library.)

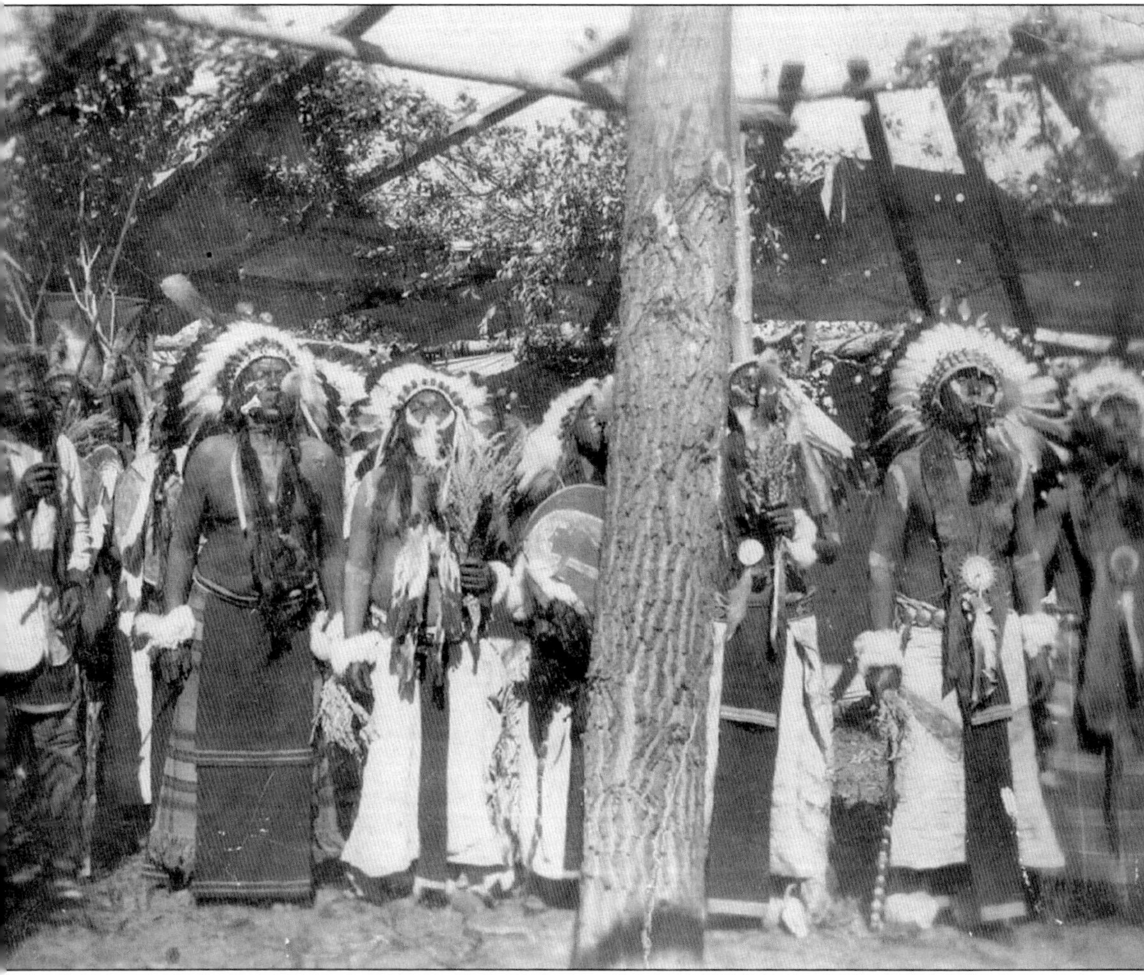

This photograph of the Sun Dance shows the center pole, the "Tree of Life." The rites of the ceremony have been passed down from generation to generation, along with their sacred meanings.

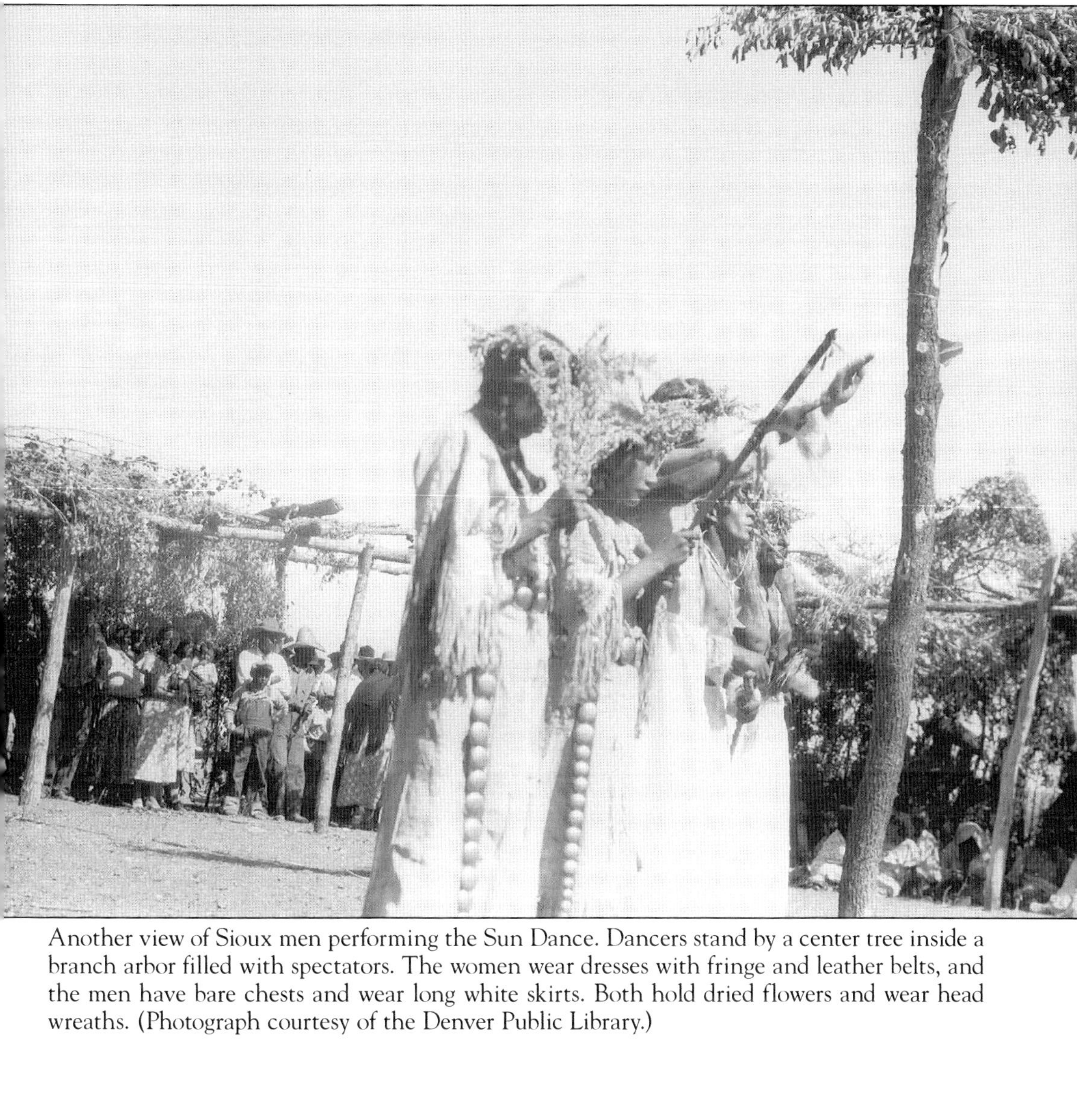

Another view of Sioux men performing the Sun Dance. Dancers stand by a center tree inside a branch arbor filled with spectators. The women wear dresses with fringe and leather belts, and the men have bare chests and wear long white skirts. Both hold dried flowers and wear head wreaths. (Photograph courtesy of the Denver Public Library.)

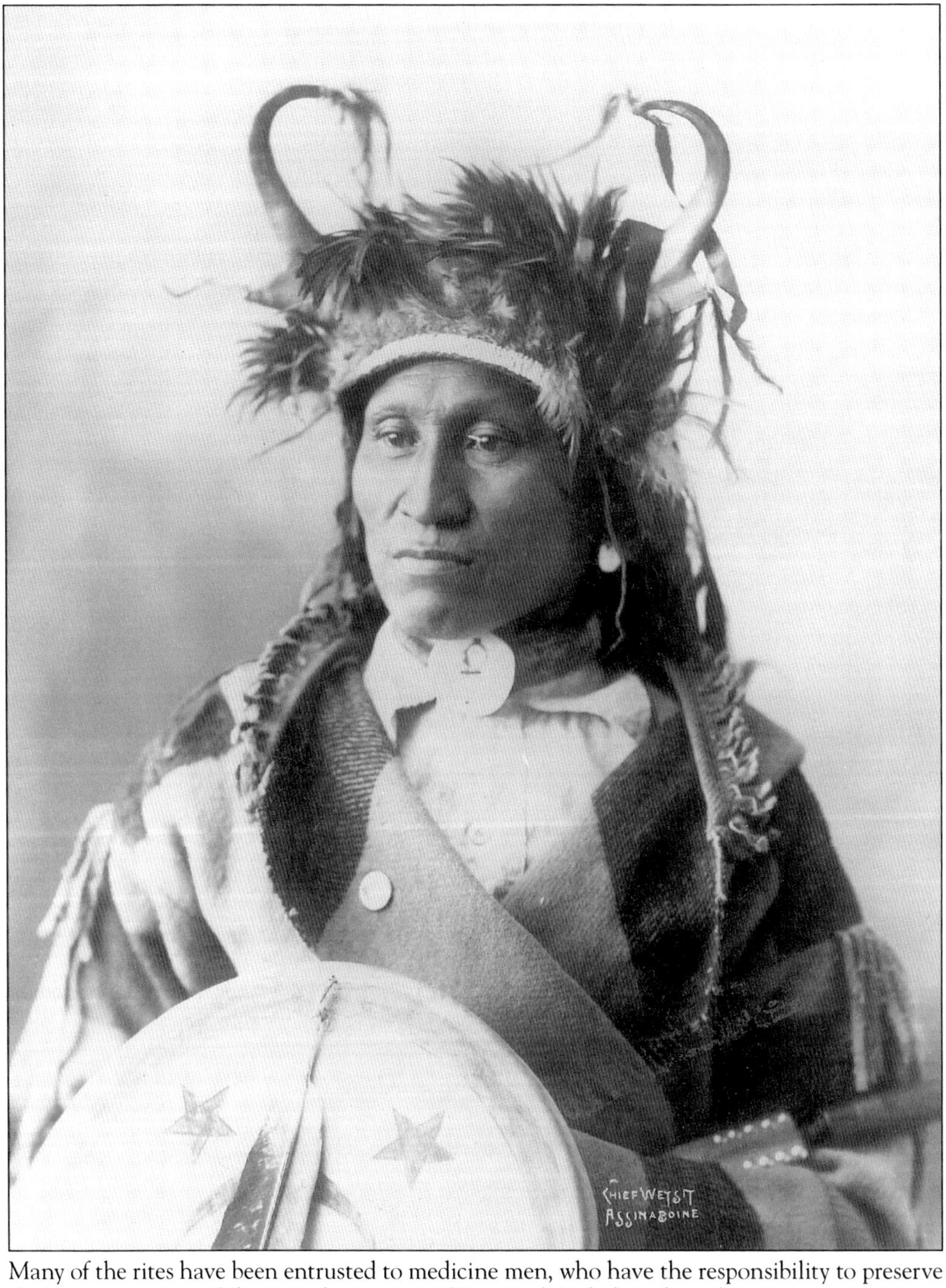

Many of the rites have been entrusted to medicine men, who have the responsibility to preserve their true meanings. (Photograph courtesy of Fort Peck Tribal Archives.)

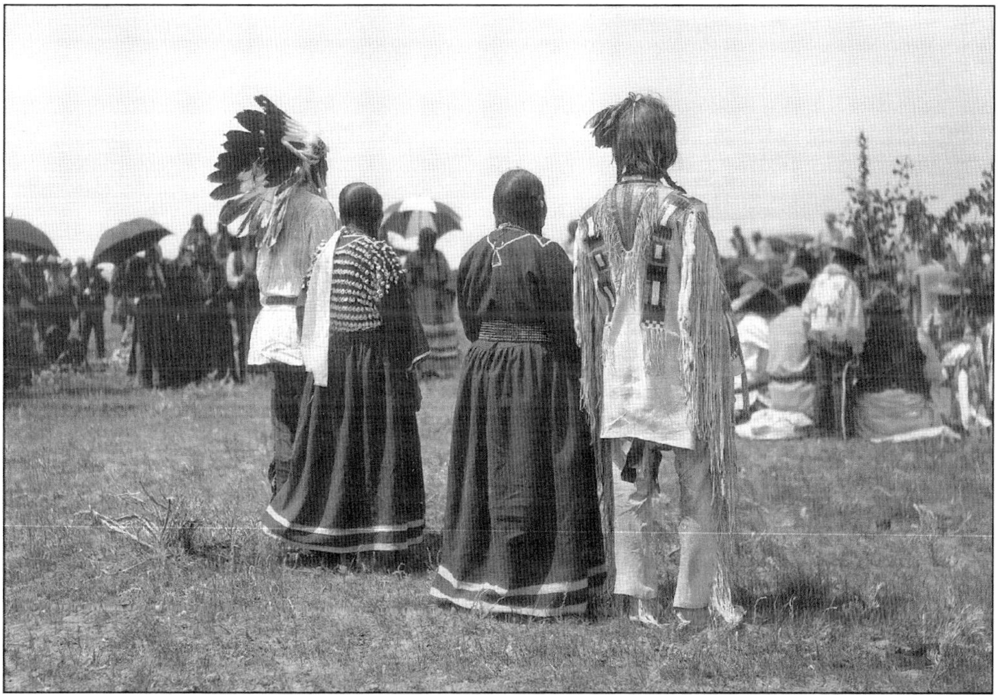

Here is a photograph of the celebration that has everyone focused on the drum and the dancers. Both men and women wear ceremonial dress and take part. (Photograph courtesy of Fort Peck Tribal Archives.)

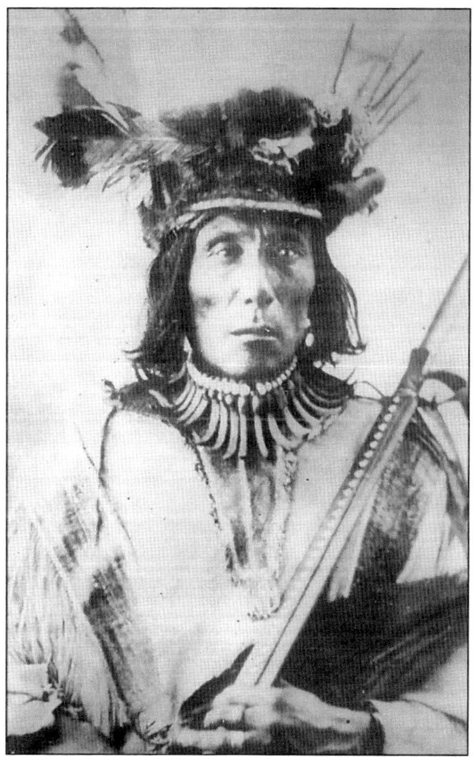

This is a photograph of Medicine Bear, a member of the Yanktonai band. (Photograph courtesy of the National Park Service, Little Bighorn Battlefield National Monument.)

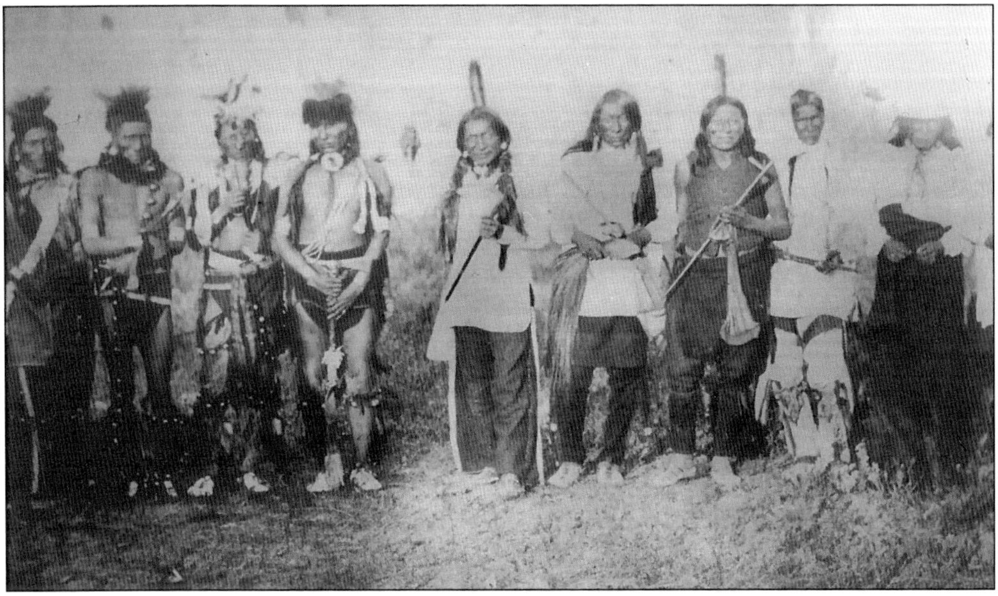

Pictured are young men preparing to participate in the celebration. (Photograph courtesy of the National Park Service, Little Bighorn Battlefield National Monument.)

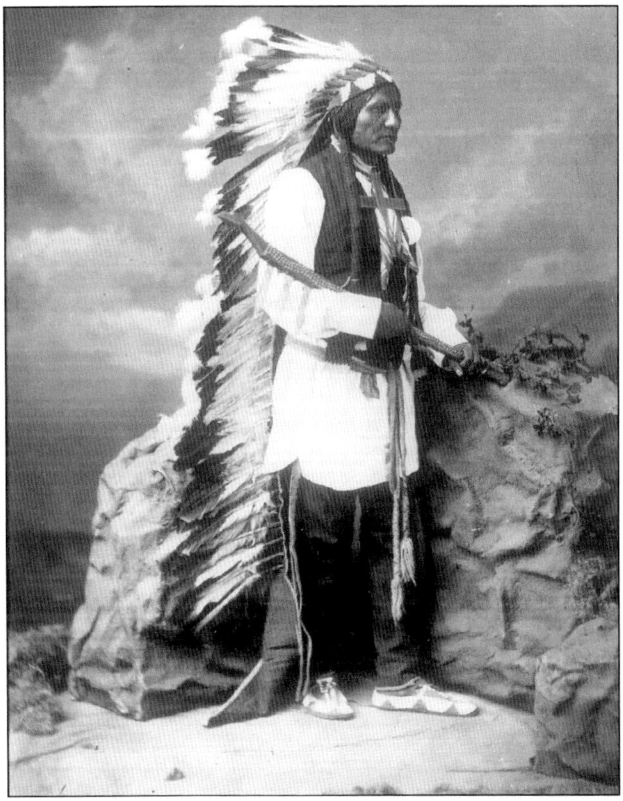

Pictured here is Shunka-Bloka, He Dog, a noble Oglala. His magnificent headdress was a symbol of bravery and importance. (Photograph courtesy of Fort Peck Tribal Archives.)

The Oglala ceremonial rite as part of the Sun Dance has Slow Bull, fire-carrier, lifting the skull from the dry, grassy plains. (Photograph courtesy of Fort Peck Tribal Archives.)

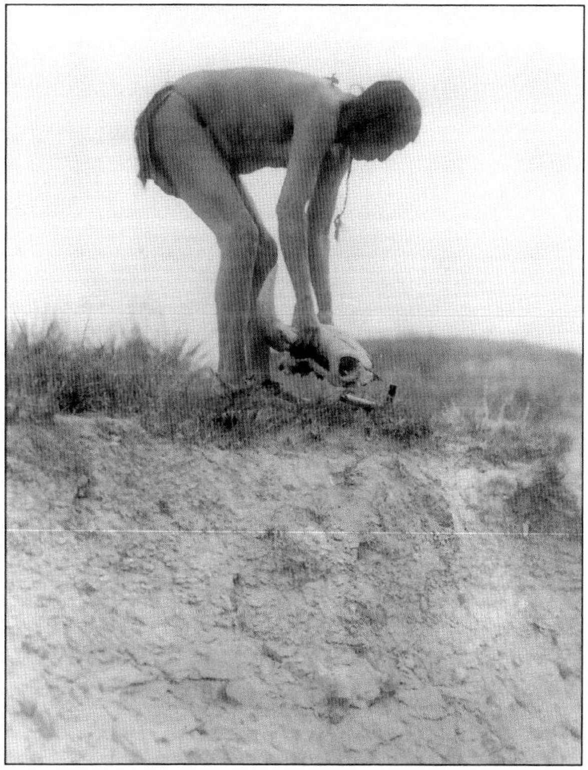

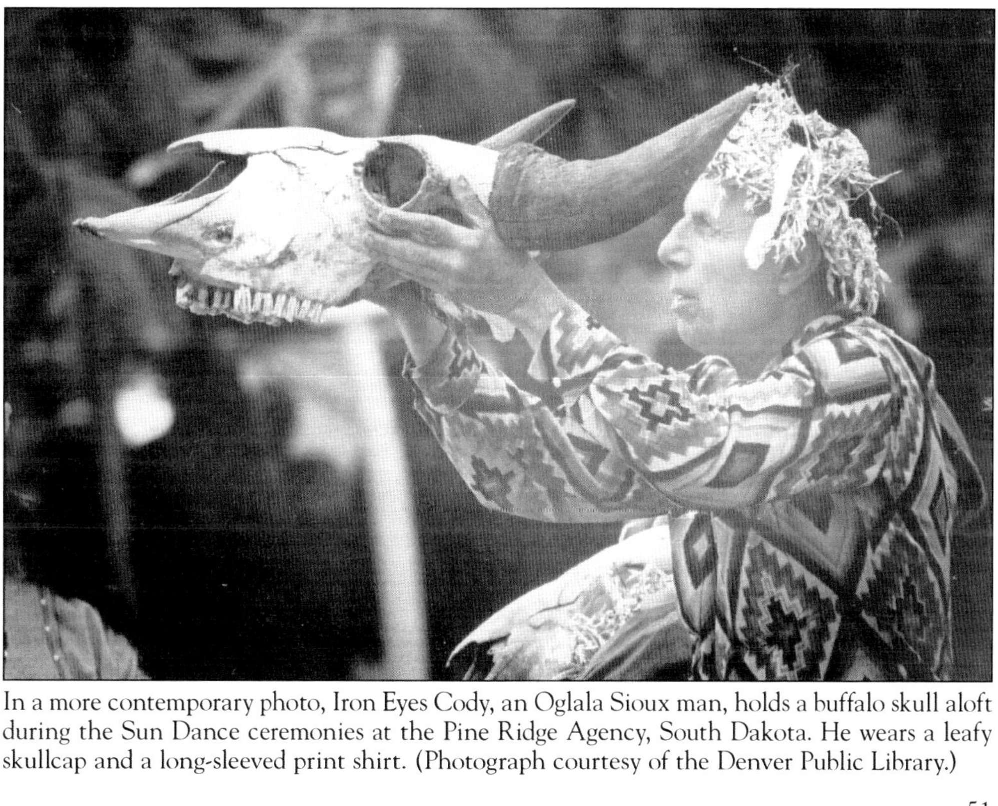

In a more contemporary photo, Iron Eyes Cody, an Oglala Sioux man, holds a buffalo skull aloft during the Sun Dance ceremonies at the Pine Ridge Agency, South Dakota. He wears a leafy skullcap and a long-sleeved print shirt. (Photograph courtesy of the Denver Public Library.)

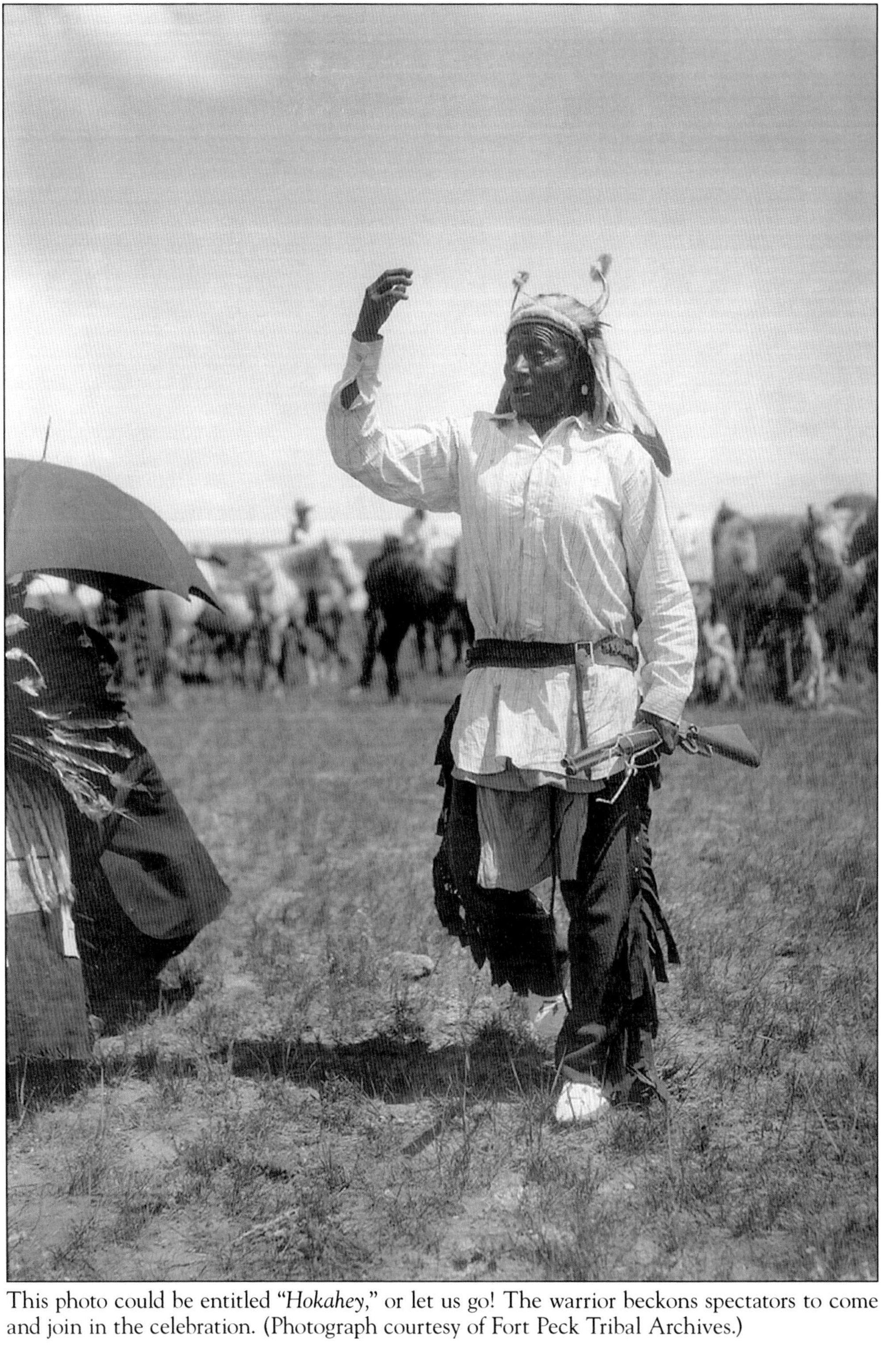

This photo could be entitled "*Hokahey*," or let us go! The warrior beckons spectators to come and join in the celebration. (Photograph courtesy of Fort Peck Tribal Archives.)

Pictured is *Mato wakan*, or Medicine Bear, also known as Medicine Bear Track. He was a member of the Cut Head Band of the Yanktonai. (Photograph courtesy of Fort Peck Tribal Archives.)

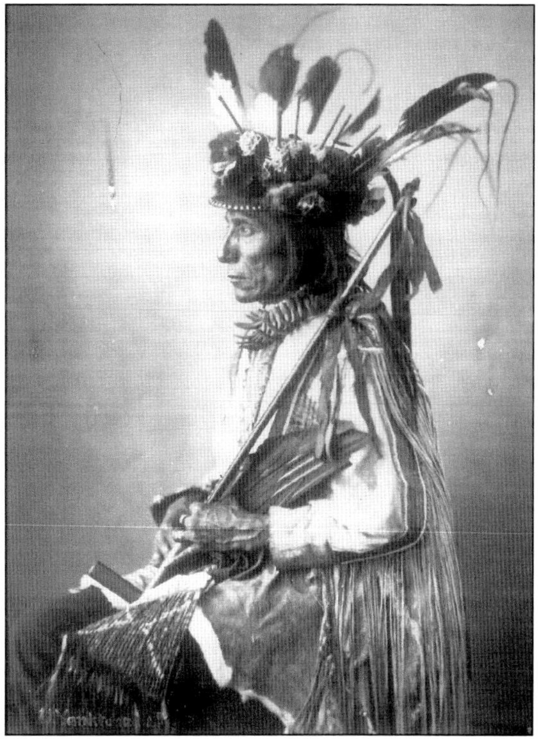

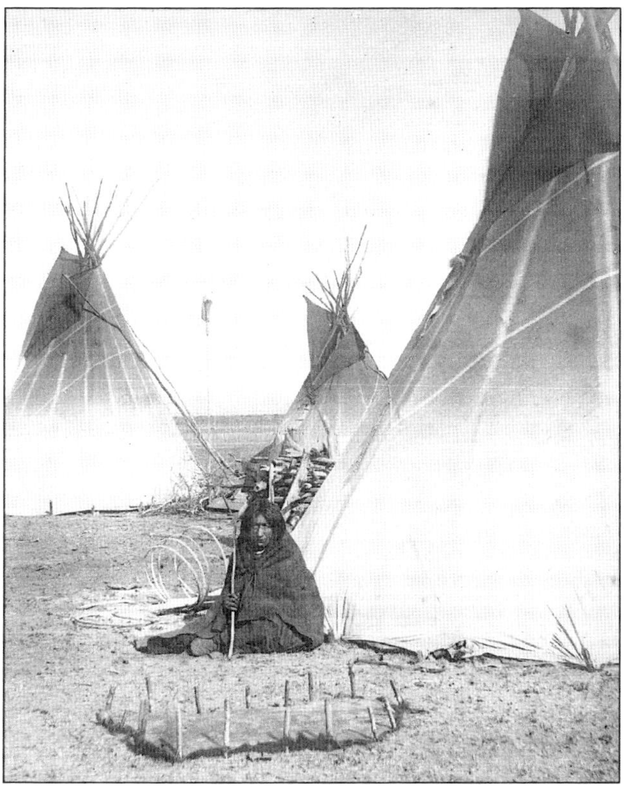

An elderly Dakota woman sits in front. Nearby is an animal skin staked for tanning. This is the largest tipi, called the medicine tipi, belonging to the medicine man. Here the people would assemble in the evenings. Singing and dancing occurred until the medicine man, who sits by the side of a drum, calls out that he has made his medicine, 'in thoughts,' and they can retire to their lodges to await the morning dawn. (Photograph courtesy of the Denver Public Library.)

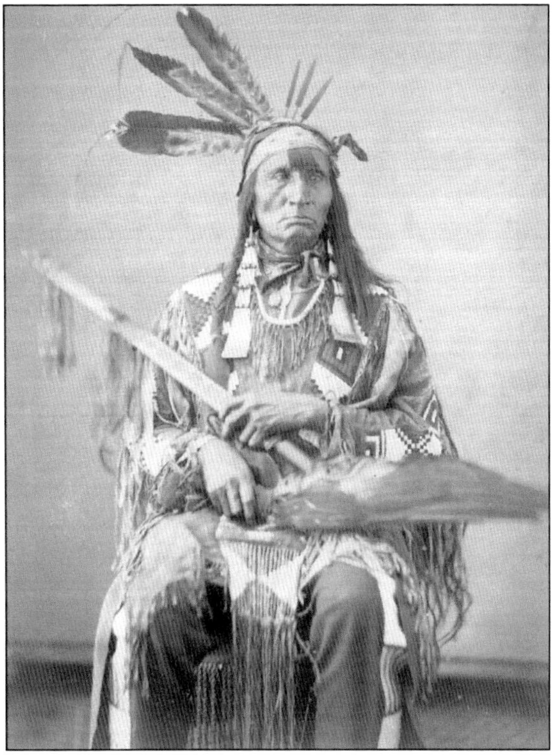

Seated in this portrait is a Hunkpapa, Walking Shooter. He wears three eagle feathers and three arrows attached to a scarf around his head, long metal earrings, a kerchief, a fringed buckskin shirt with beaded bands, a fringed breechcloth, and leggings. In one hand he holds a fan of feathers, in the other hand is a sword with a decorated sheath. (Photograph courtesy of the Denver Public Library.)

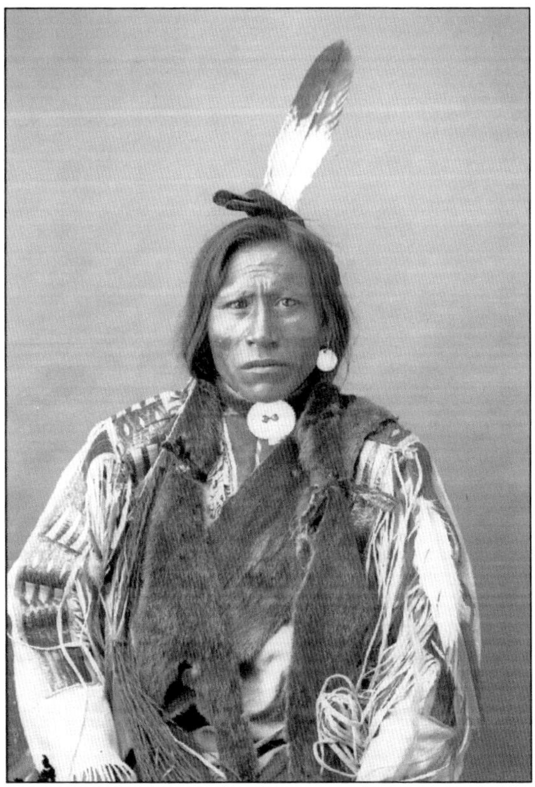

Frisking Elk, a Dakota, wears one feather in his hair, one earring, and a necklace. The braids are wrapped in fur, with a fur sash, and the embroidered shirt has fringed sleeves. (Photograph courtesy of the Denver Public Library.)

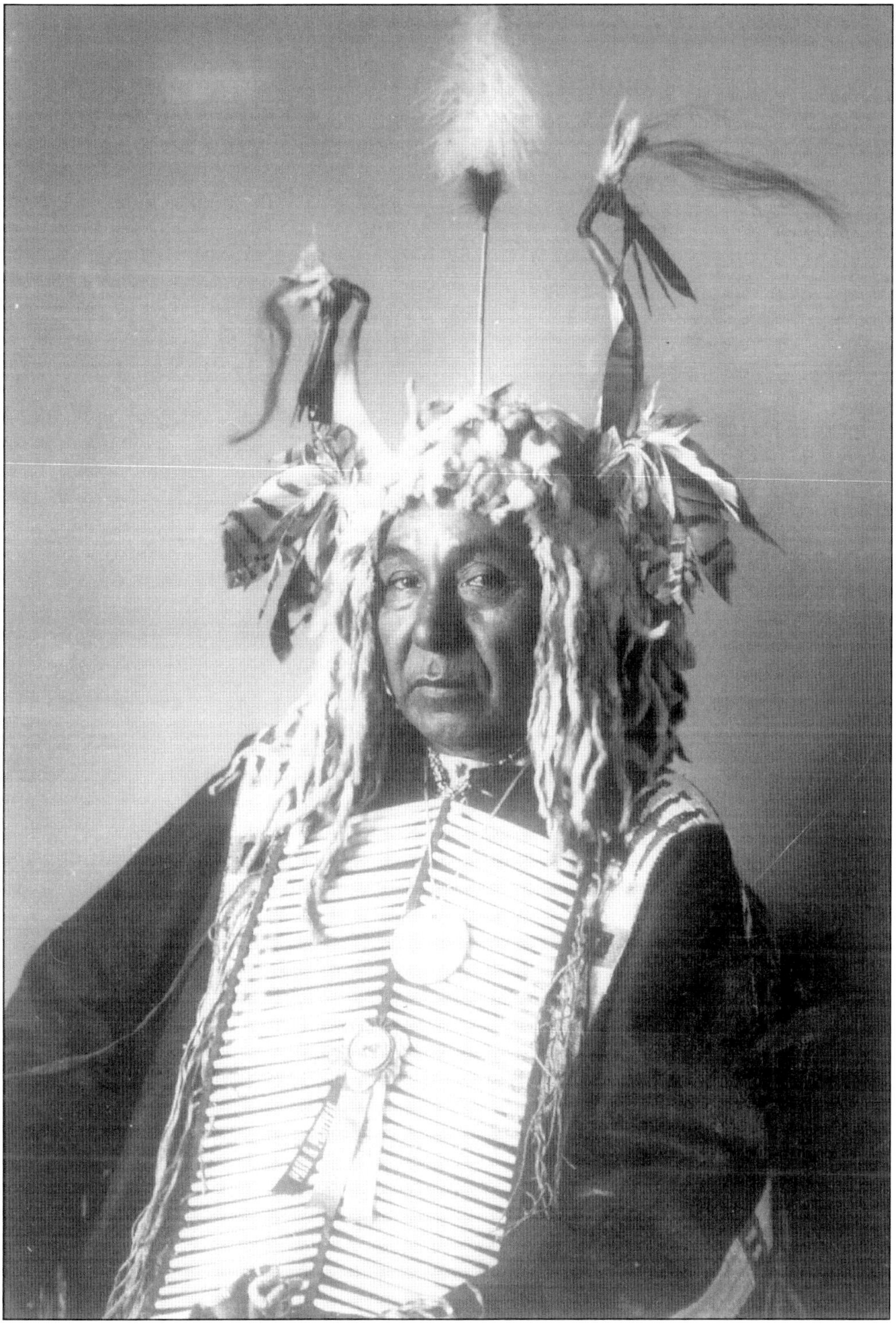

Pictured here is Yellow Earth, also known as John Lone Dog. (Photograph courtesy of Fort Peck Tribal Archives.)

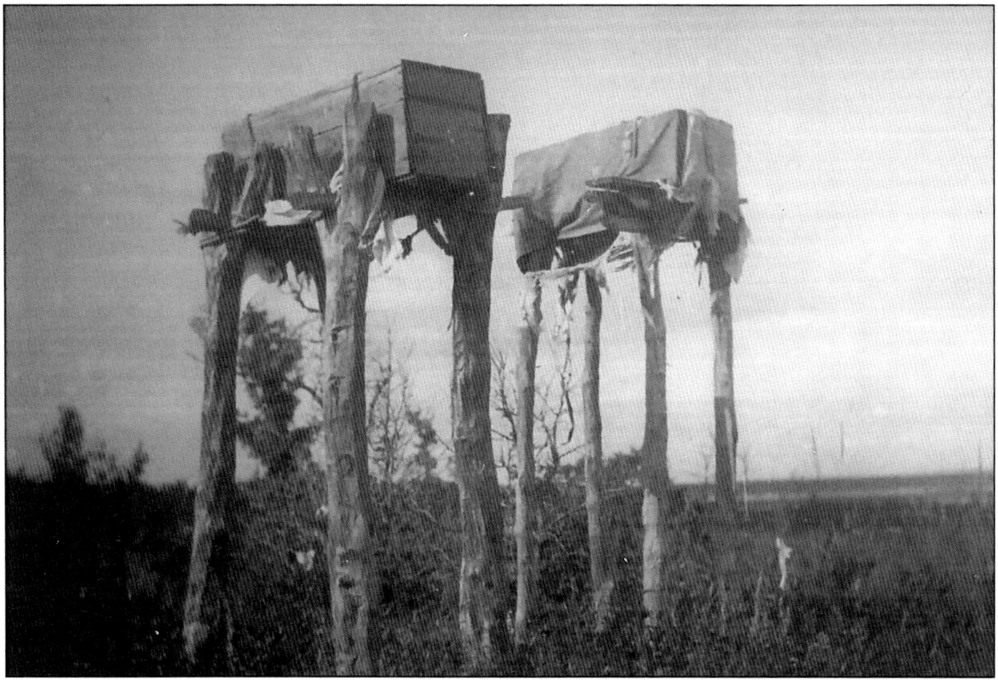

Life and death were part of the never-ending circle, just as the sun rose and set. Life continued after death. The dead were not buried under ground. They were placed upon high scaffolds where their spirits could escape into the spirit world. (Photograph courtesy of the National Park Service, Little Bighorn Battlefield National Monument.)

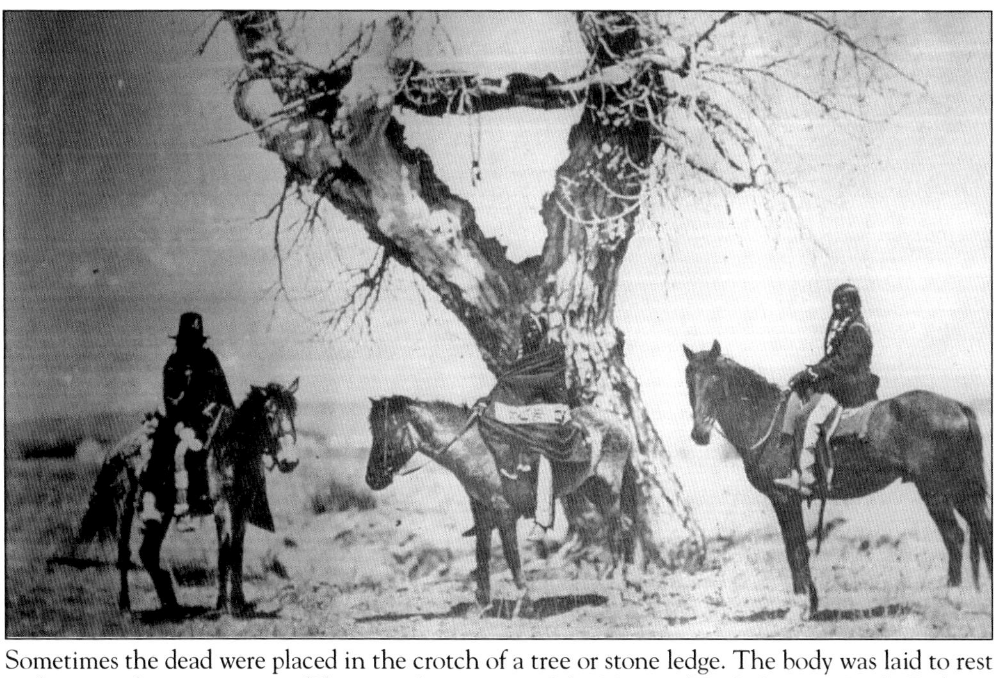

Sometimes the dead were placed in the crotch of a tree or stone ledge. The body was laid to rest with some of its possessions. (Photograph courtesy of the National Park Service, Little Bighorn Battlefield National Monument.)

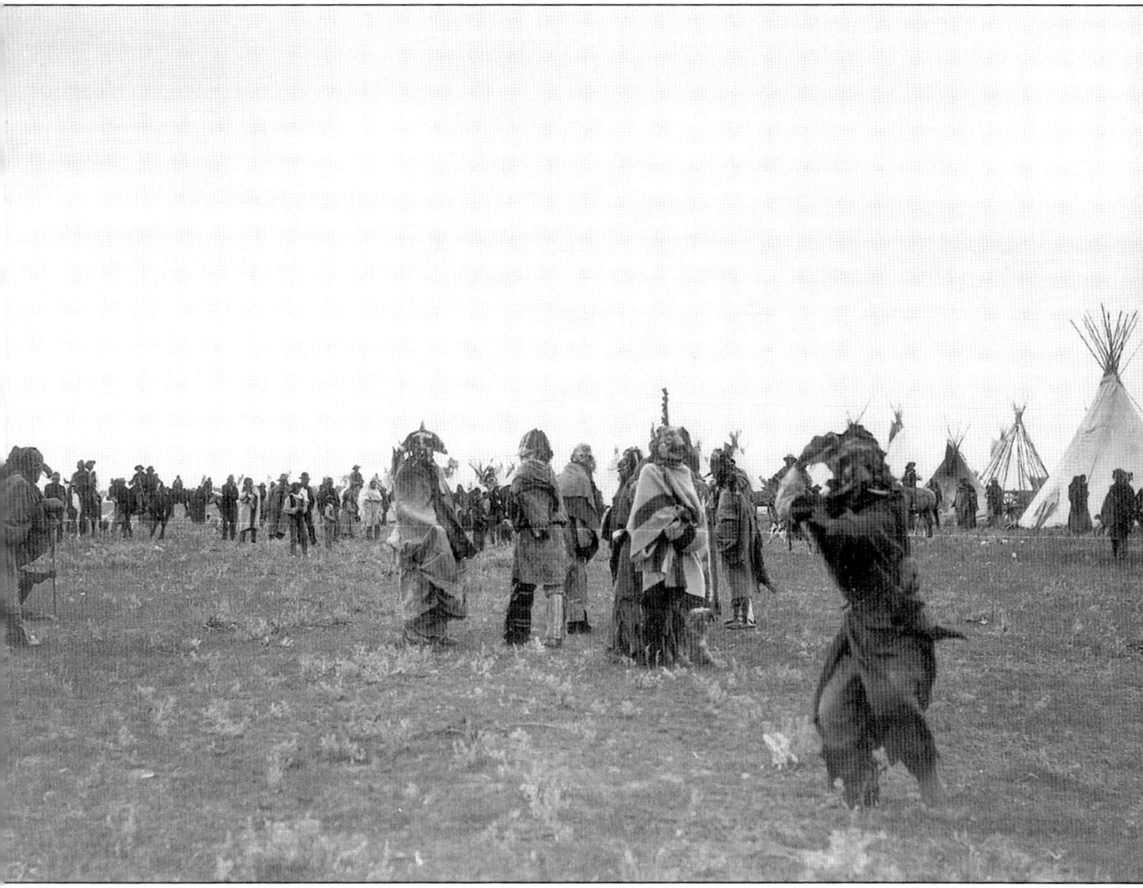

The Heyoka Society was a group for holy men. Members dressed in this fashion to perform certain rites. It is believed by the Indian people that they possess certain powers. (Photograph courtesy of Fort Peck Tribal Archives.)

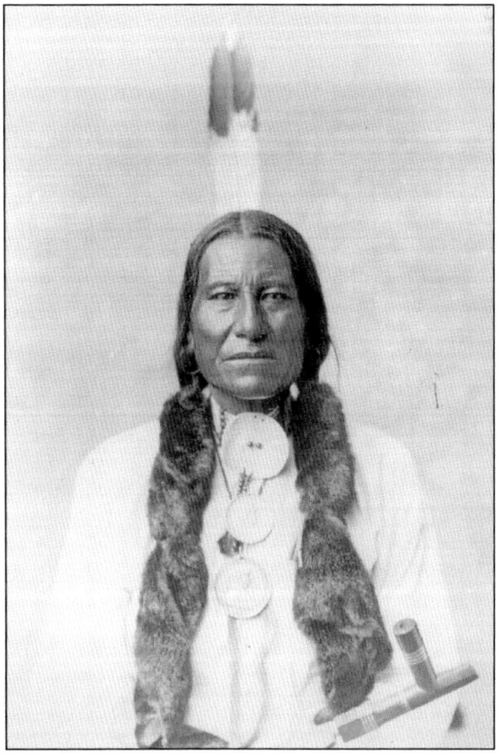

This is a photograph of White Ghost, a member of the Yanktonai band. (Photograph courtesy of Fort Peck Tribal Archives.)

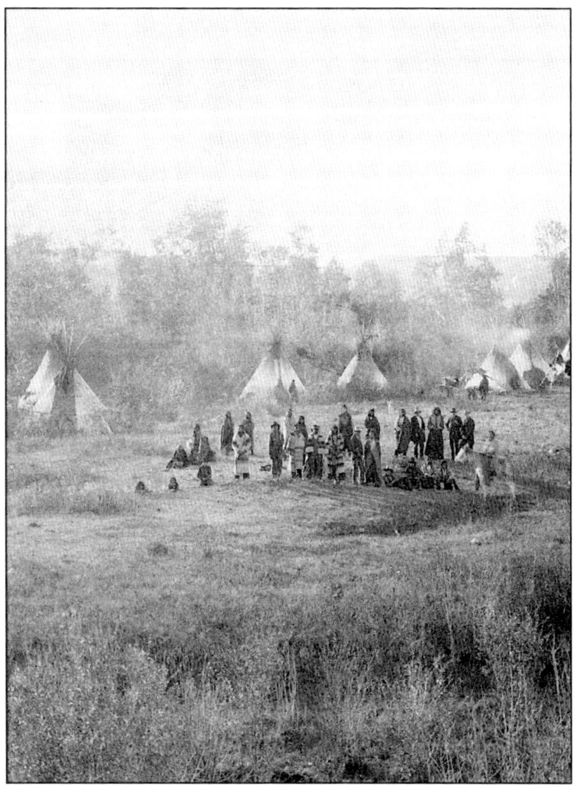

Distant view of Sioux gathered at the bottom of a hill near lodges. (Photograph courtesy of the Denver Public Library.)

Spotted Eagle, medicine man of the Sans Arc Sioux, wears a buffalo cape, metal arm bands, feathers, and a fur hat with horns. He carries a hoop, has white lines painted on his face, and shell disks on his forehead. People in the background include men with feather headdresses. (Photograph courtesy of the Denver Public Library.)

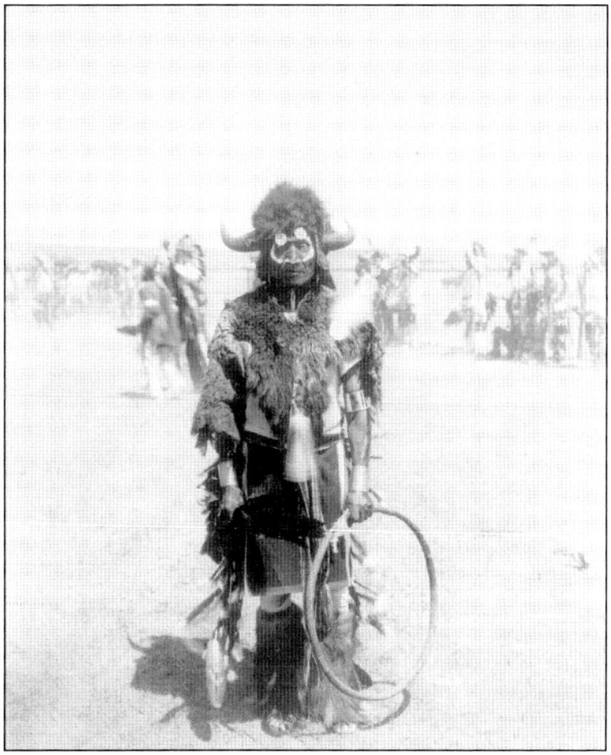

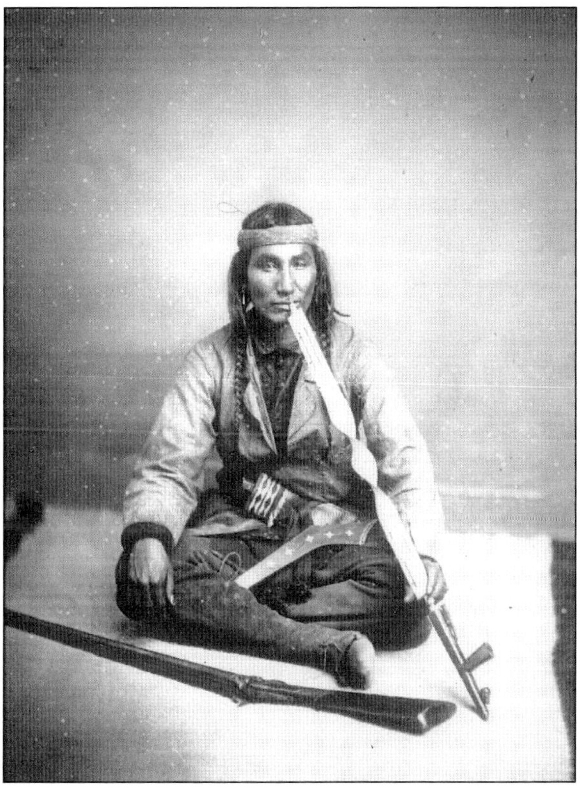

Pictured here is a Santee Sioux sitting with a ceremonial pipe, club, knife in a sheath, and rifle. He wears a headband, checked jacket, leggings, and moccasins. (Photograph courtesy of the Denver Public Library.)

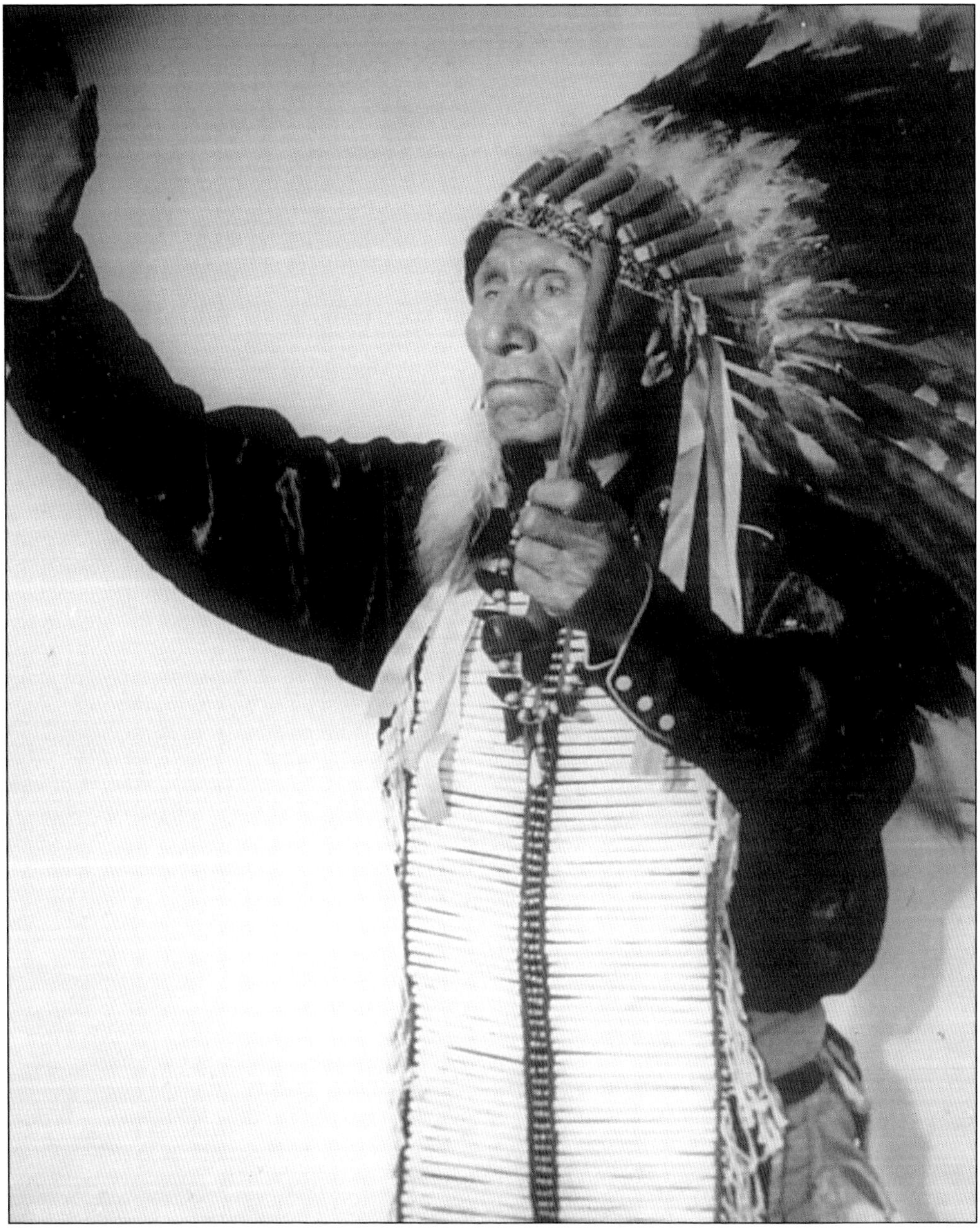

Pictured here is *Hehaka Sapa*, Black Elk, a Holy Man of the Oglala Sioux, who was 13 years old during the Tiospaye encampment at the Little Bighorn. Black Elk's father and Crazy Horse's father were cousins, having the same grandfather. Black Elk's concern for the vanishing Sioux culture and the preservation of the rites and ceremonies of his people led him to assist in the writing of several texts on the subject.

In remote parts of the world remain hidden things. Civilizations containing natural wealth and wonders lie concealed from scholars. These cryptic treasures await discovery, hopeful that learned man will interpret them to enrich the heritage of humanity and reveal extensive knowledge of a people past. (Photograph courtesy of the National Park Service, Little Bighorn Battlefield National Monument.)

Four

The Silent Strength of Winyan (Women)

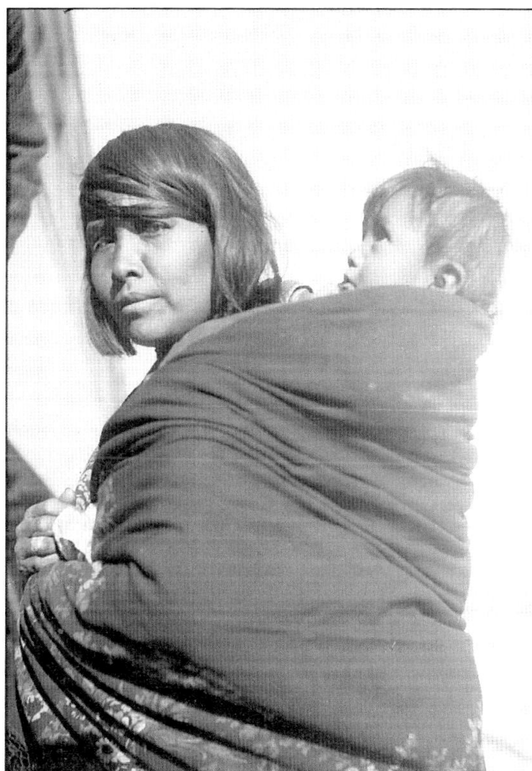

For this spiritual account to be considered complete, words must be said about the important role women had in the life of their tribe. The Dakota word for woman, common to many dialects, is *Winyan*. The tribes traveled in bands and they were a family. Striving and living off the land, they only took what was needed. They always offered thanks and supplication to the Great Creator for all things.

Since the format of this book focuses on pictures rather than words, this chapter presents a photographic portrayal of the Indian woman's provision of clothing and shelter, child rearing, and the preparation of food for her family. In this photograph, a Dakota woman has her baby safely wrapped in a blanket on her back. (Photograph courtesy of the Denver Public Library.)

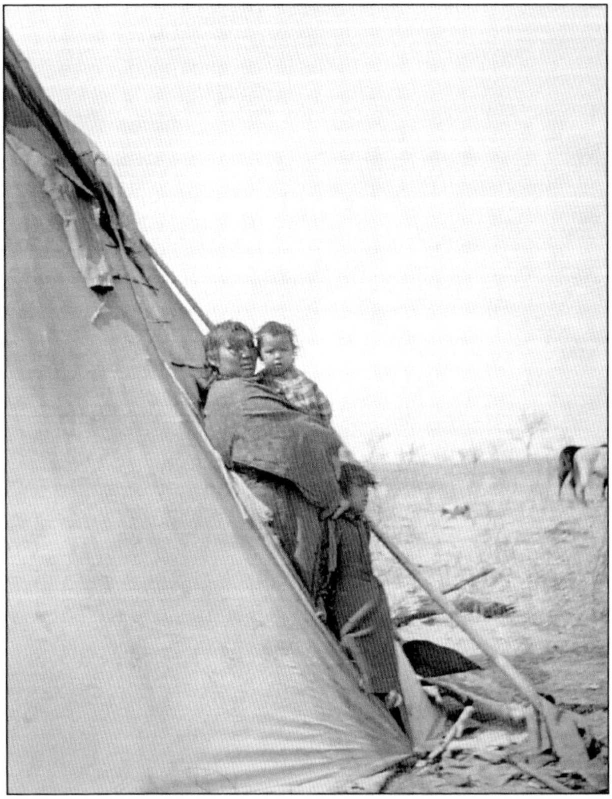

Raising children was a primary responsibility of women. It was helpful to busy mothers that child raising was an extended-family affair. Here, a woman stands near the entrance to a tipi with two children. She holds one wrapped in a blanket shawl. The other child is wrapped in a blanket. Two horses and a dog stand in the distance. (Photograph courtesy of the Denver Public Library.)

A woman and child sit inside a brush-covered summer shelter. The woman holds a large piece of cloth, and the child looks at an animal hide. Hides, a blanket, and other fur pelts lie on the floor. Others hang from a wooden pole placed horizontally along the brush-covered walls of the shelter. (Photograph courtesy of the Denver Public Library.)

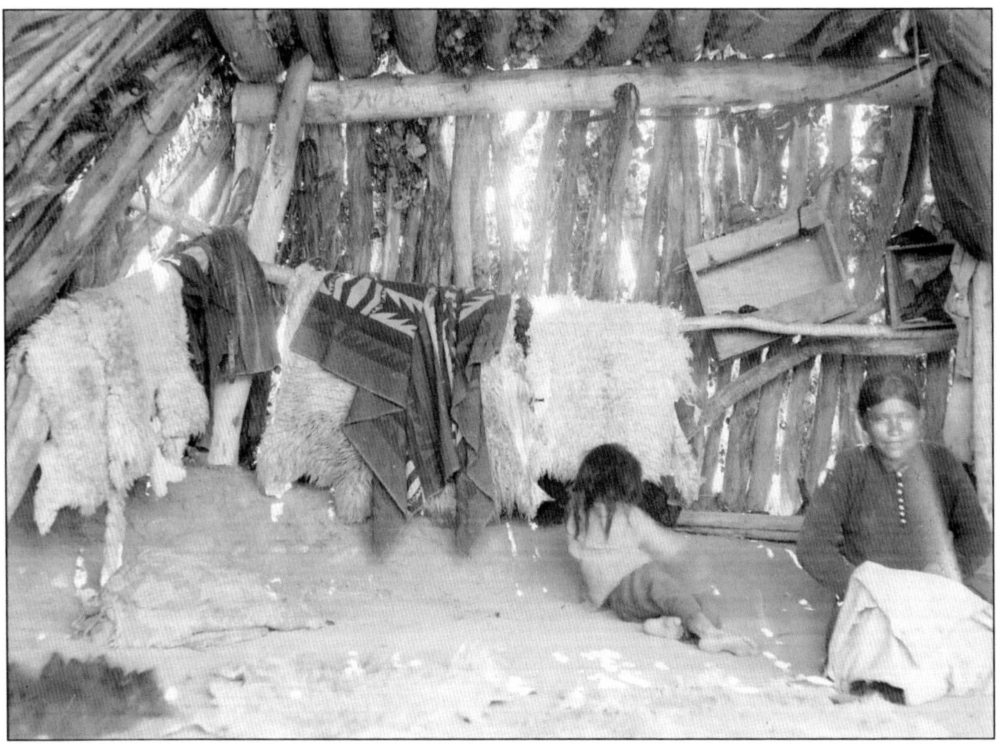

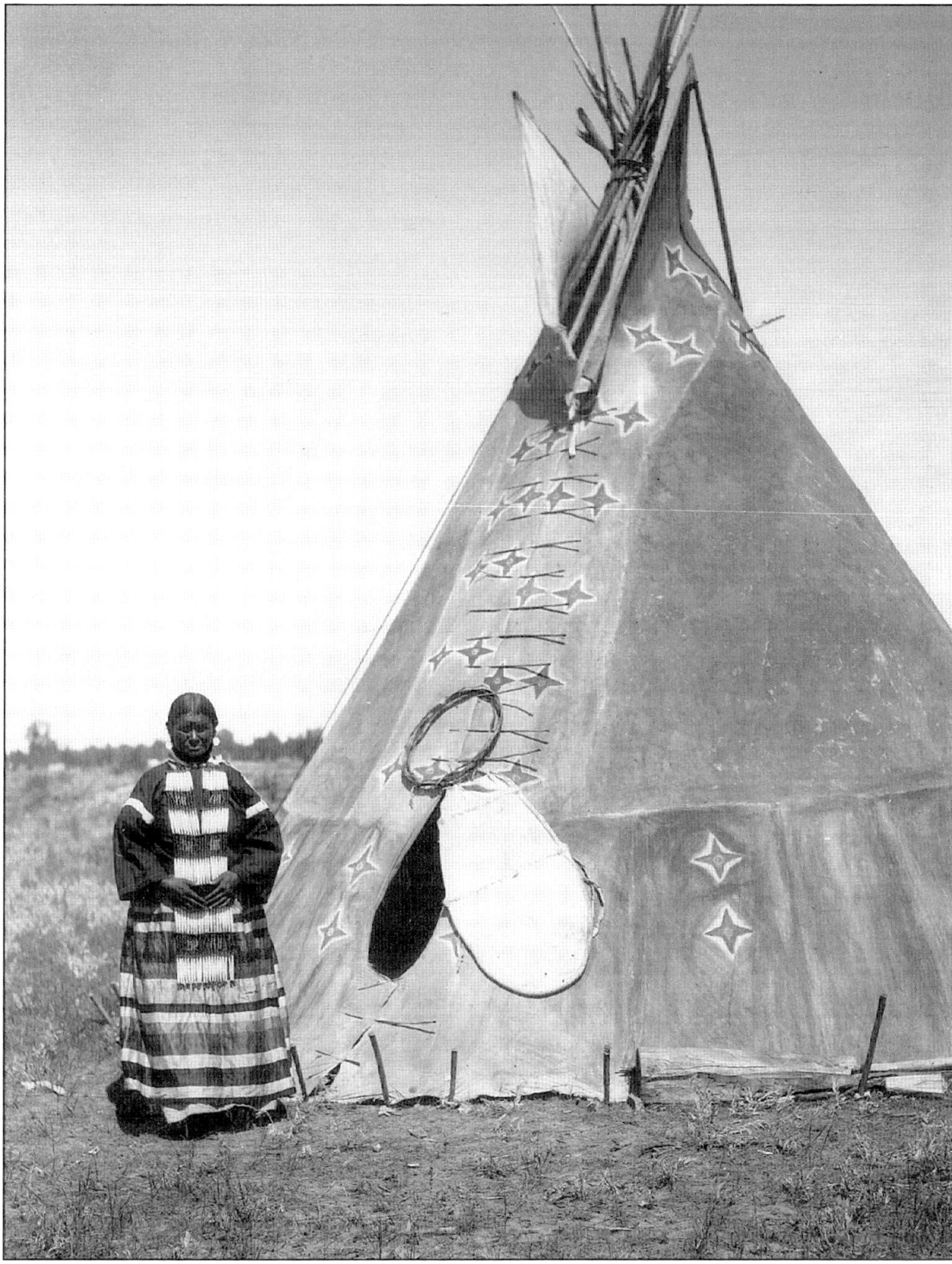

It was the last of the month of June, the time of the "Moon" for the women. A change occurs that no man breaches. A woman was regarded as very powerful during that time and remained in the lodge alone, in peace, for the duration of that time. Recalling Sitting Bull's prophecy, he saw many soldiers falling head first into camp. They were invading a sacred place and time for the women. The men were out hunting or gathering certain objects for worship, collecting sage, sweetgrass, and stones for the *Inipi*, the sweat bath. Sitting Bull saw the soldiers falling into camp, where the women were. He saw a camp with lodges, not a battlefield. (Photograph courtesy of Fort Peck Tribal Archives.)

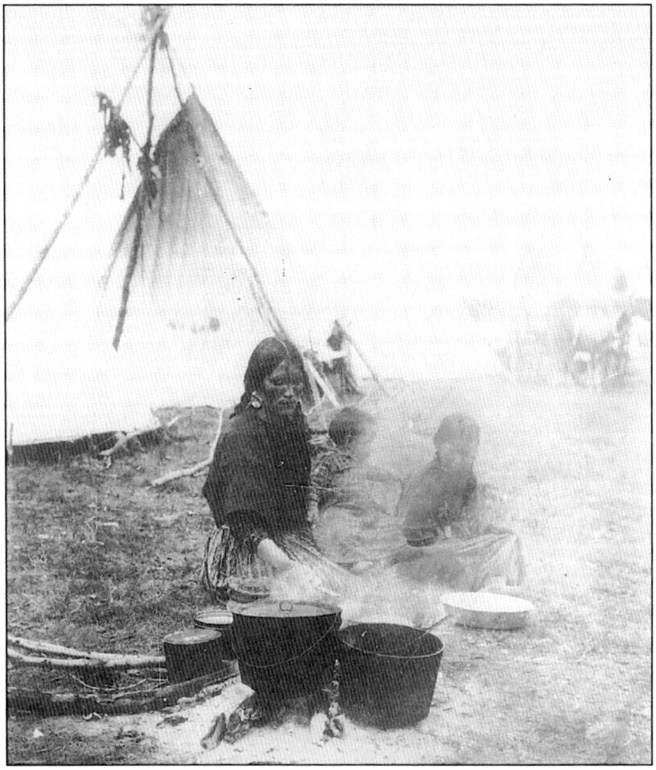

Indian women centered their lives around food, clothing, and shelter. A woman sits on the ground in front of a tipi and tends cooking pots on an open fire. She holds an infant in her lap, and another child sits next to her. (Photograph courtesy of the Denver Public Library.)

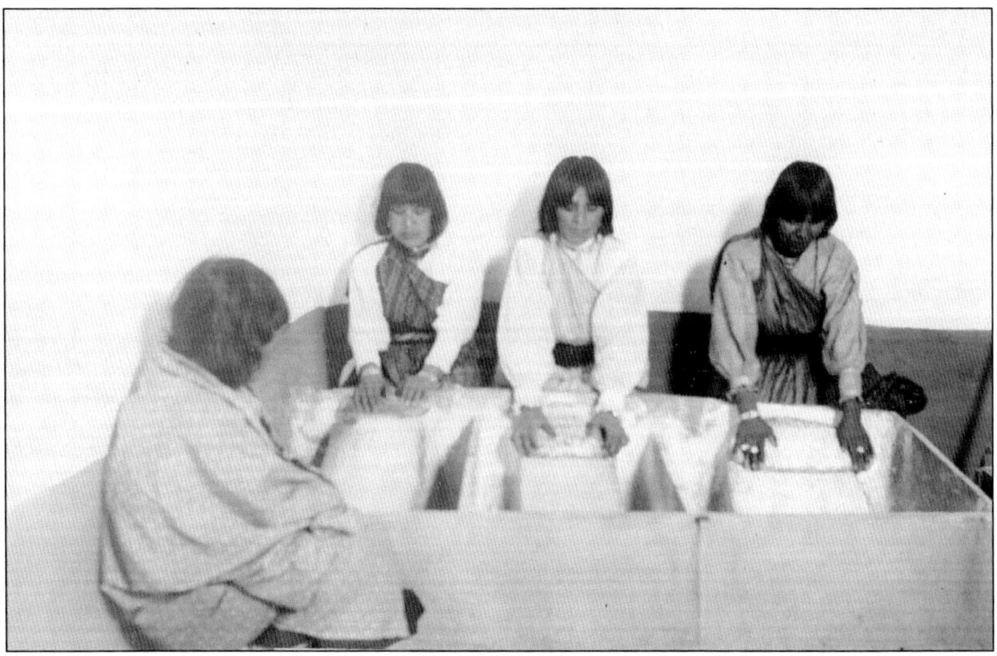

The Indian woman's role was less glamorous than that of the beautifully dressed warrior. She spent much of her time with the older women learning her responsibilities and perfecting her skills. A young girl learned to do all these things well so she could become a good wife and mother. (Photograph courtesy of the Denver Public Library.)

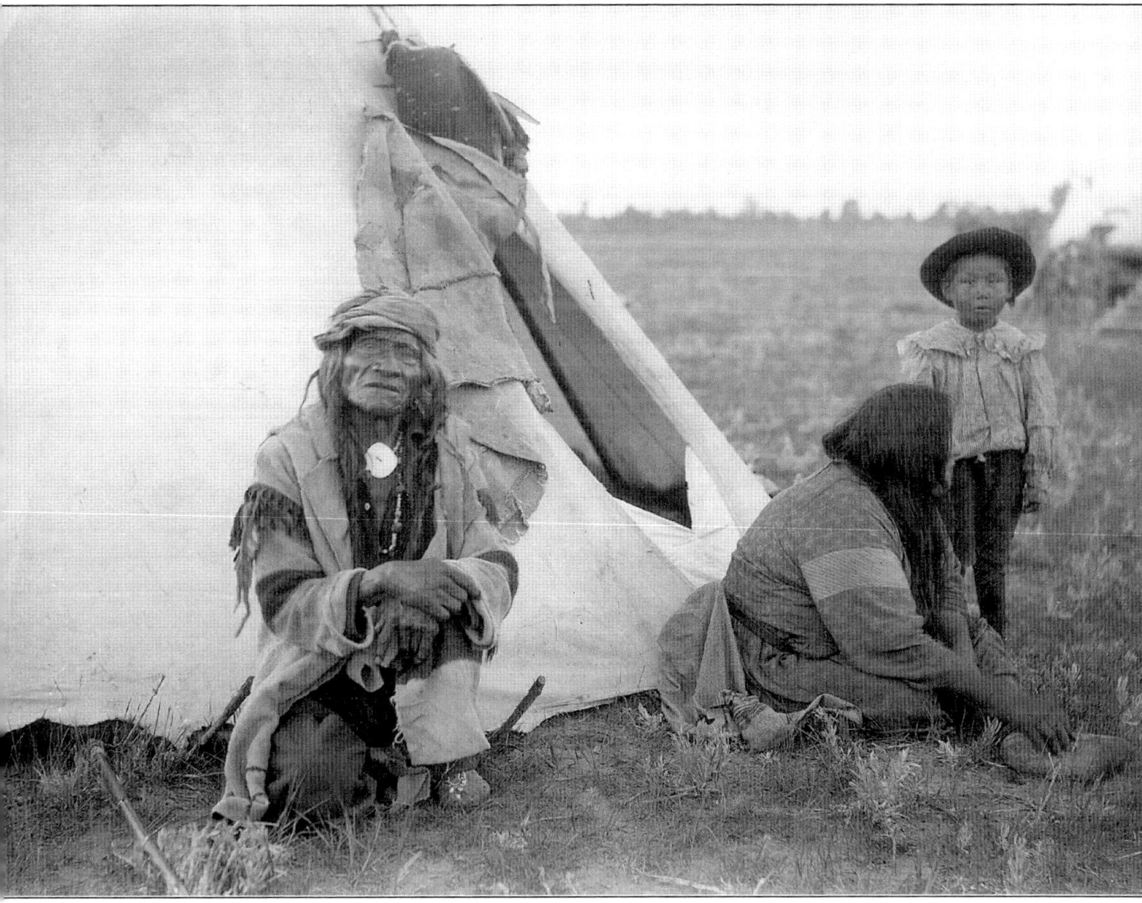

In the social structure of the tribe, the contributions of the women proved a valuable asset. The women knew their responsibilities and considered them essential to the welfare of their people. Women also helped with arranging marriages, consulting on peace and war, leading special ceremonies, and directing tribe movements. (Photograph courtesy of Fort Peck Tribal Archives.)

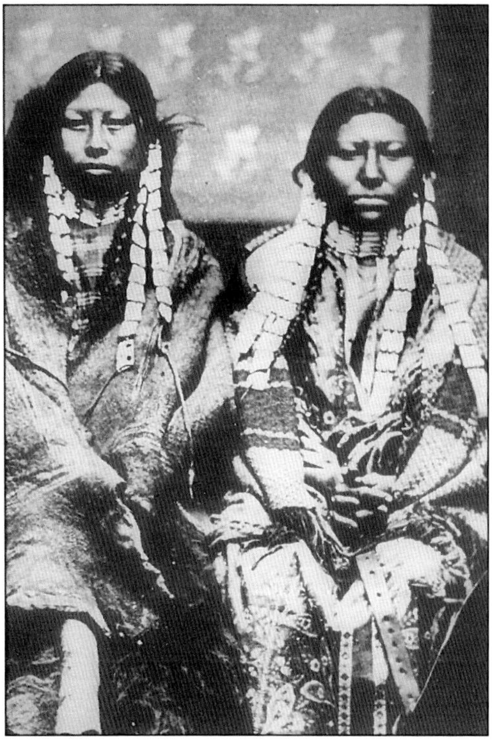

Often history does not fully comprehend the honor, status, and wealth accorded Indian women for their industry and expertise. Nor does it recognize the less visible powers that involved the silent strengths women contributed to the survival of their people. (Photograph courtesy of the National Park Service, Little Bighorn Battlefield National Monument.)

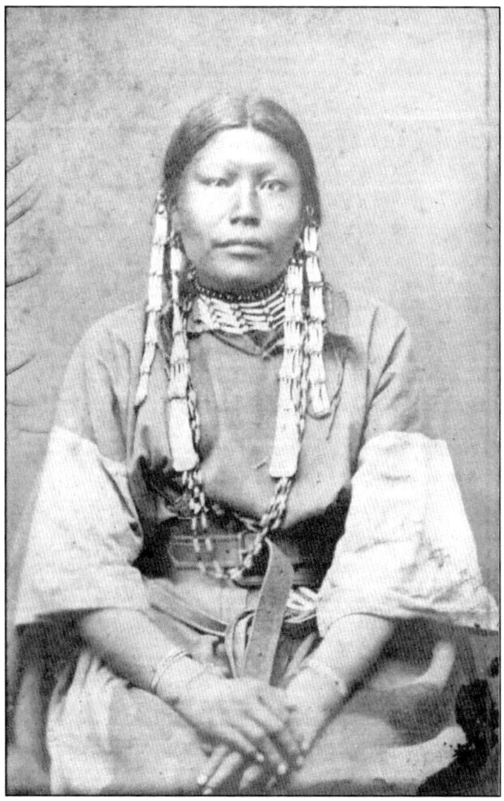

Here is a portrait of a Dakota Sioux woman wearing a dress with a leather belt, bracelets, a hair bone choker, and earrings. In the life of the tribe, women were highly respected and although they had no active role in the government of the tribe, their opinion, especially that of the elderly, was sought and heeded. (Photograph courtesy of the Denver Public Library.)

An Indian woman sits on horseback in front of a tipi. A small child rests in a cradleboard adorned with beaded flowers on the side of the horse. Cradleboards were a functional way of carrying babies. They could be stood up against rocks or trees, attached to saddles for easy transport, or worn on one's back. They protectively restrained children while a woman worked. This woman wears a patterned scarf tied around her head and has a plaid, wool blanket wrapped around her legs. She sits on a striped, wool blanket. (Photograph courtesy of the Denver Public Library.)

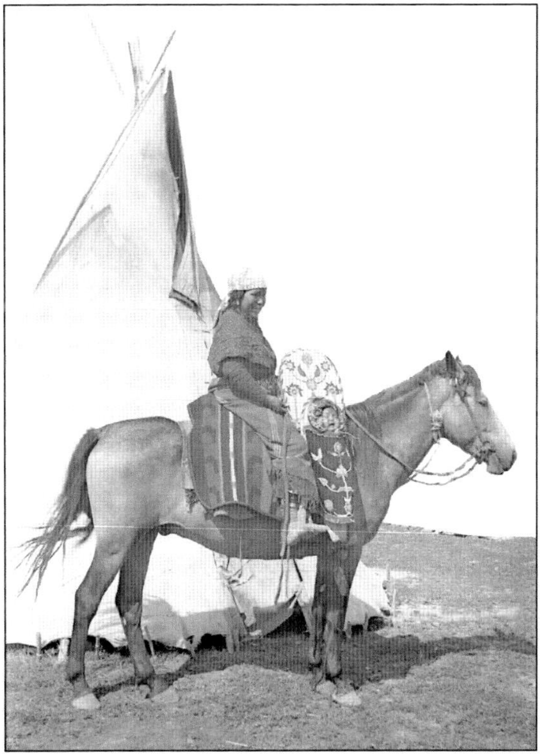

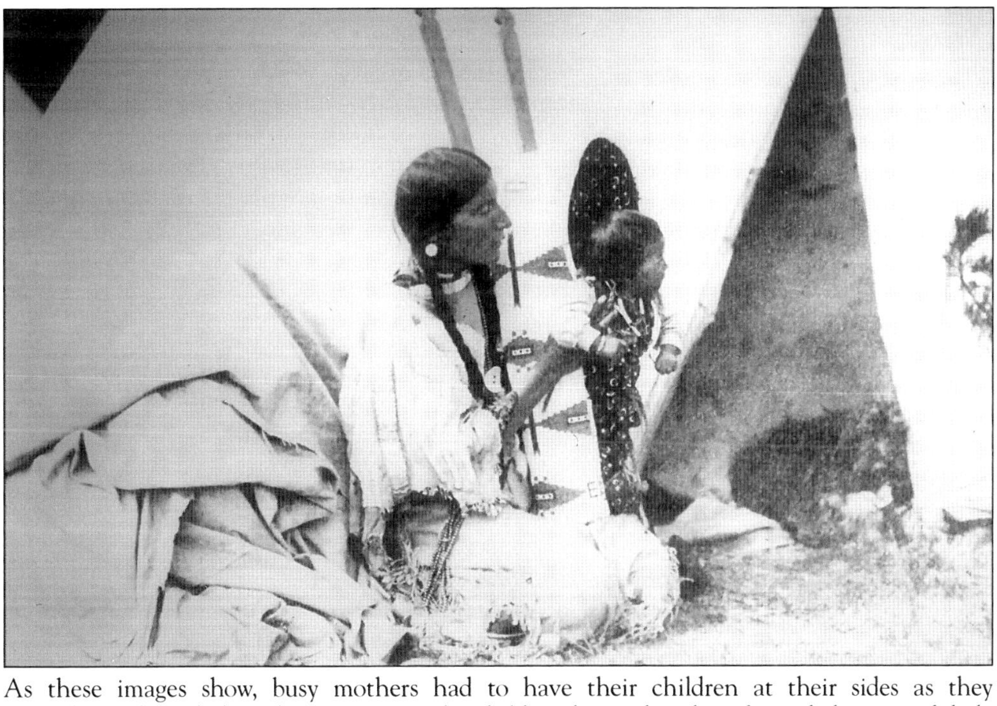

As these images show, busy mothers had to have their children at their sides as they carried out their daily tasks. Consequently, children learned and performed the arts of daily living at an early age. (Photograph courtesy of the National Park Service, Little Bighorn Battlefield National Monument.)

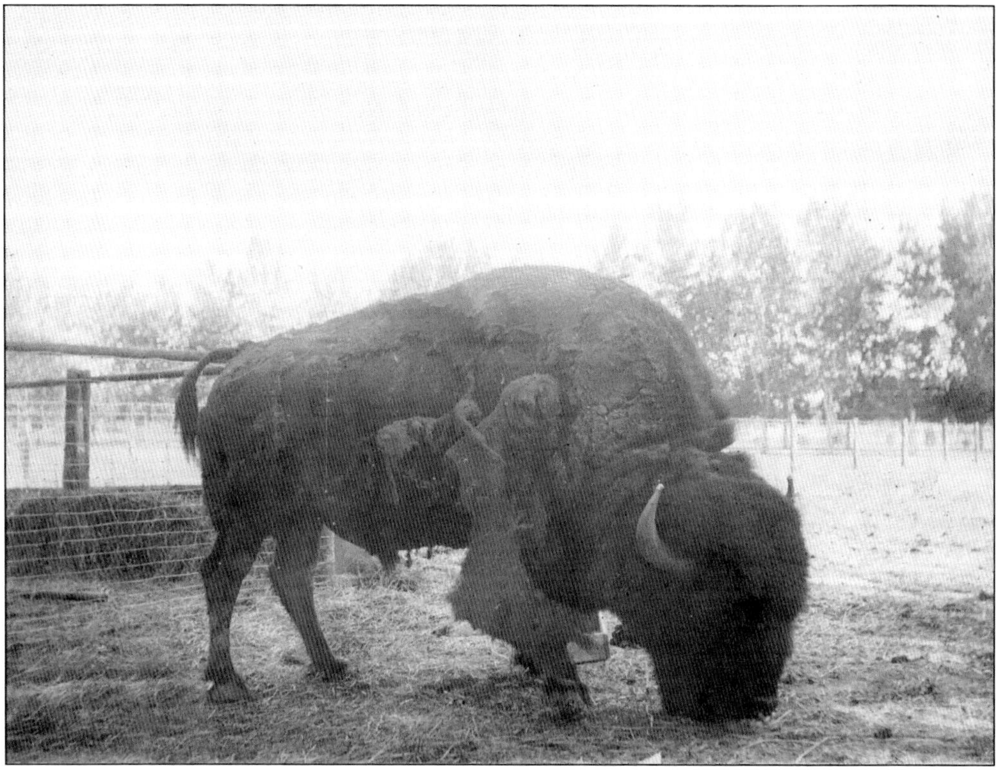

Women were responsible for butchering the buffalo and other game, and then dressing the hides. (Photograph courtesy of the Denver Public Library.)

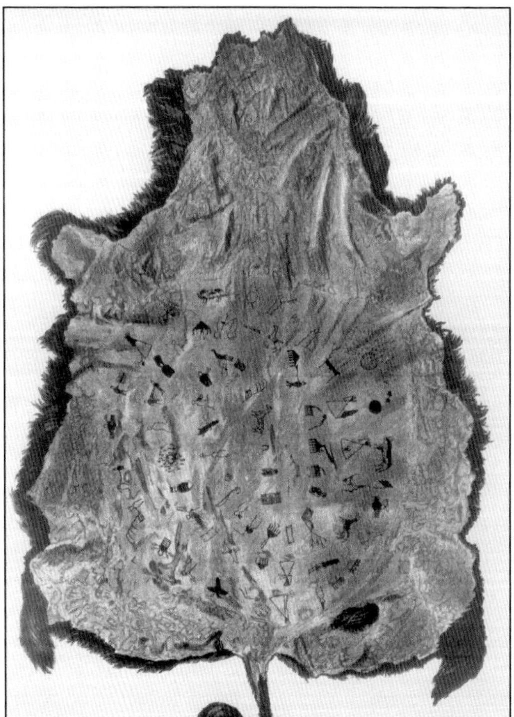

Shown here is a buffalo hide belonging to Lone Dog, dating from c. 1800. Paint marks are those of Lone Dog's "Winter Count." This is a pictorial record of events that happened to the tribe, including a record of births and deaths. (Photograph courtesy of Fort Peck Tribal Archives.)

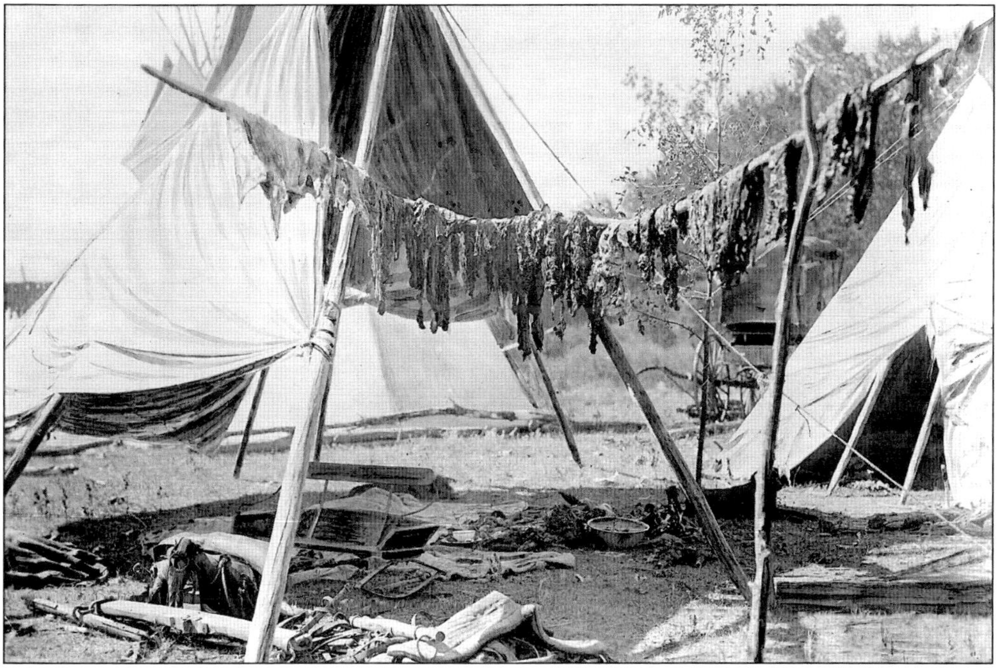

Women of the buffalo-hunting tribes made full use of the animals hunted. They skinned and scraped a hide while it was warm. Then they stripped the meat and set it out to dry. A proficient woman could process three buffalo a day totaling 300 pounds of dried meat and pemmican. Pemmican, sun-dried meat used by the Dakota, is shown hanging in strips on a crossbar supported by two timber stands. (Photograph courtesy of the Denver Public Library.)

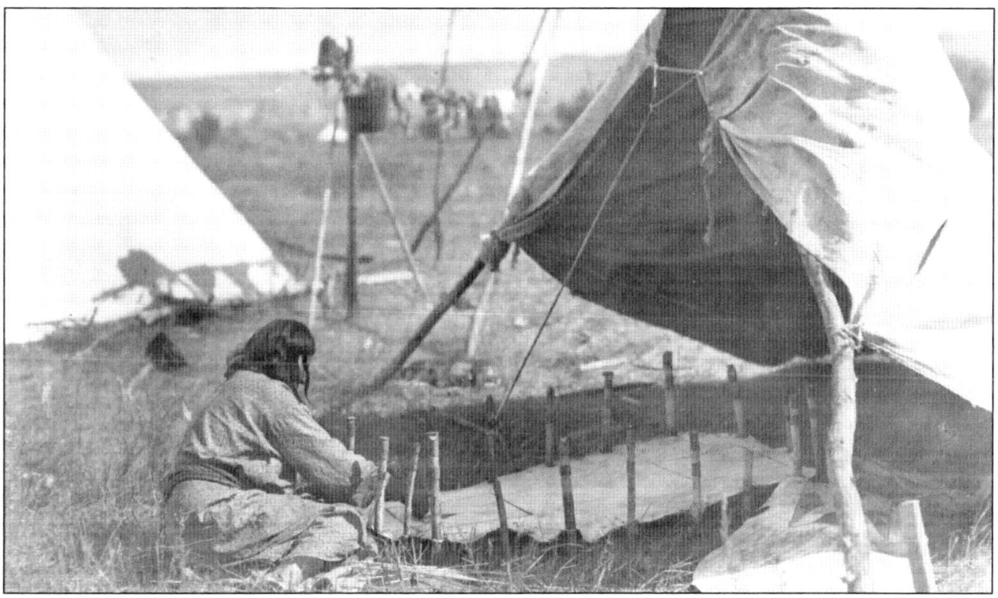

This is a view of a woman wearing a long dress and sitting on the ground as she paints an animal hide. The hide is secured to the ground by stakes and lies in shade created by a canvas covered frame. A tipi, tipi frames, and a drying rack with furs draped over it are nearby. (Photograph courtesy of the Denver Public Library.)

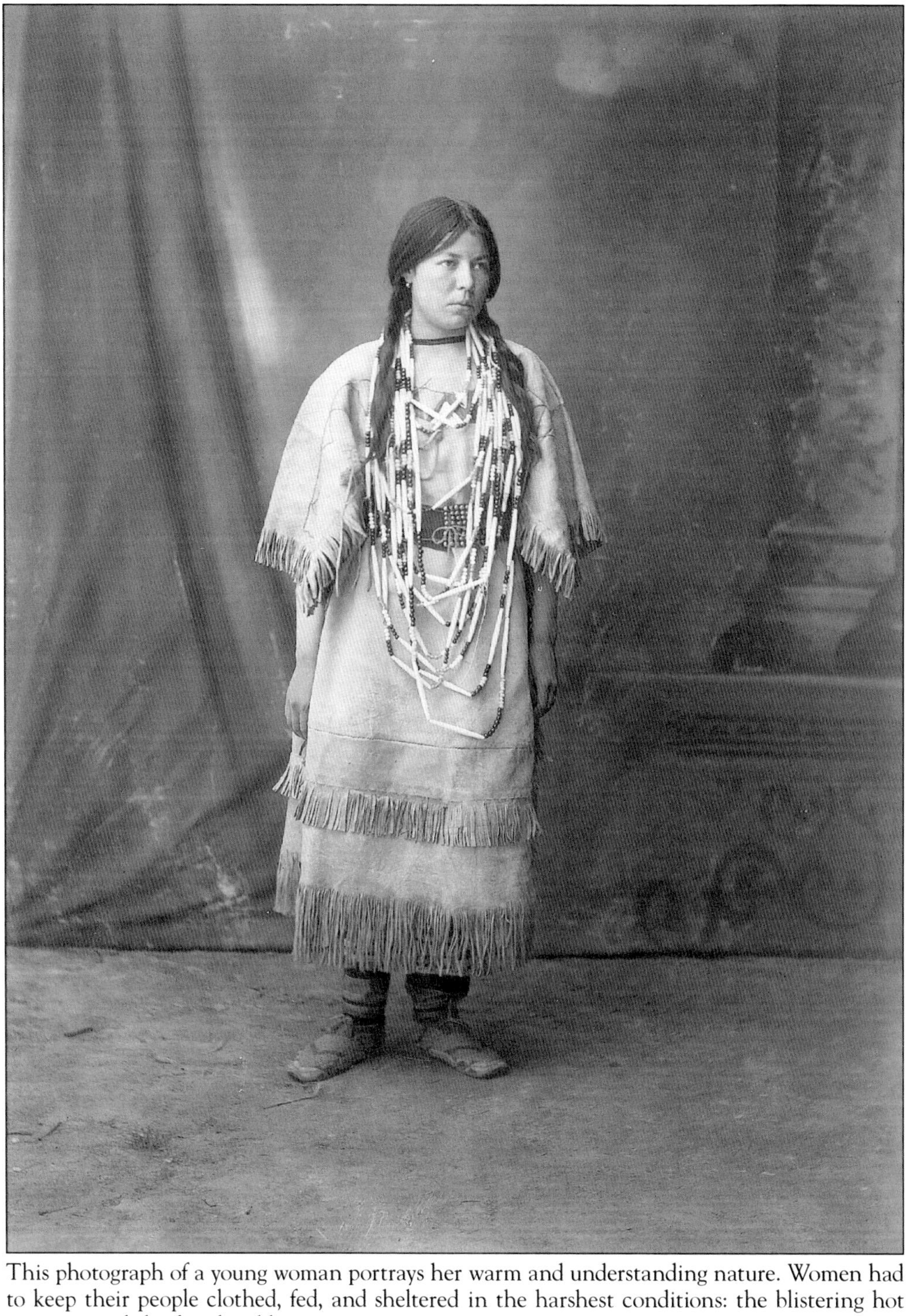

This photograph of a young woman portrays her warm and understanding nature. Women had to keep their people clothed, fed, and sheltered in the harshest conditions: the blistering hot summers and the frigid, cold winters.

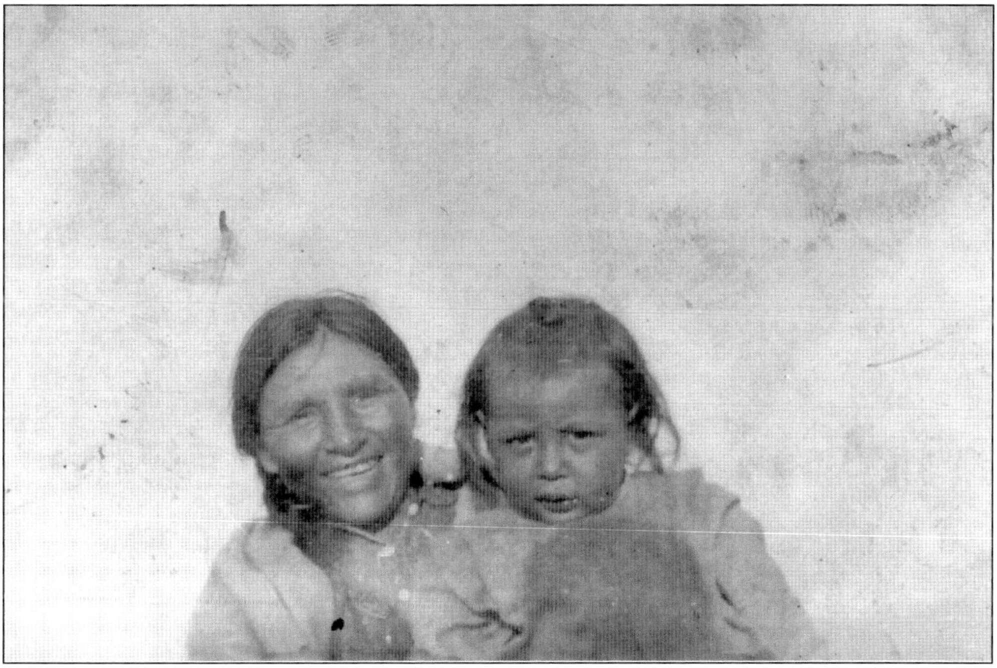

Grandmothers directly participated in child-rearing, teaching morals, tribe histories, and sacred ceremonial rituals. (Photograph courtesy of Fort Peck Tribal Archives.)

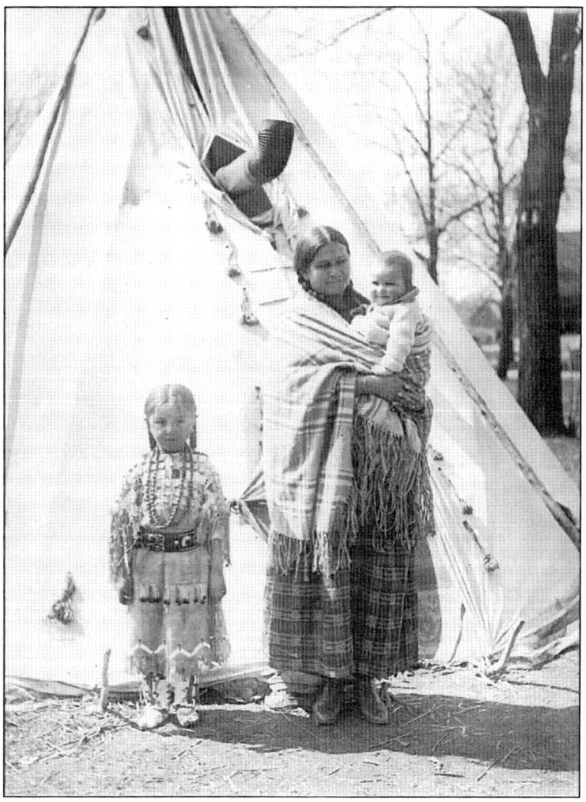

A Dakota Sioux mother holds a baby and poses next to a young girl in front of a tipi with a stove pipe. The woman and baby are wrapped in a shawl, and the girl wears a buckskin dress decorated with beads and shells, beaded moccasins, and a necklace. (Photograph courtesy of the Denver Public Library.)

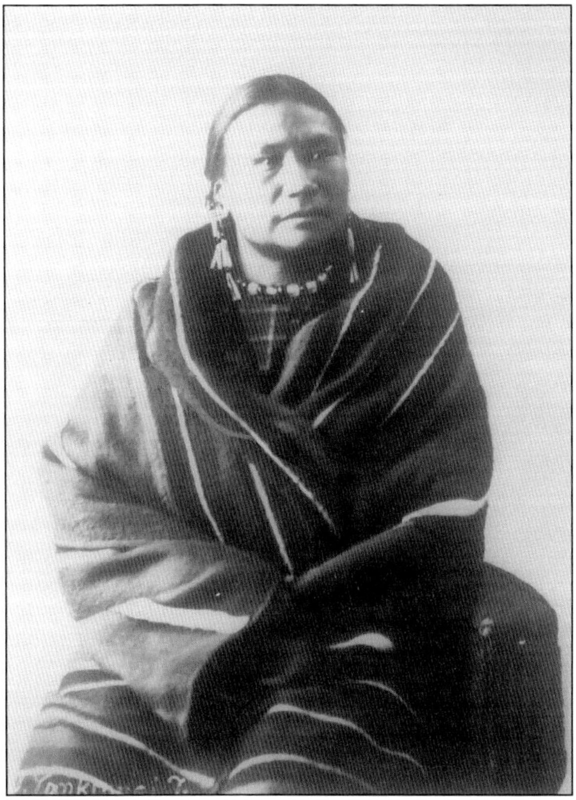

This woman is the wife of Eagle Man, from the Cut Head Band of the Yanktonai. (Photograph courtesy of Fort Peck Tribal Archives.)

Some Indians chose to stay for a time at the Trading Post. Here a family rests for a moment before setting out to follow game.

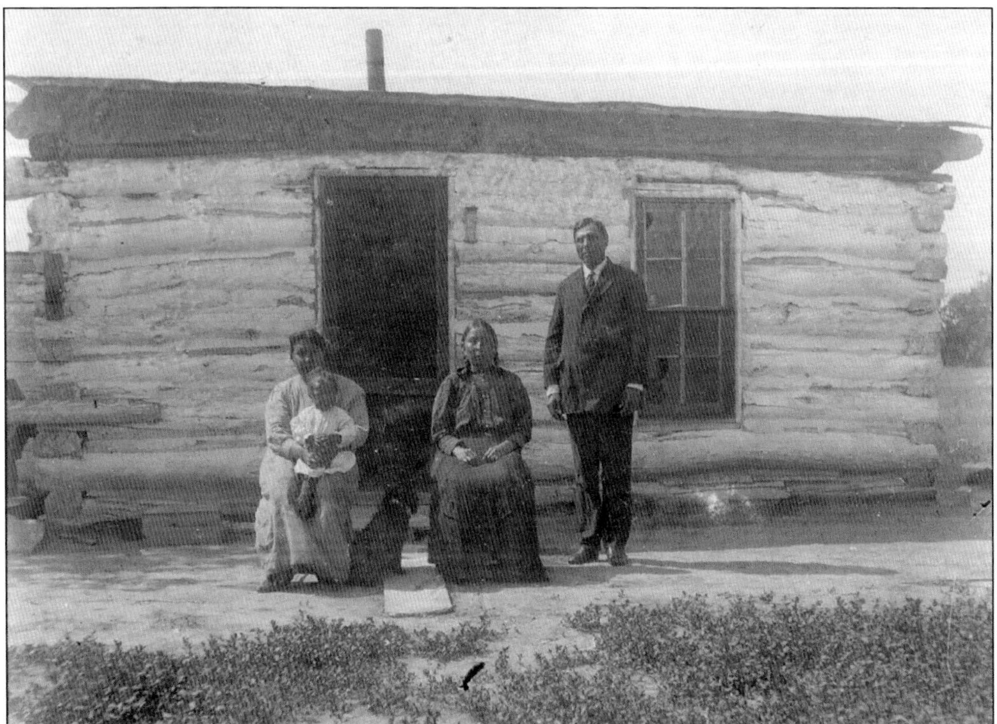

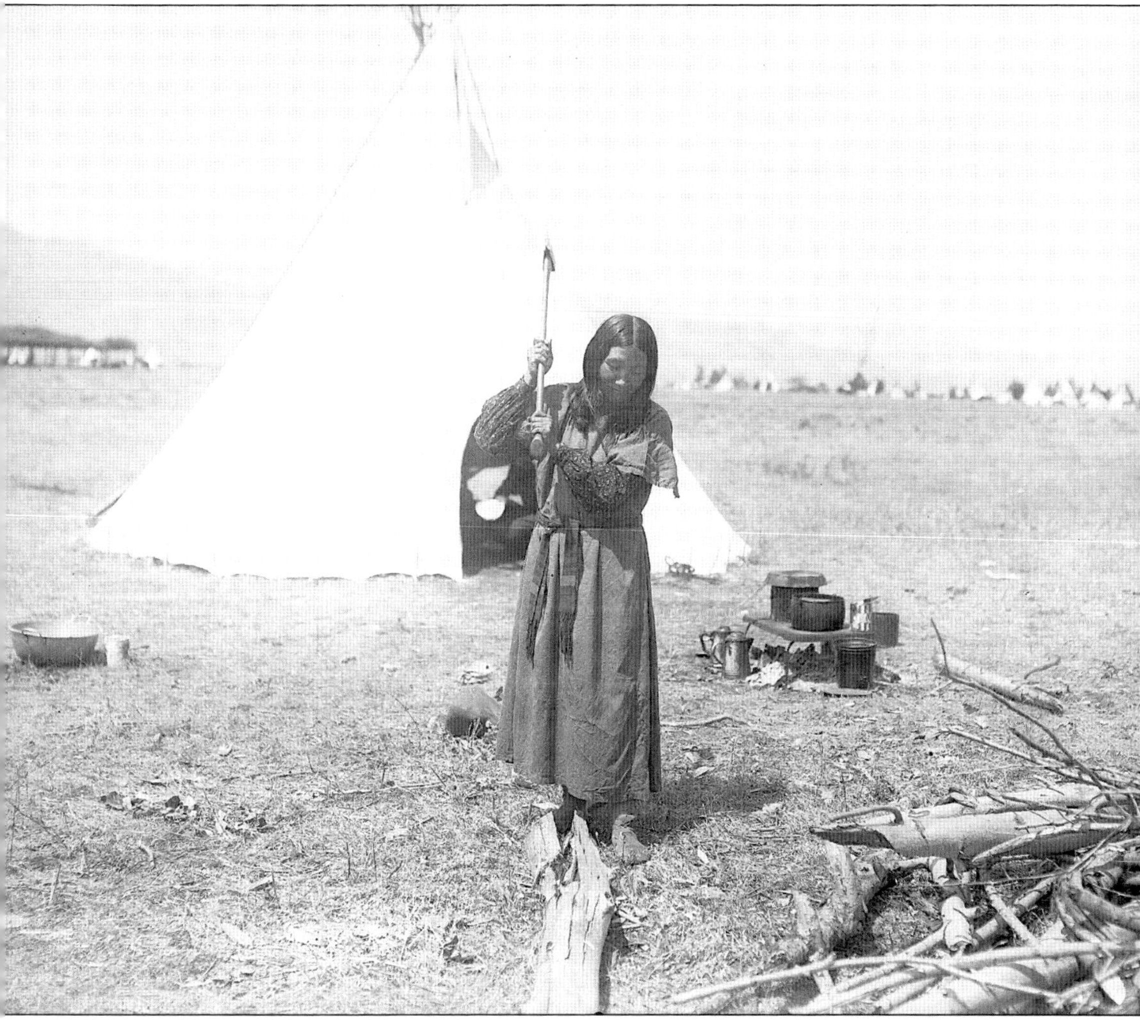

Mary Walk in Water, also known as Mary Inhoosta Woodcock, chops a log with an ax in front of a tipi. Pots cook over a campfire; a mixing bowl is in the left mid-ground; a man sits on a wood crate; additional tipis are in the distance. (Photograph courtesy of the Denver Public Library.)

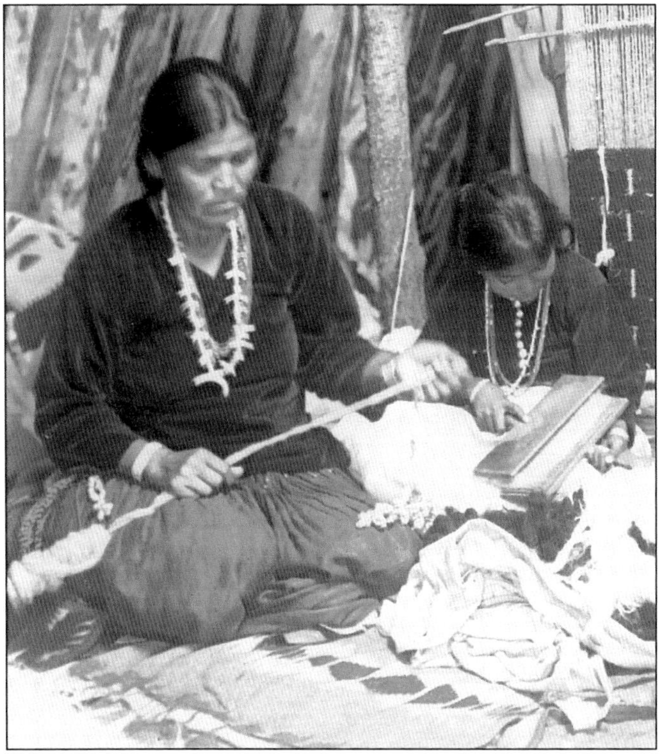

A woman and a young girl weave blankets from wool. The young girl combs out wool with a large, flat brush. The other woman spools the wool onto a spindle. Patterned blankets lie on the ground where they work. (Photograph courtesy of the Denver Public Library.)

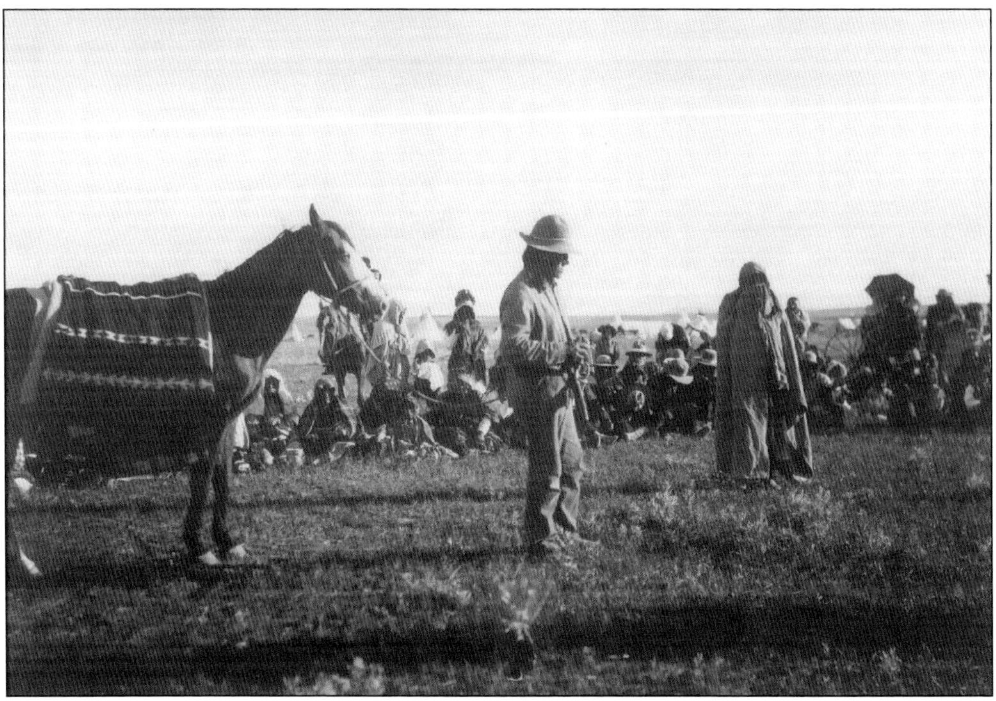

Among their many tasks, women were responsible for fetching water daily, preparing and cooking food, making pots, tools and baskets, processing animal hides, and especially raising children. (Photograph courtesy of Fort Peck Tribal Archives.)

Two Dakota women sit next to wood bundles and tipis on a damp and cloudy day. The women are preparing to make a fire for cooking the evening meal. (Photograph courtesy of the Denver Public Library.)

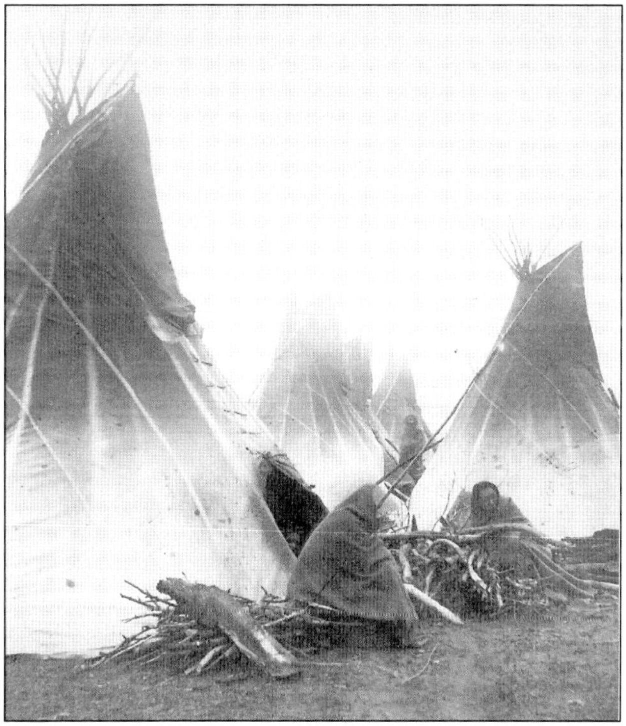

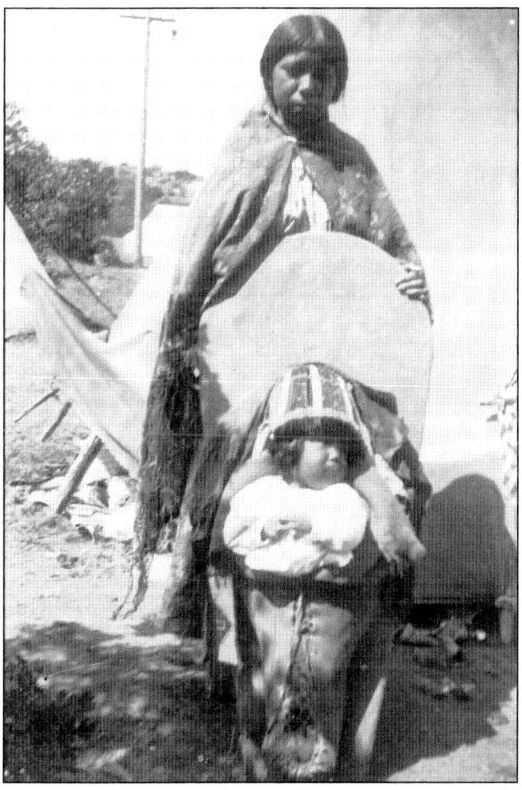

An Indian woman stands holding a cradleboard with a tightly secured baby. A bonnet protects the baby's head. The board is made of a branch doubled back on itself and bound by a stretched animal skin. (Photograph courtesy of the Denver Public Library.)

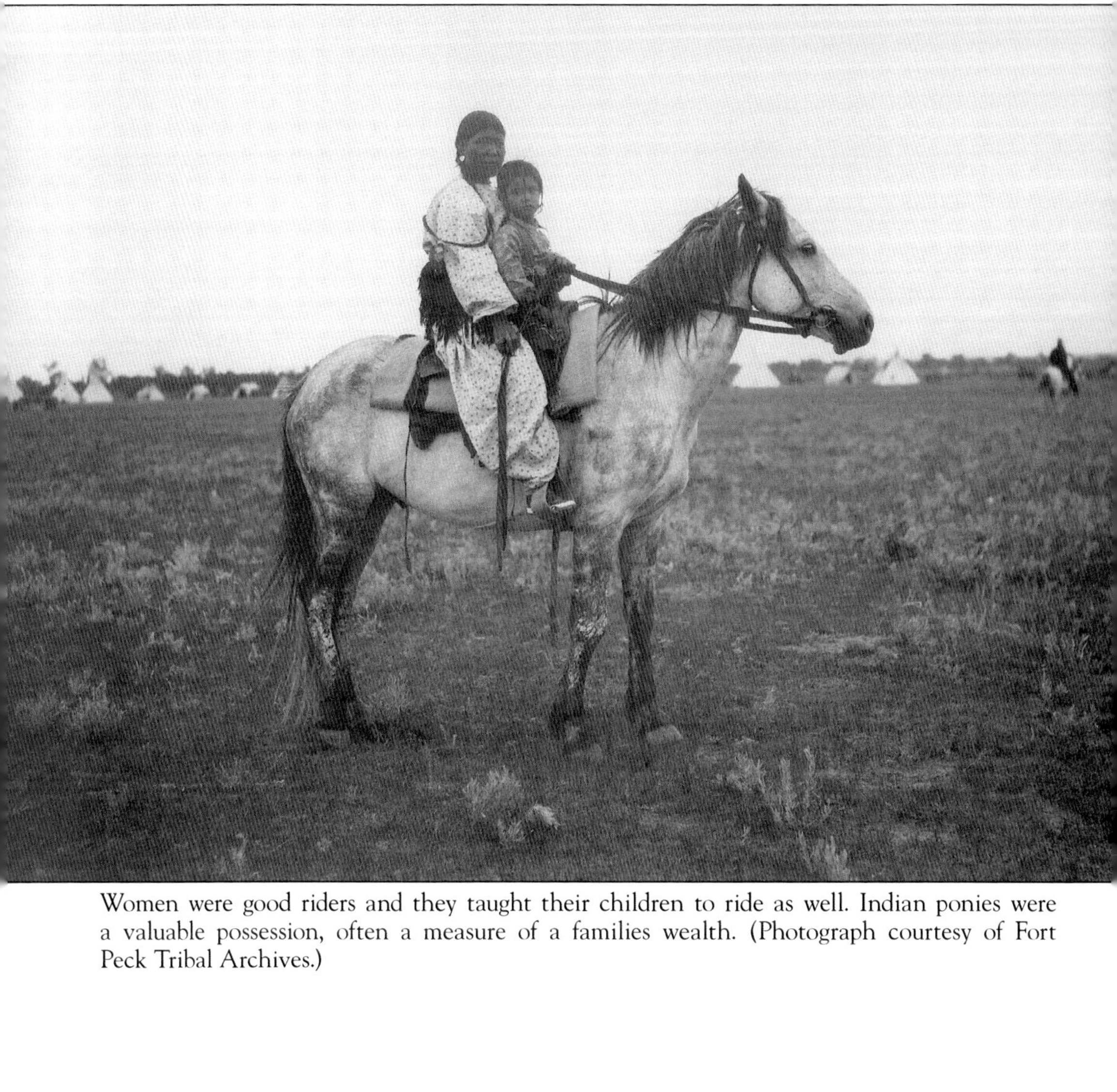

Women were good riders and they taught their children to ride as well. Indian ponies were a valuable possession, often a measure of a families wealth. (Photograph courtesy of Fort Peck Tribal Archives.)

Five

DANCING TO THE SONG OF FREEDOM

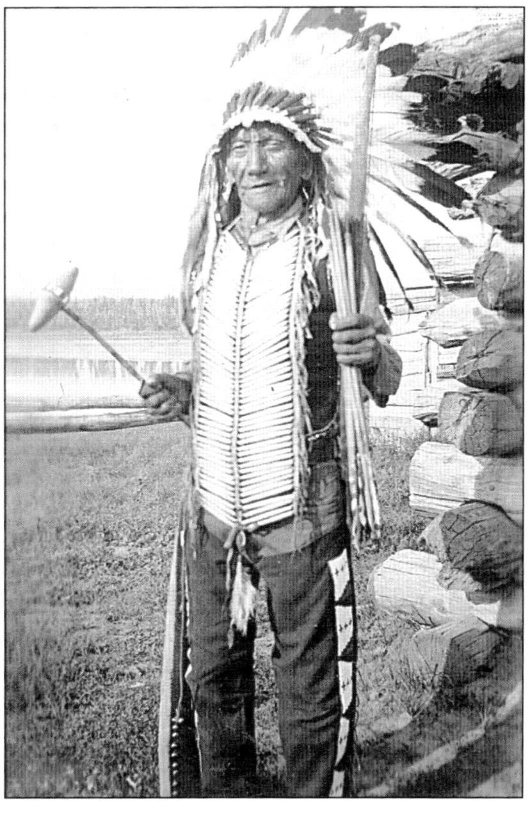

Feather Earring, this author's great-great-grandfather, was a Minneconjou who received his name from the many feathers he wore on his clothes and in his headdress. Feather Earring and his brother, Dog With Horn, were present at the Tiopsaye village.

In the evening, the celebration of freedom continued as the campfires of the village burned brightly. The dancing and feasting would go on late into the night, along with stories of victory and the hunt. (Photograph courtesy of the State Historical Society of North Dakota.)

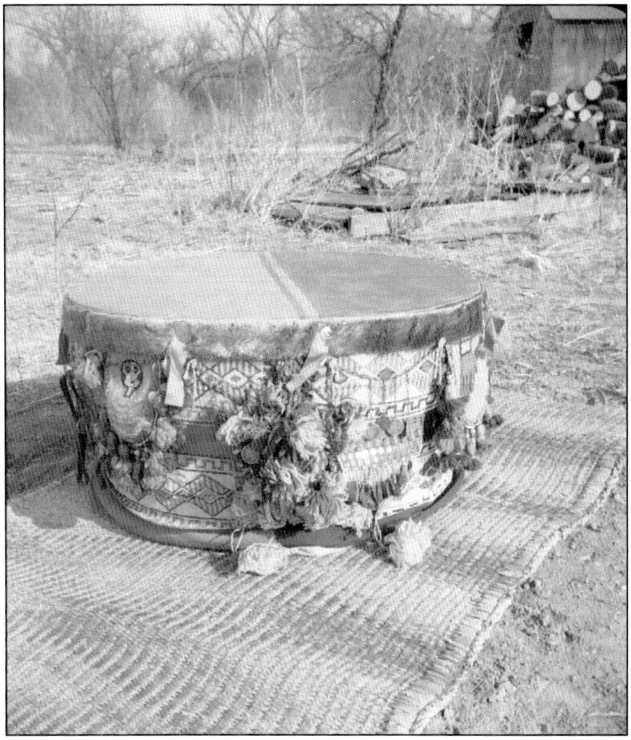

This is a close-up view of a Potawatomi Prairie Band drum. The drum is decorated with beads, fur pelts, conchos, and yarn. (Photograph courtesy of the Denver Public Library.)

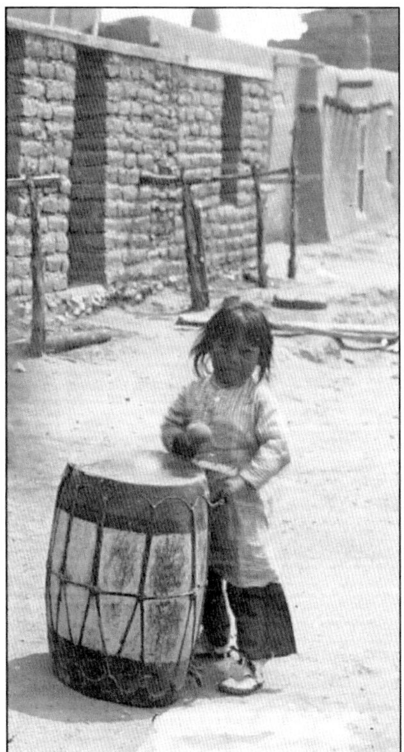

Pictured is a little girl with a drum. (Photograph courtesy of the Denver Public Library.)

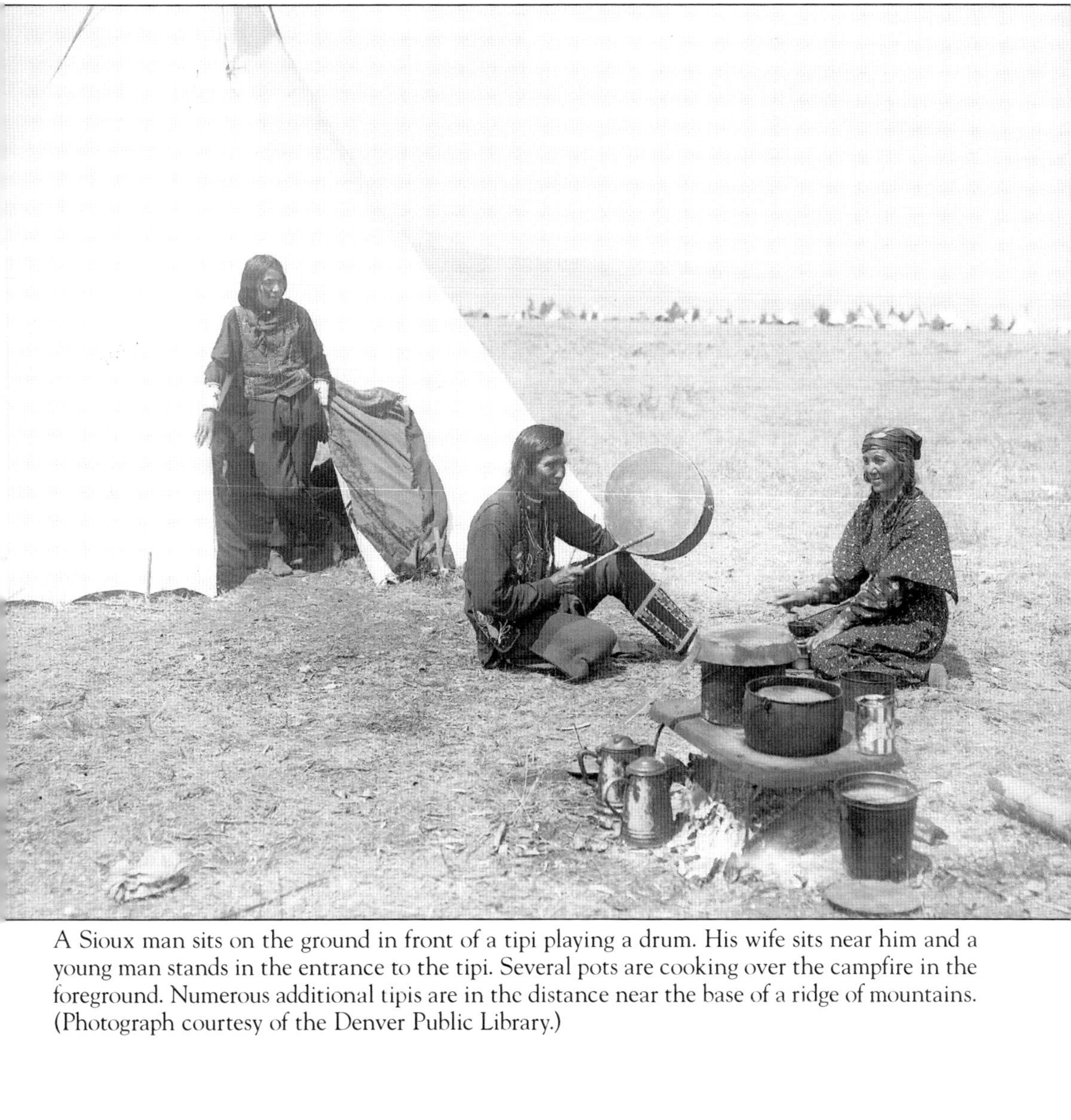

A Sioux man sits on the ground in front of a tipi playing a drum. His wife sits near him and a young man stands in the entrance to the tipi. Several pots are cooking over the campfire in the foreground. Numerous additional tipis are in the distance near the base of a ridge of mountains. (Photograph courtesy of the Denver Public Library.)

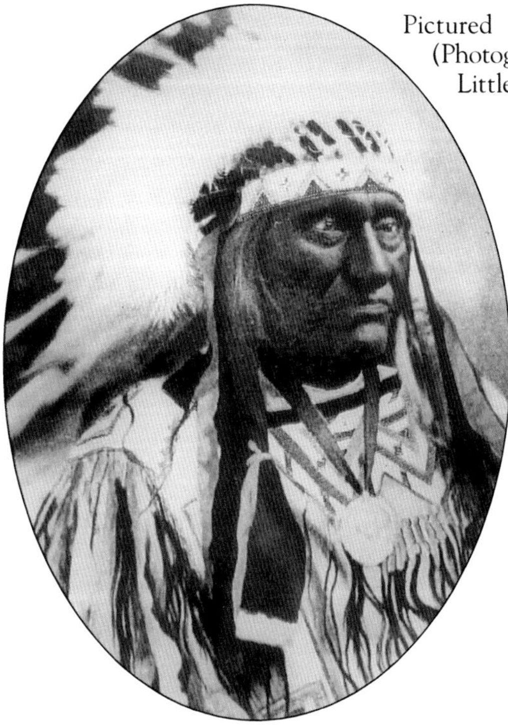

Pictured is Chief Little Wound, a Sioux warrior. (Photograph courtesy of the National Park Service, Little Bighorn Battlefield National Monument.)

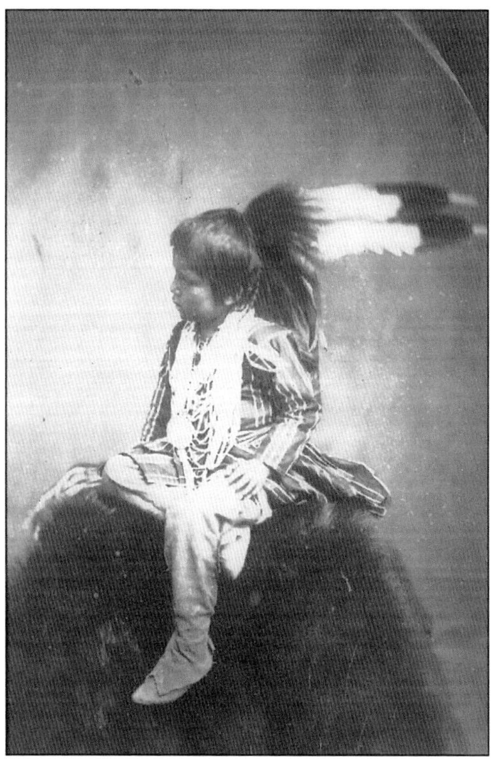

Here is a portrait of Ma-za-oo-me, Little Bird Hunter, a Santee Sioux boy, seated on a animal fur. This son of a chief wears a headdress, striped cotton tunic, leggings, and bead necklaces. (Photograph courtesy of the Denver Public Library.)

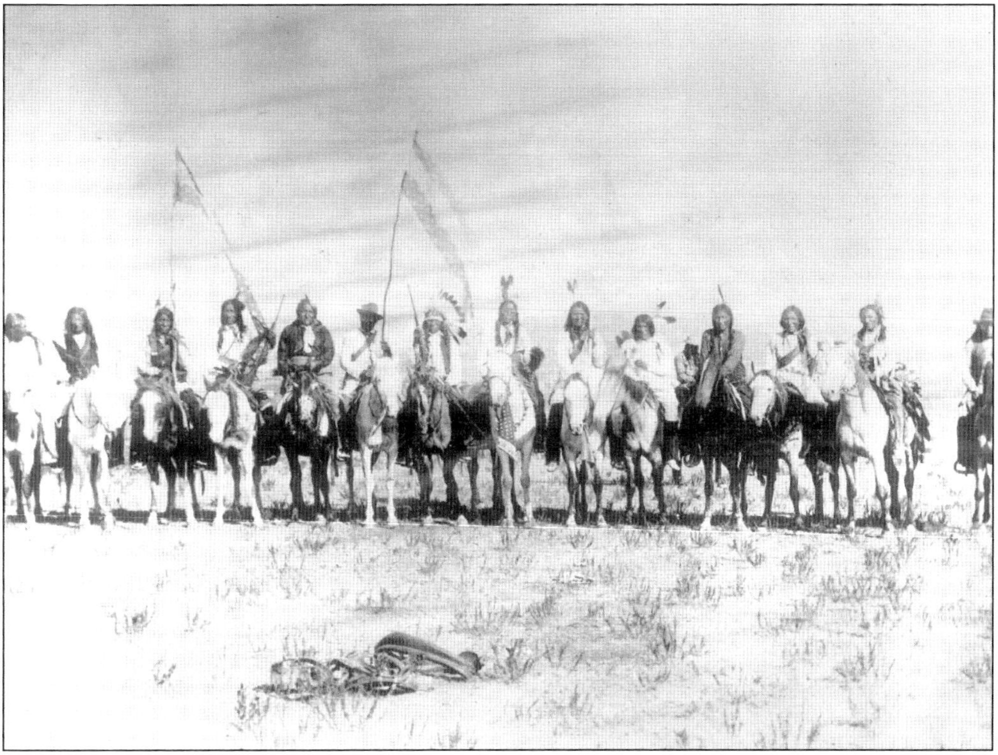

A group of Sioux chiefs rest on horseback. They wear cotton shirts, head feathers—one with headdress. (Photograph courtesy of the Denver Public Library.)

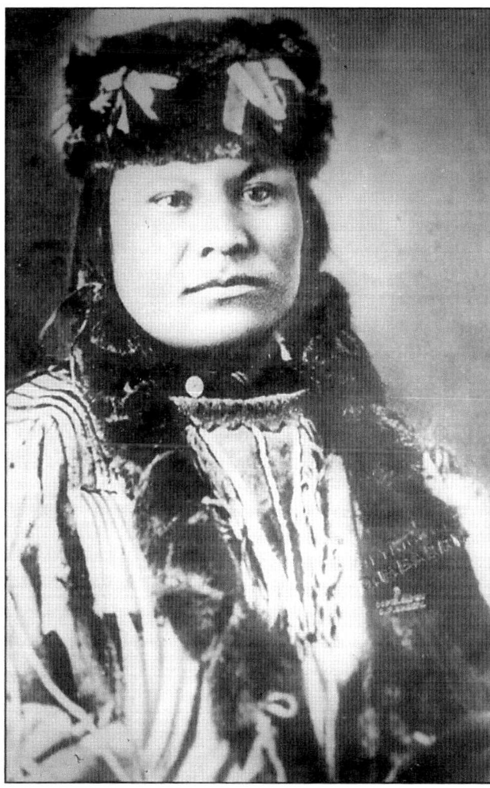

Pictured is Brave Bear. (Photograph courtesy of the National Park Service, Little Bighorn Battlefield National Monument.)

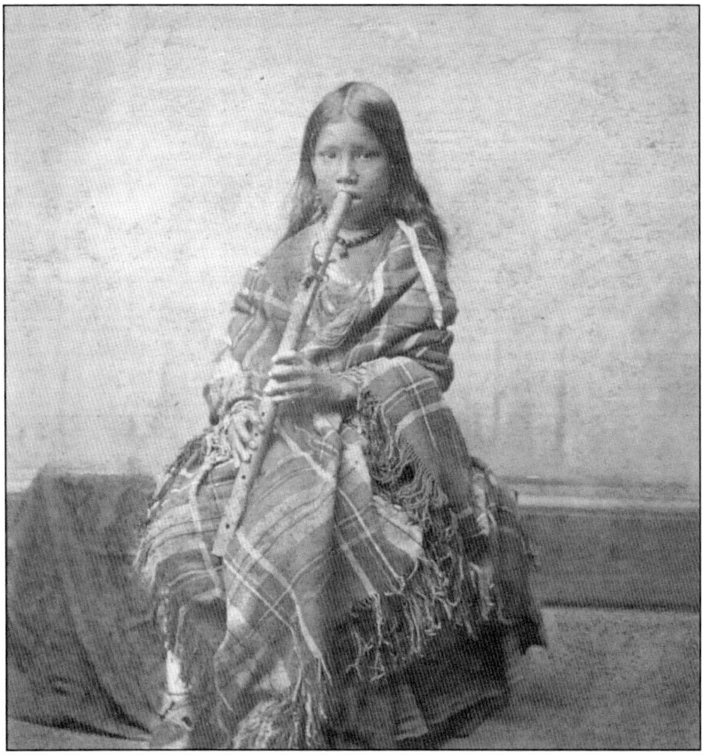

In this photograph, a Sioux girl is shown wrapped in a plaid blanket and playing a flute. (Photograph courtesy of the Denver Public Library.)

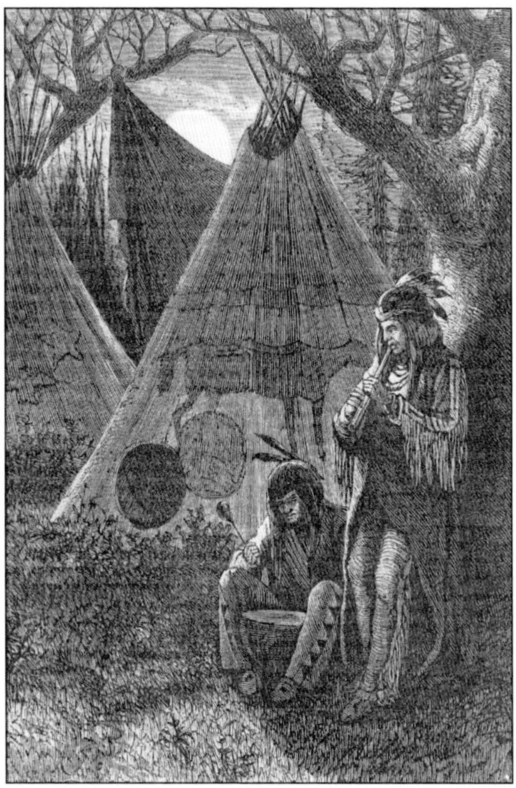

Men are outside a tipi on a moonlit night. One man sits on the ground playing a drum, the other leans against a tree and plays a flute. Source: Appleton's Journal, August 20, 1870, p. 215. (Photograph courtesy of the Denver Public Library.)

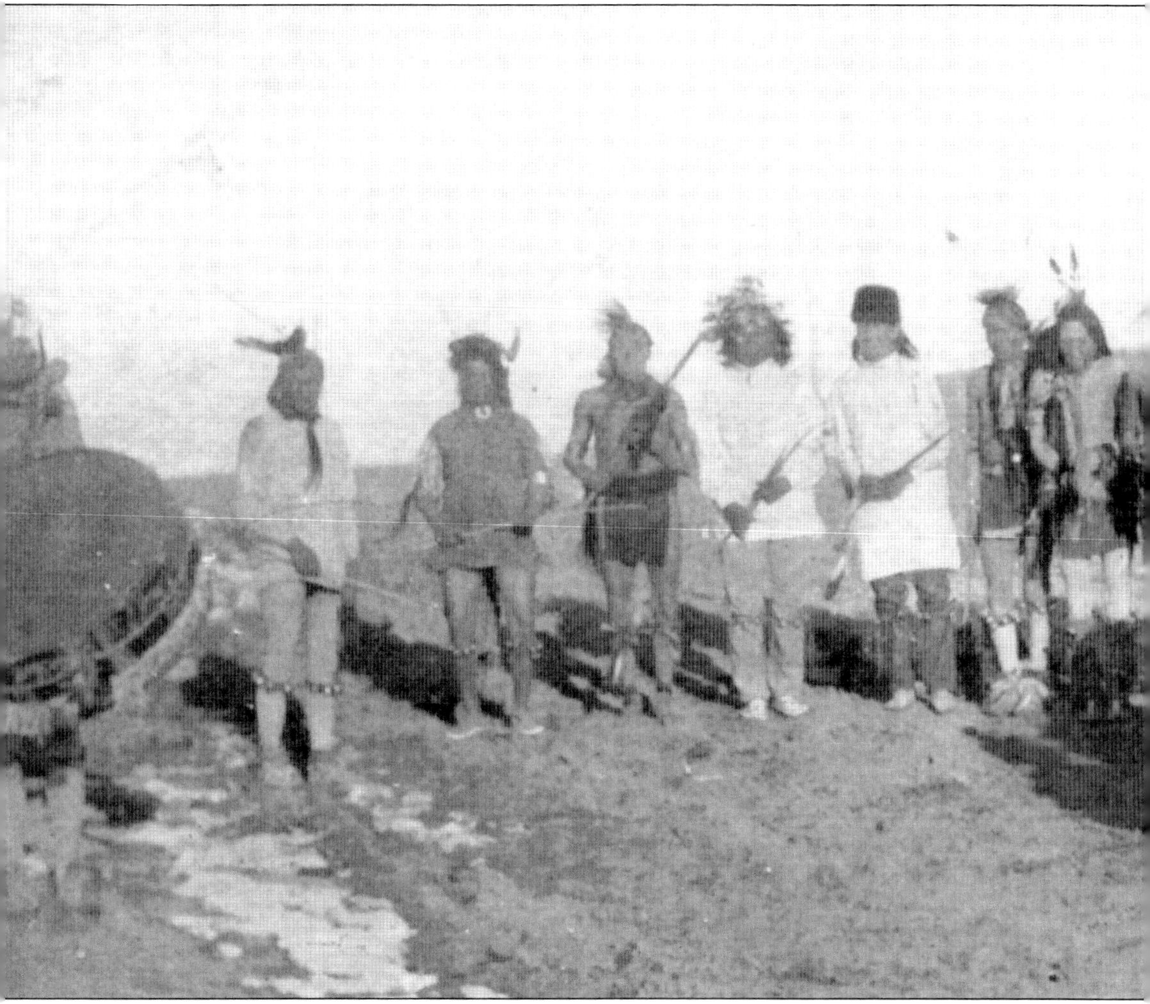

This is a postcard of a group of Sioux men performing a Grass Dance. The man on the far left holds a large drum. Most of the men wear feathers on their heads and some hold feathers in their hands. (Photograph courtesy of the Denver Public Library.)

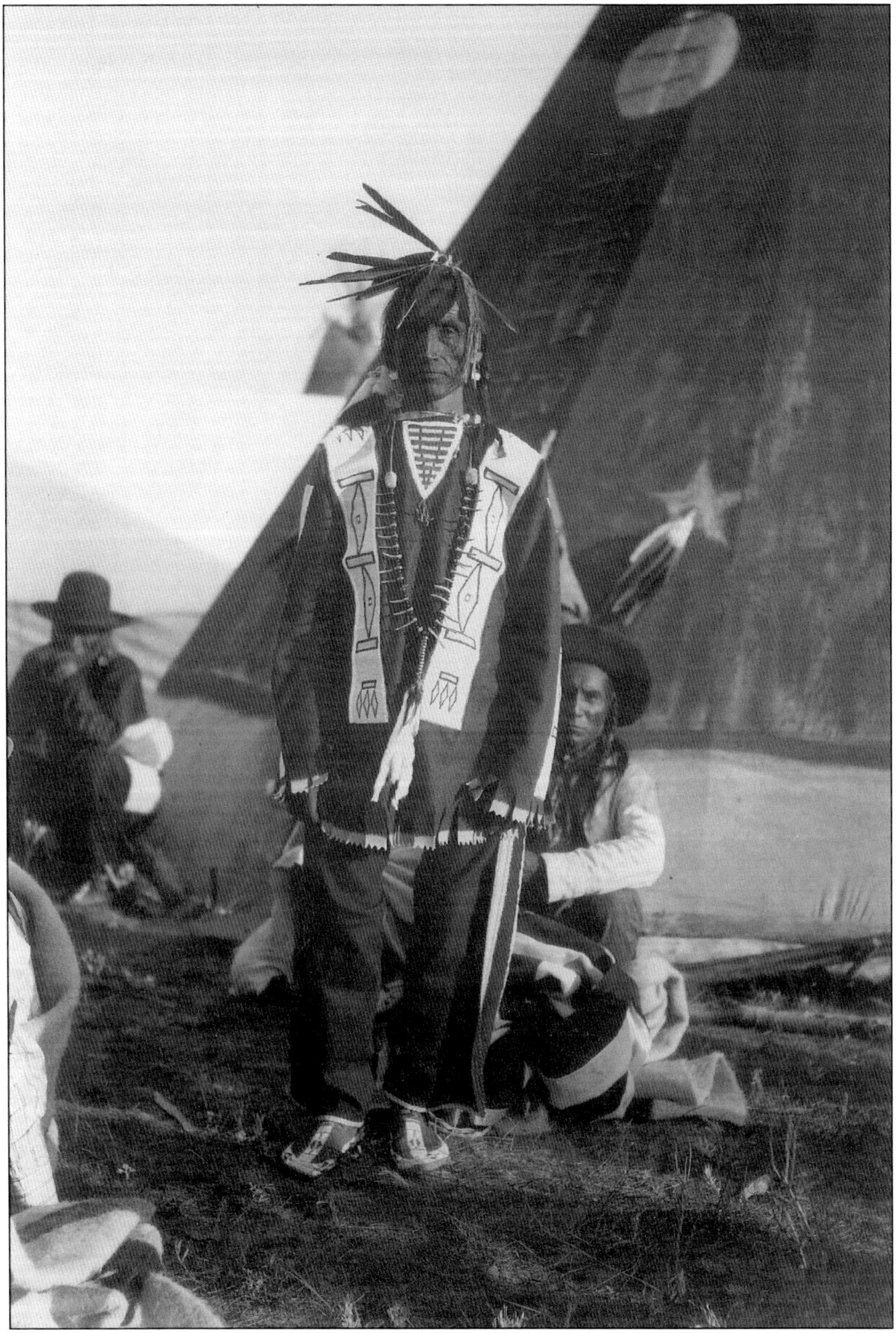

Here is a photograph of a warrior who is ready to join the celebration. (Photograph courtesy of Fort Peck Tribal Archives.)

This is a photograph of Red Fish, a prominent and highly respected chief. (Photograph courtesy of Fort Peck Tribal Archives.)

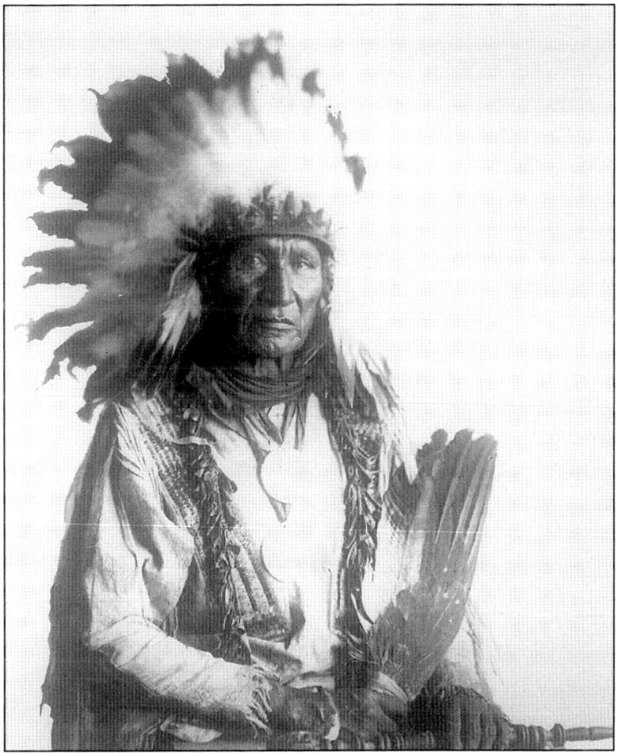

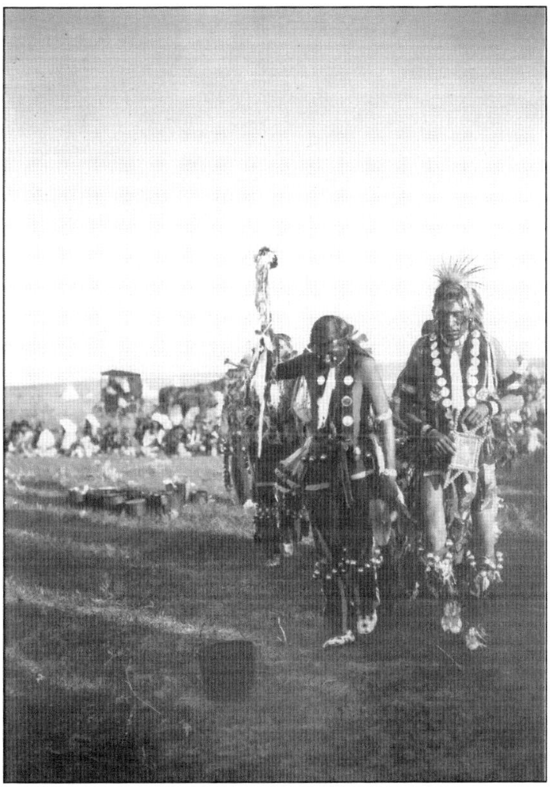

The sound of the drum invited everyone to join the dance and become part of the festivities. (Photograph courtesy of Fort Peck Tribal Archives.)

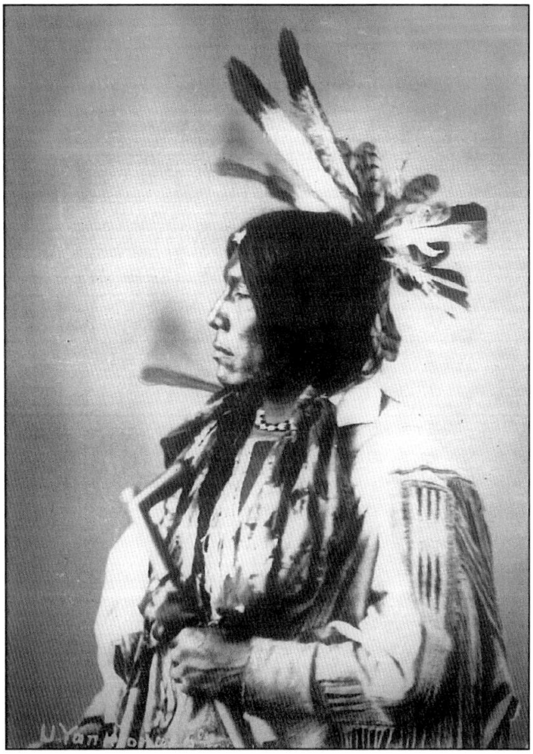

Pictured is a brave warrior. (Photograph courtesy of Fort Peck Tribal Archives.)

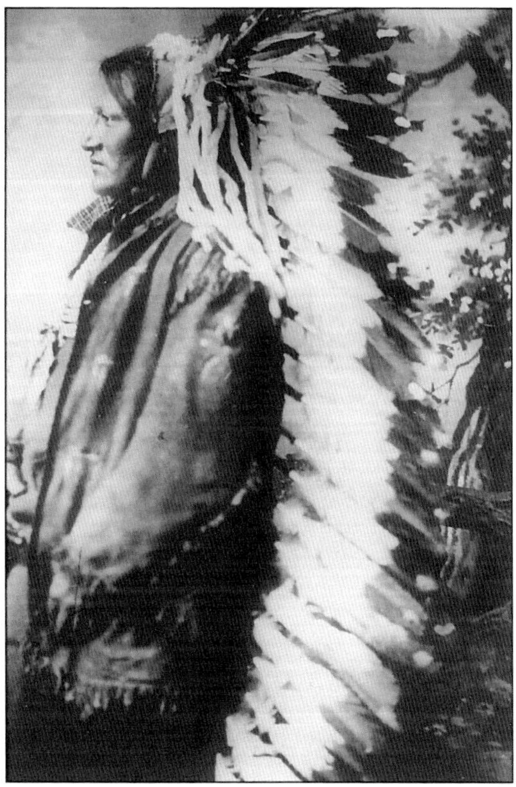

This is a photograph of Chief John Grass. (Photograph courtesy of the National Park Service, Little Bighorn Battlefield National Monument.)

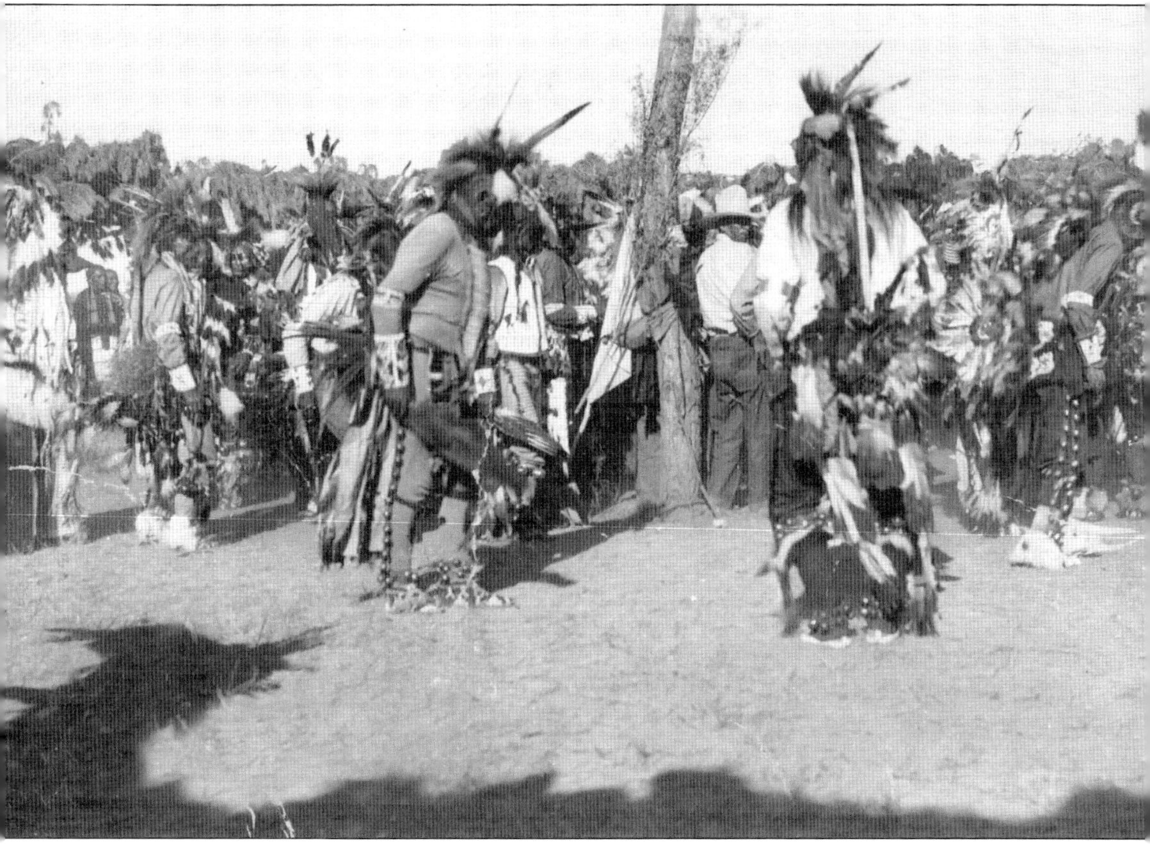

Pictured are the participants of the Sun Dance. Sioux men dance around a tree trunk decorated with cloth and branches wearing feathers, bells, leggings, shirts, and face paint. (Photograph courtesy of the Denver Public Library.)

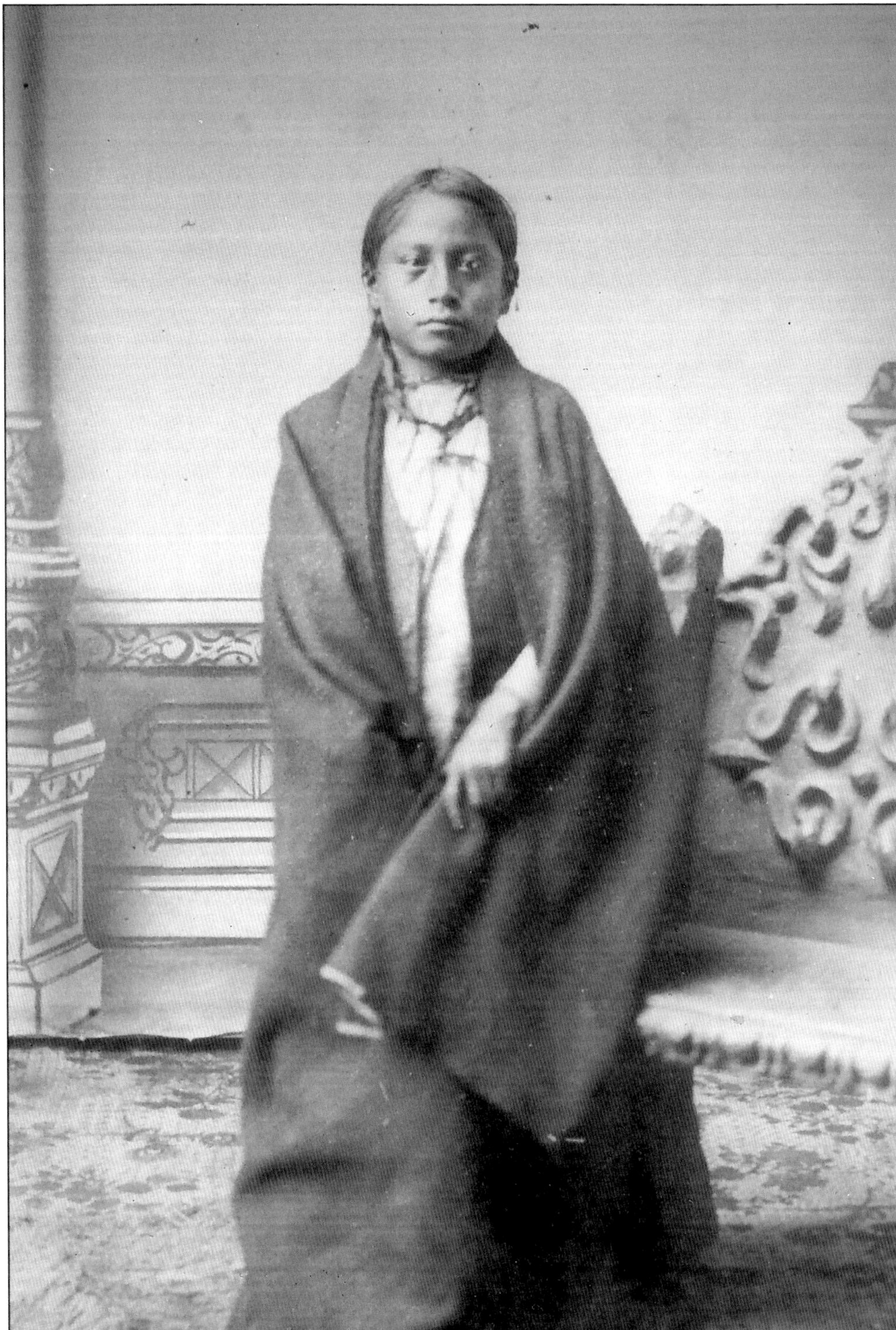

This is a photograph of Crow Foot, Sitting Bull's son. (Photograph courtesy of the National Park Service, Little Bighorn Battlefield National Monument.)

This is a photograph of Little Big Man, Oglala. (Photograph courtesy of the National Park Service, Little Bighorn Battlefield National Monument.)

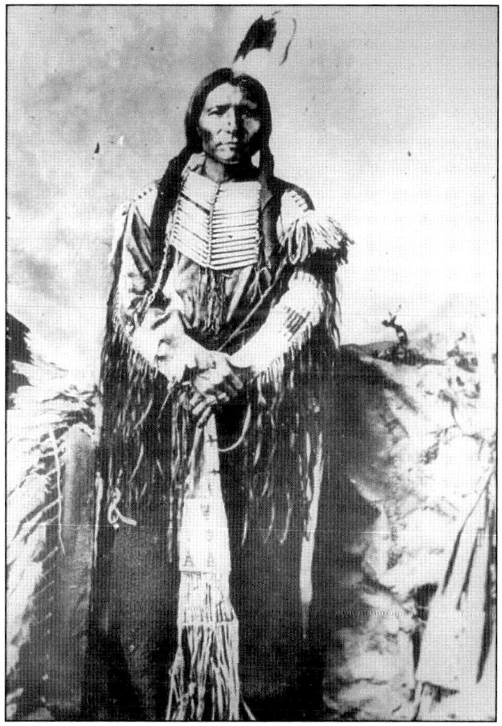

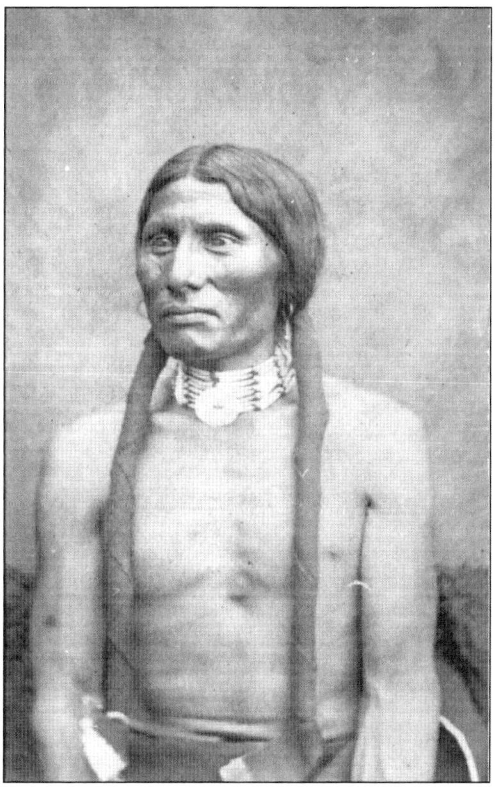

Another view of Little Big Man. He is shirtless with a hair pipe choker and cloth bound braids. (Photograph courtesy of the Denver Public Library.)

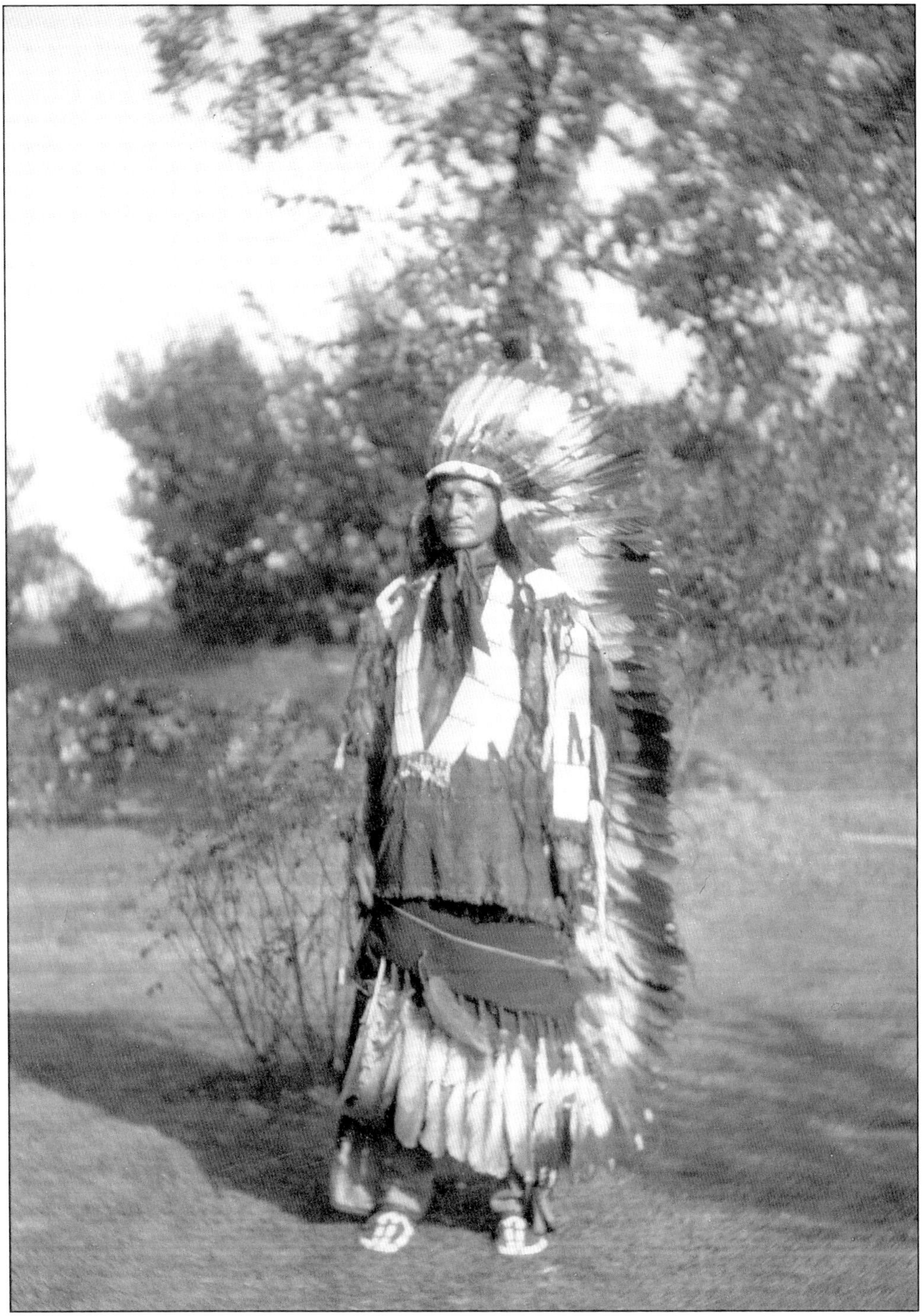

A Sioux man poses outside wearing feather headdress and skirt, buckskin shirt, leggings, and moccasins. (Photograph courtesy of the Denver Public Library.)

Six

The Warriors' Redemption

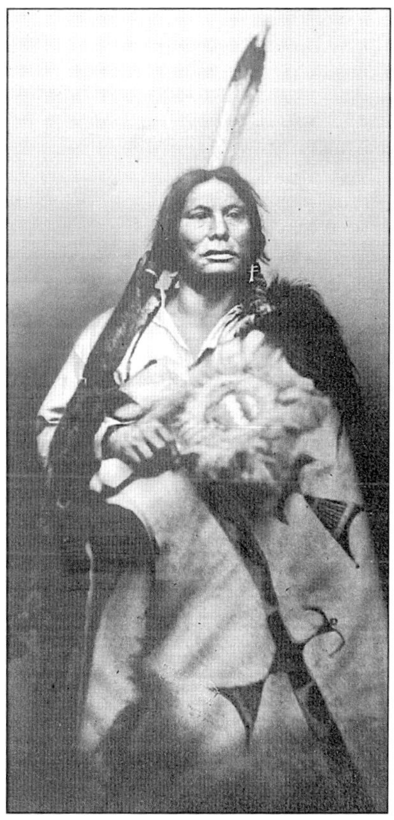

Historical accounts of the Tiospaye village on the banks of the Little Bighorn River number the warriors between 1,500 and 1,700 men—far too many to list. Instead, the author has included the pictures of the more familiar and notable warriors. Of them, the most outstanding is Crazy Horse, an Oglala Sioux, a man of mystery and passion.

Gall, a Hunkpapa Sioux, was present at the encampment, as was American Horse, a fierce warrior. Among the many were Crow King (Hunkpapa), Two Moon and White Shield (Cheyenne), He Dog and Fears Nothing (Oglala), Two Eagles (Brule), Left Hand (Arapaho), Runs the Enemy (Two Kettle), Feather Earring, and Iron Thunder (Minneconjou).

This is a photograph of Chief Gall, a Hunkpapa Sioux and notable chief. (Photograph courtesy of the Denver Public Library.)

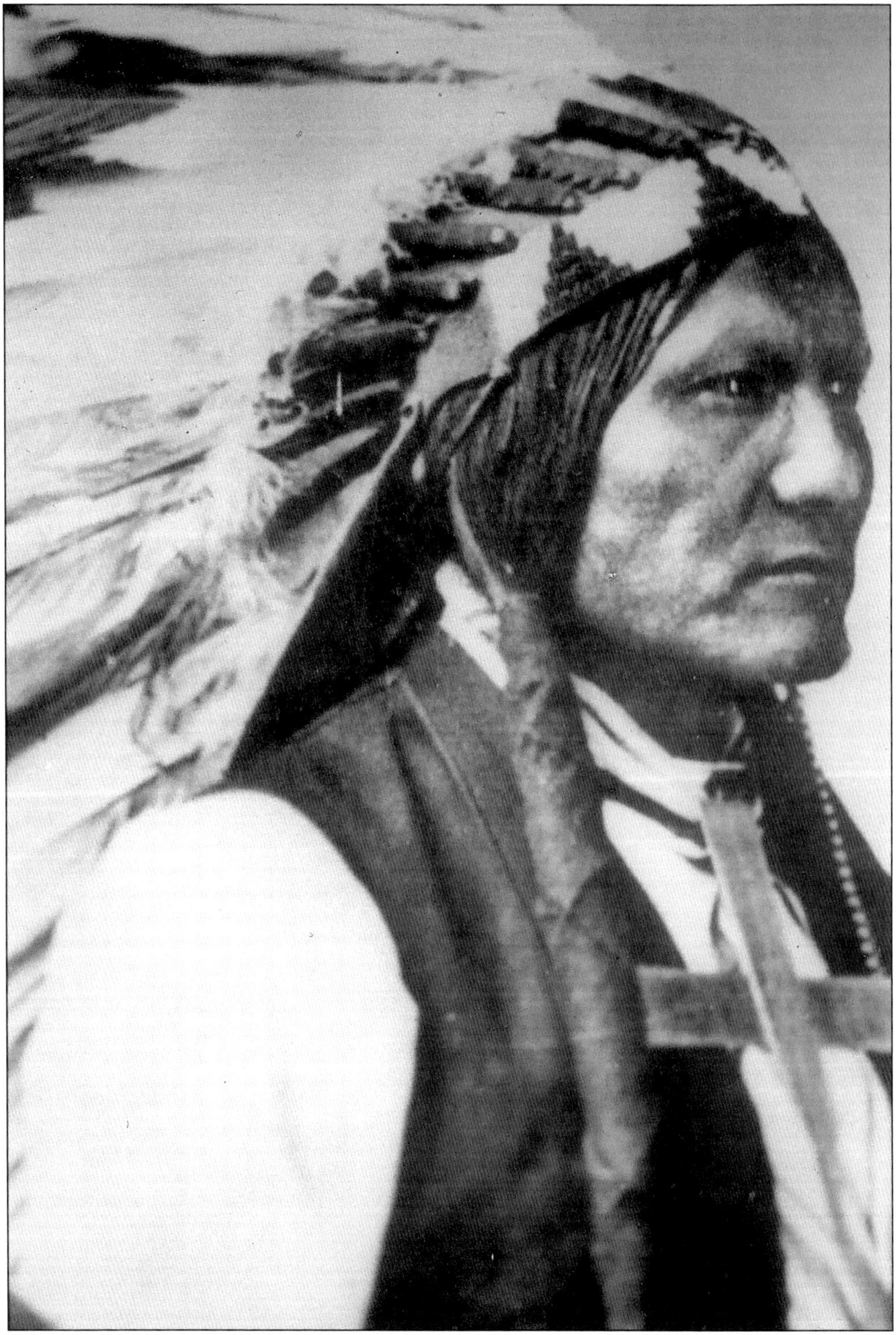

Pictured is He Dog of the Oglala Sioux, a close friend of Crazy Horse. (Photograph courtesy of the National Park Service, Little Bighorn Battlefield National Monument.)

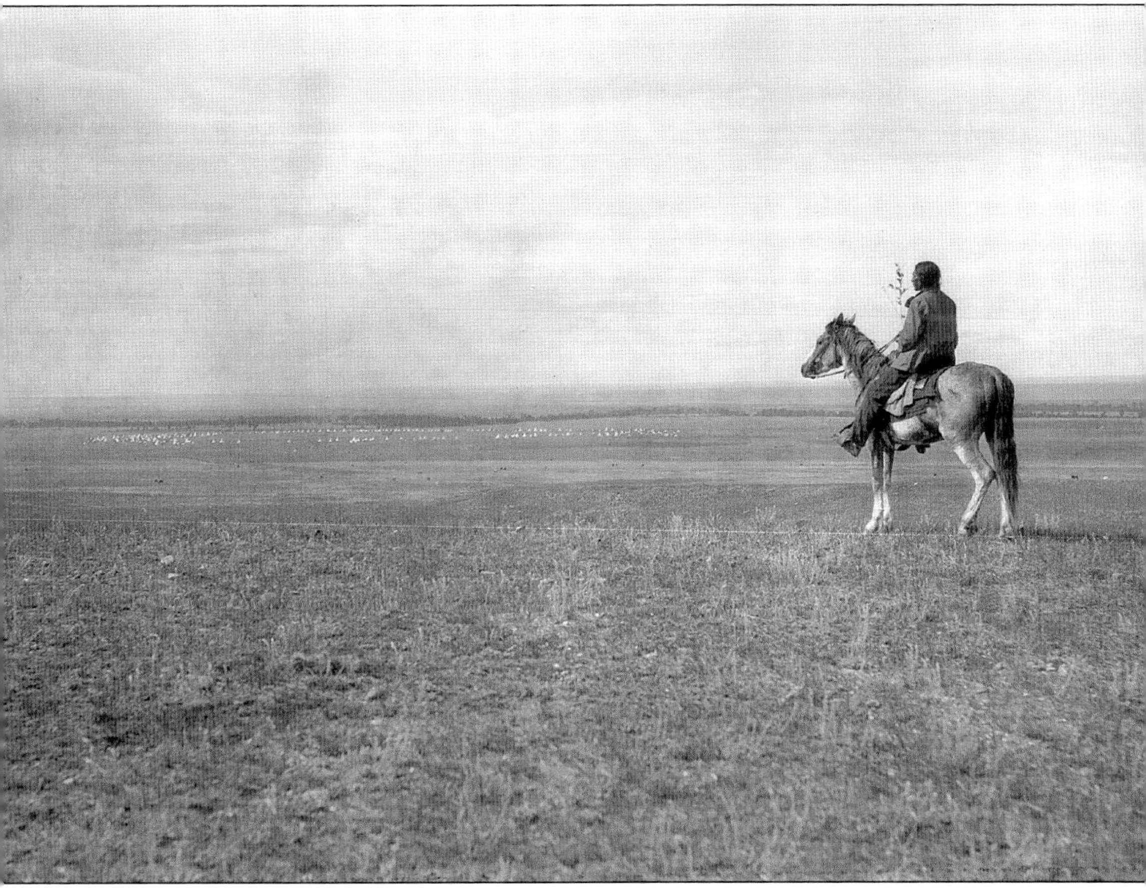

The author did not have a photograph of Crazy Horse for this book. However, this picture of a warrior represents him. Crazy Horse, for a time, achieved the rank of shirt wearer in his tribe. A shirt wearer had a high status and was responsible for the welfare of his people. He had to care for the more vulnerable such as the elderly and the orphans. (Photograph courtesy of Fort Peck Tribal Archives.)

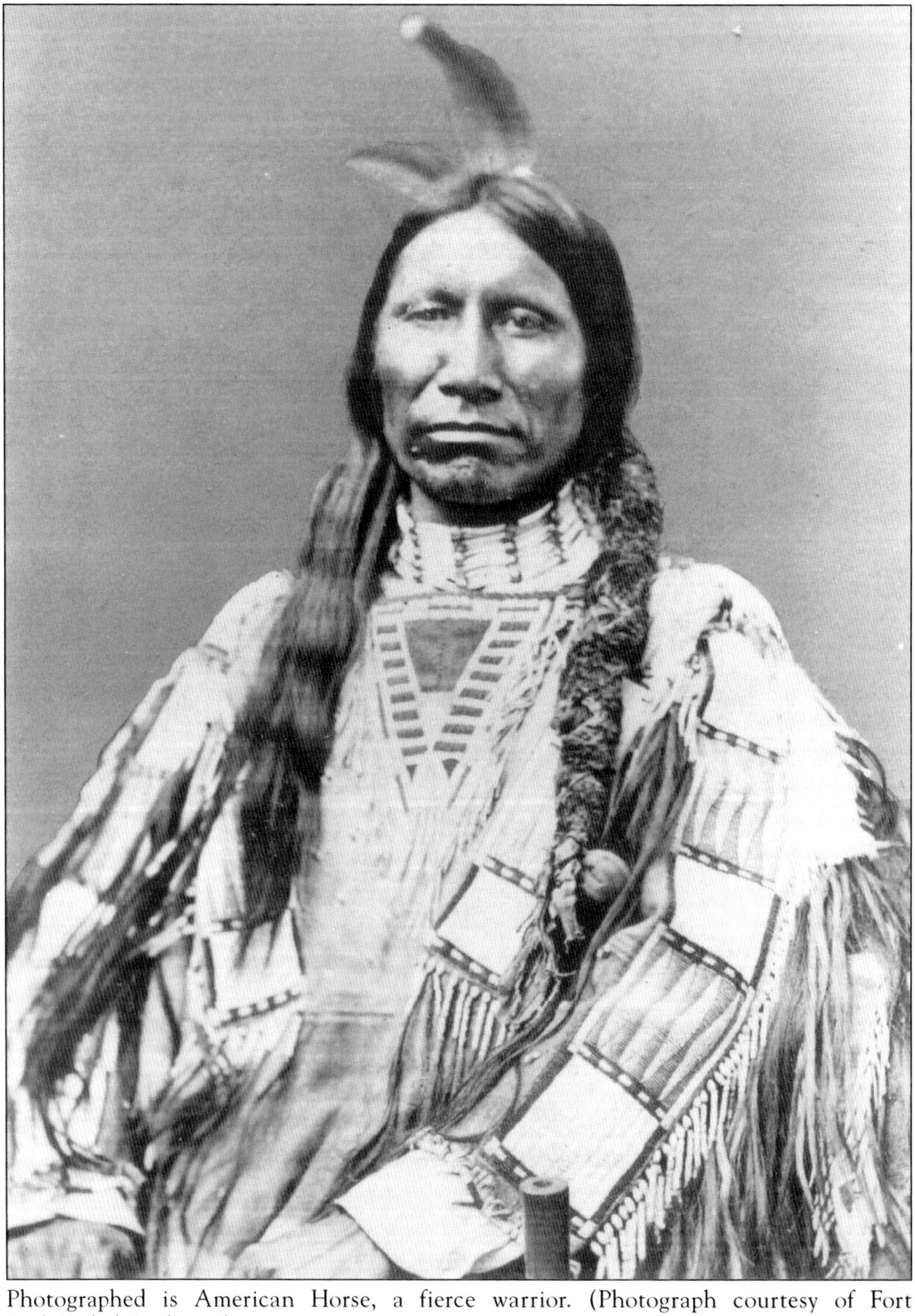

Photographed is American Horse, a fierce warrior. (Photograph courtesy of Fort Peck Tribal Archives.)

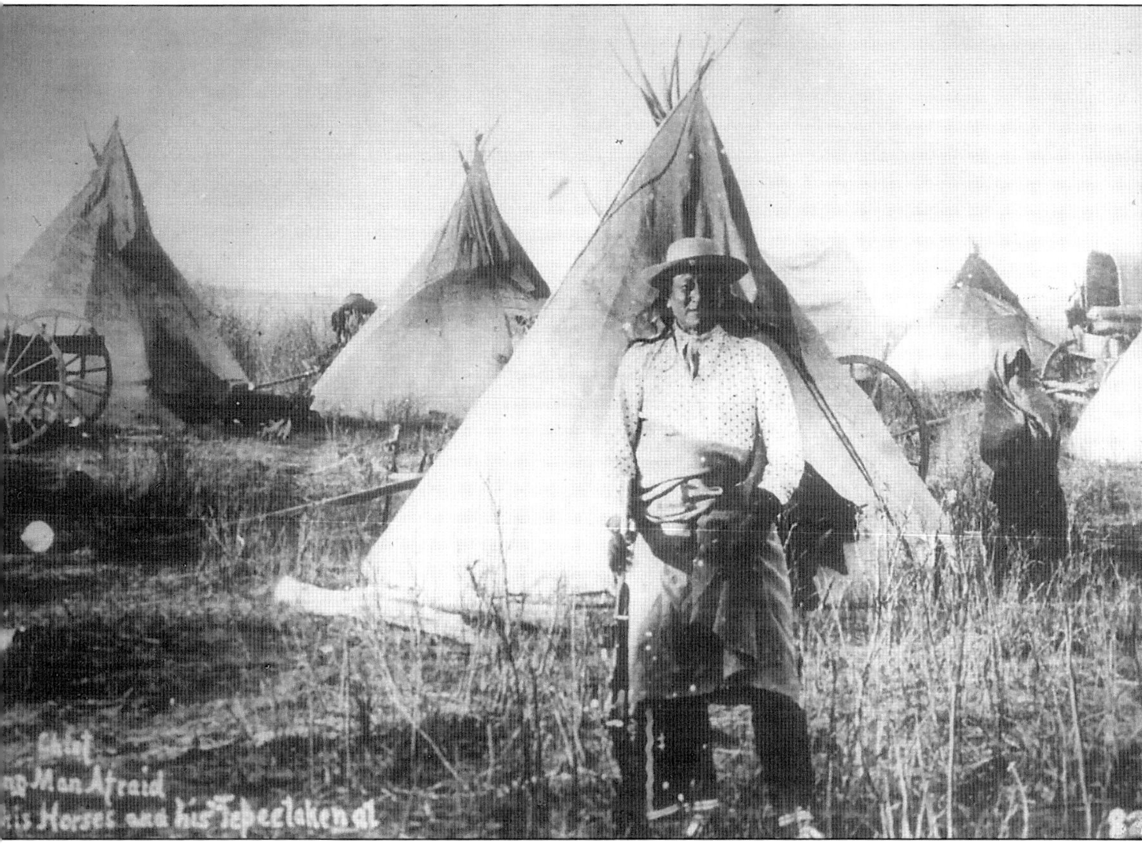

Pictured here is Man Afraid of His Horses, a Sioux warrior. (Photograph courtesy of the National Park Service, Little Bighorn Battlefield National Monument.)

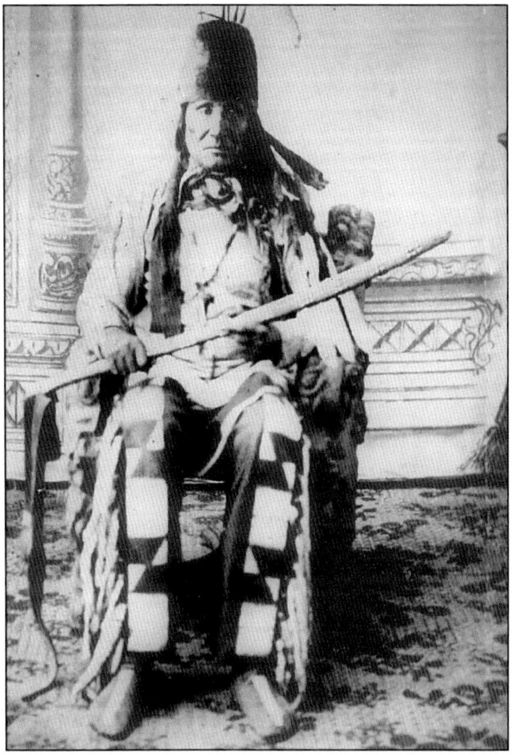

Long Dog, who rode with Sitting Bull, is pictured here. (Photograph courtesy of the National Park Service, Little Bighorn Battlefield National Monument.)

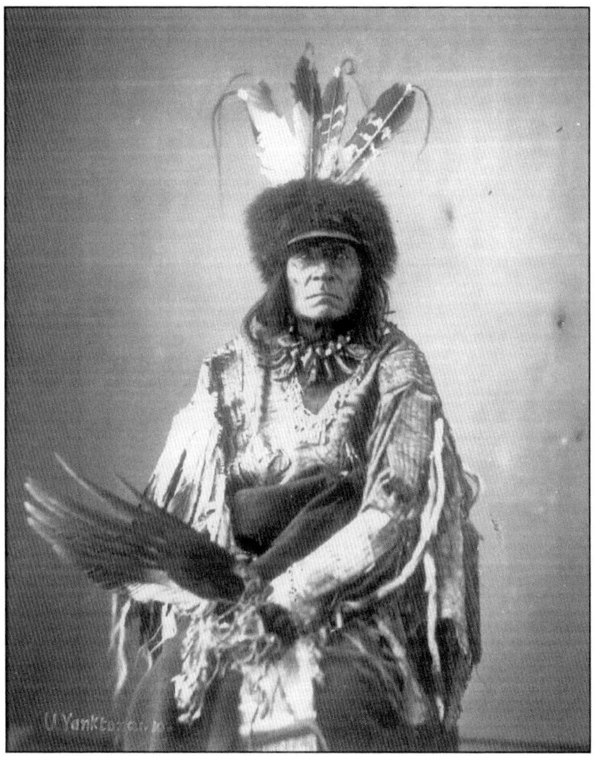

Big Razor, a Yanktonai warrior, is pictured here. (Photograph courtesy of Fort Peck Tribal Archives.)

Mato Sibacha, a Yanktonai warrior, is pictured here. (Photograph courtesy of Fort Peck Tribal Archives.)

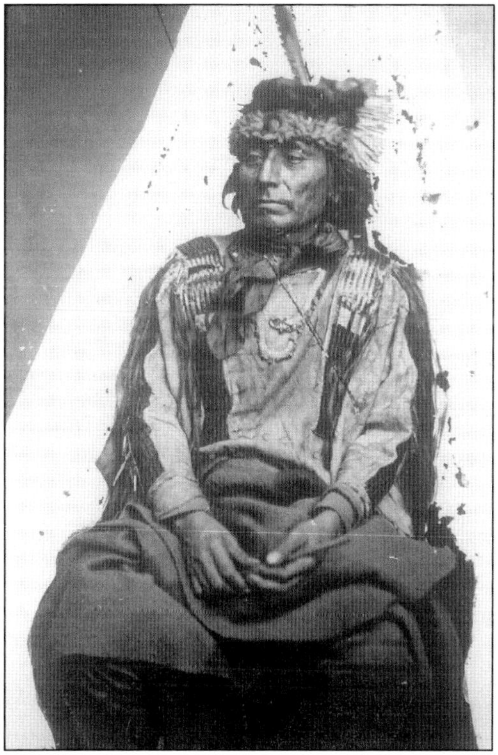

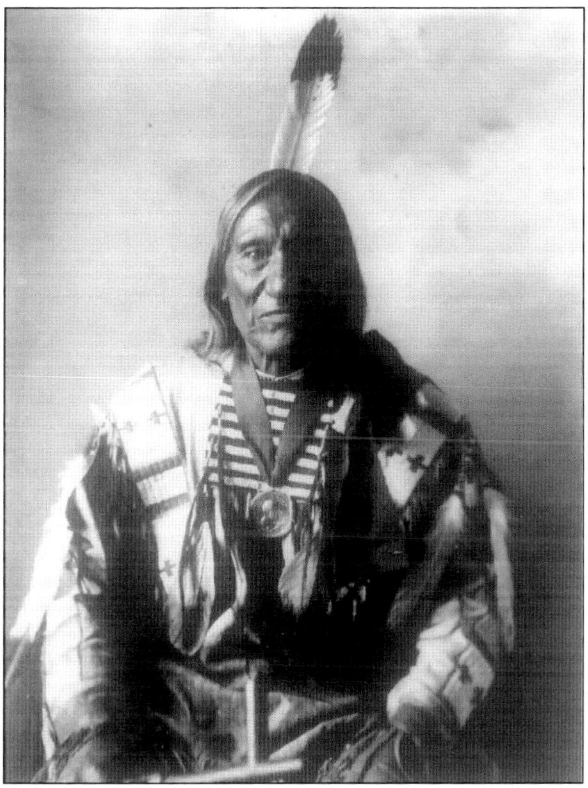

Seen here is Little Wound of the Oglala Sioux. (Photograph courtesy of Fort Peck Tribal Archives.)

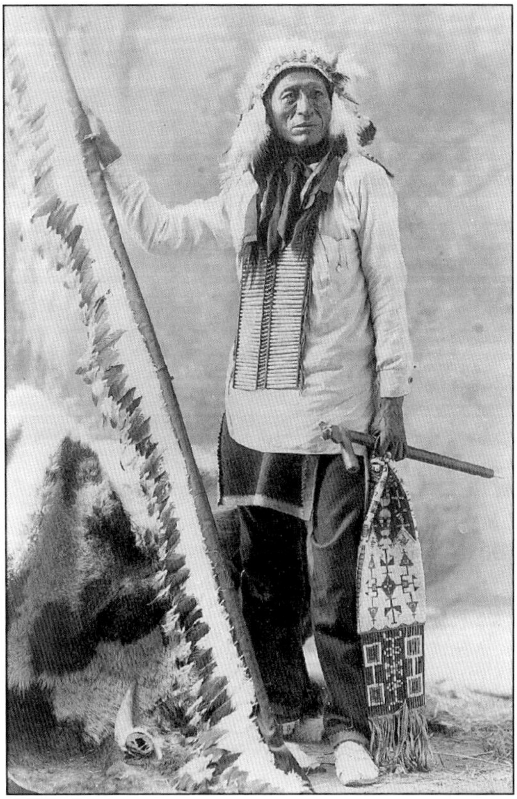

Iron Tall of the Oglala Sioux is seen here. (Photograph courtesy of Fort Peck Tribal Archives.)

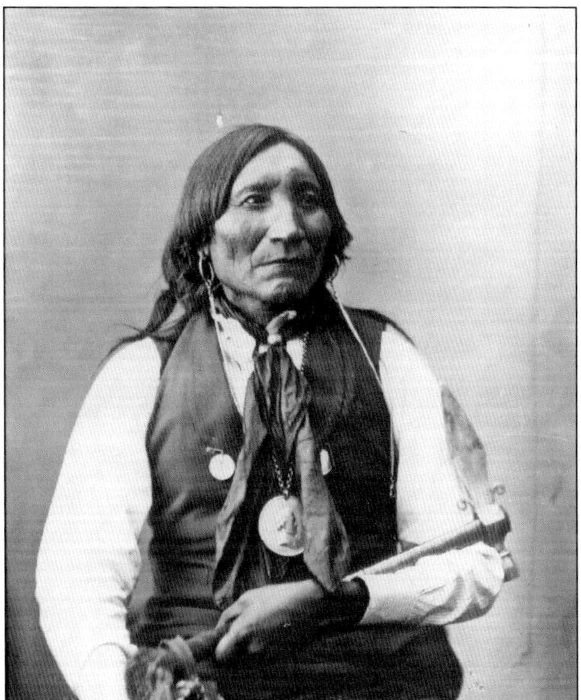

A head chief and leader, Lone Wolf was succeeded at the time of his death in 1879 by his adopted son who bears the same name. (Photograph courtesy of Fort Peck Tribal Archives.)

Two Grizzly Bears, a Yanktonai warrior, is photographed here. (Photograph courtesy of Fort Peck Tribal Archives.)

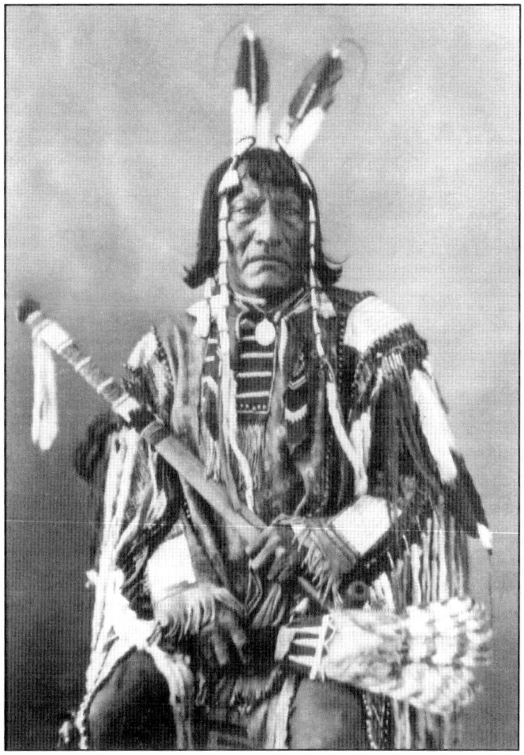

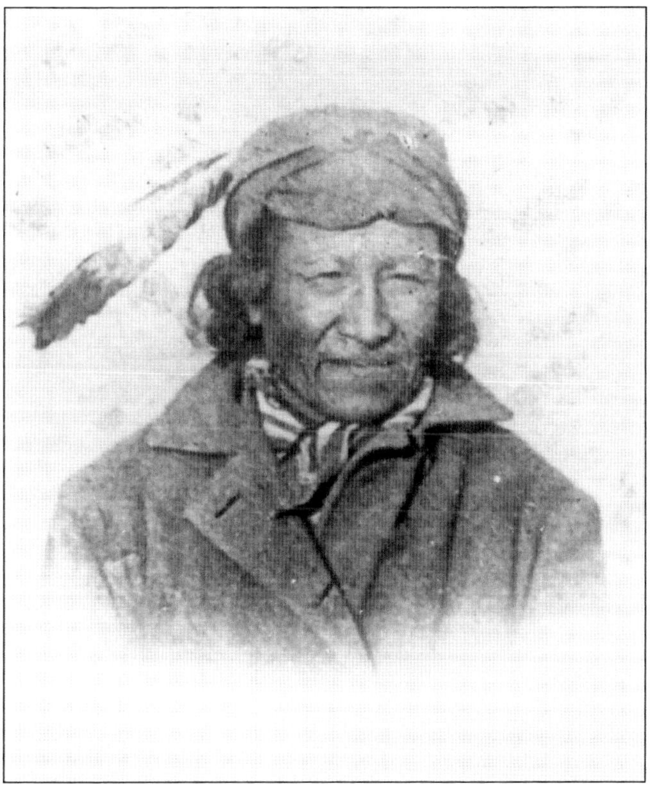

Seen here is Crow Dog, a Brule warrior. (Photograph courtesy of Fort Peck Tribal Archives.)

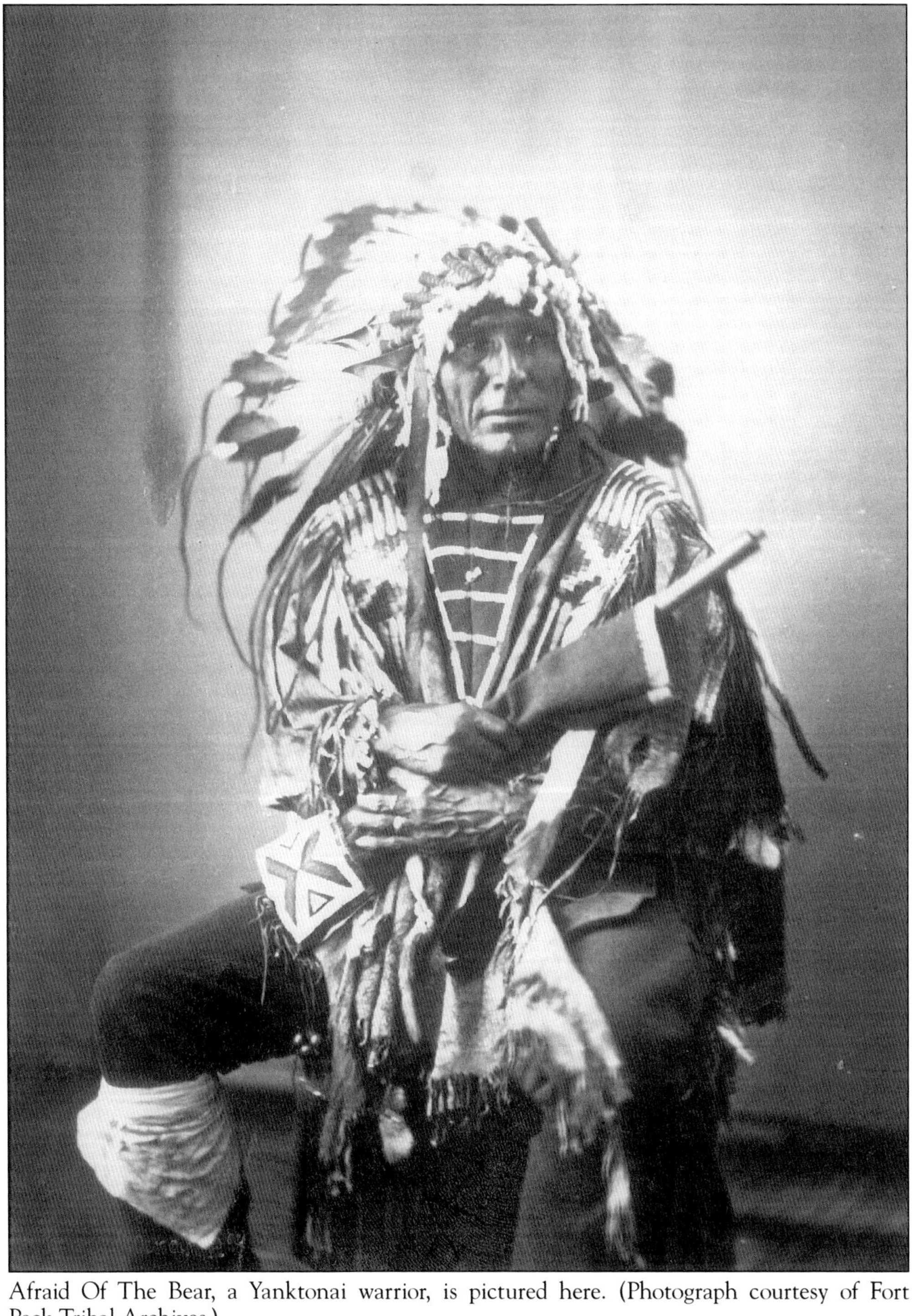

Afraid Of The Bear, a Yanktonai warrior, is pictured here. (Photograph courtesy of Fort Peck Tribal Archives.)

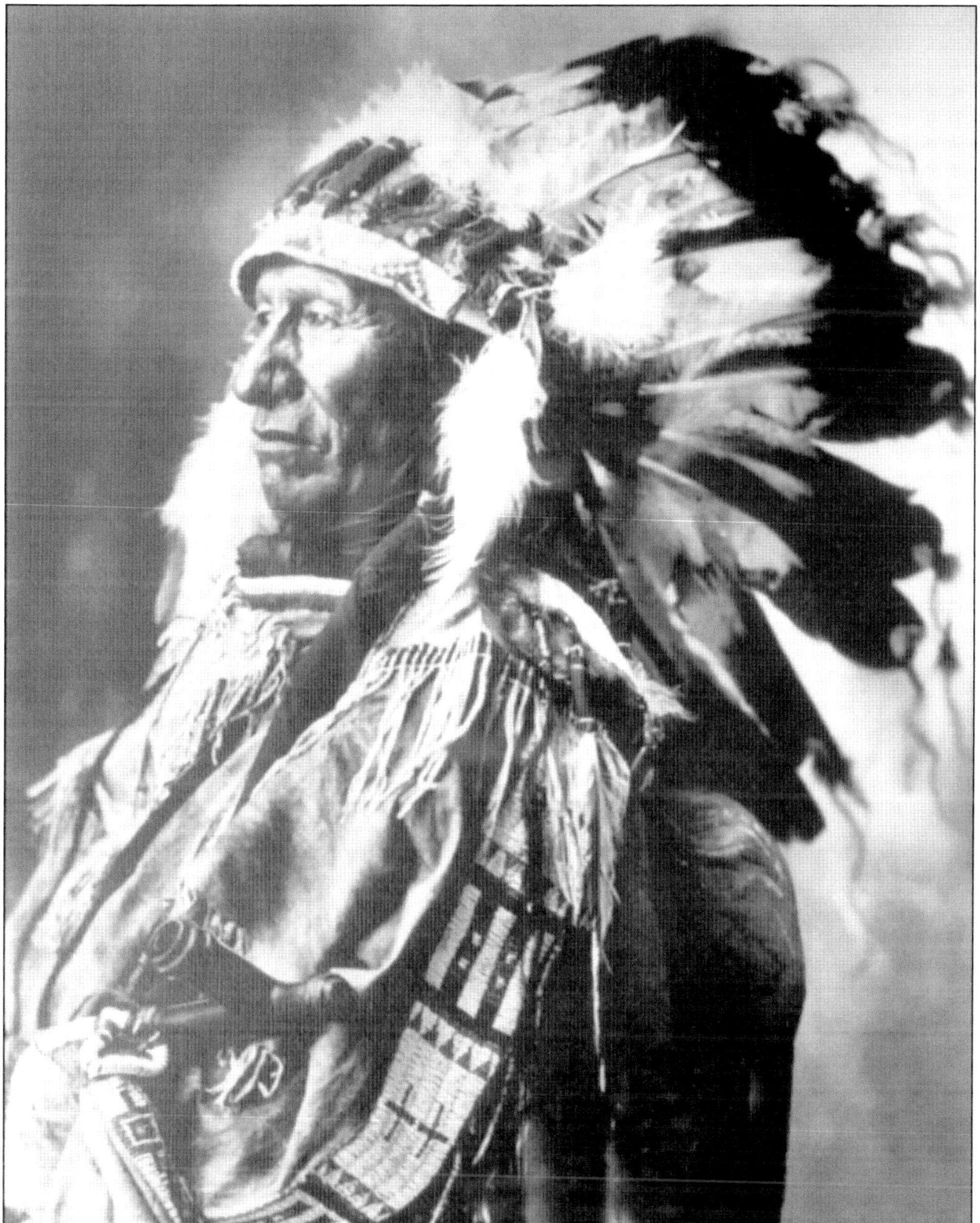

Pictured here is Chief Black Bear, a noble warrior. (Photograph courtesy of the Denver Public Library.)

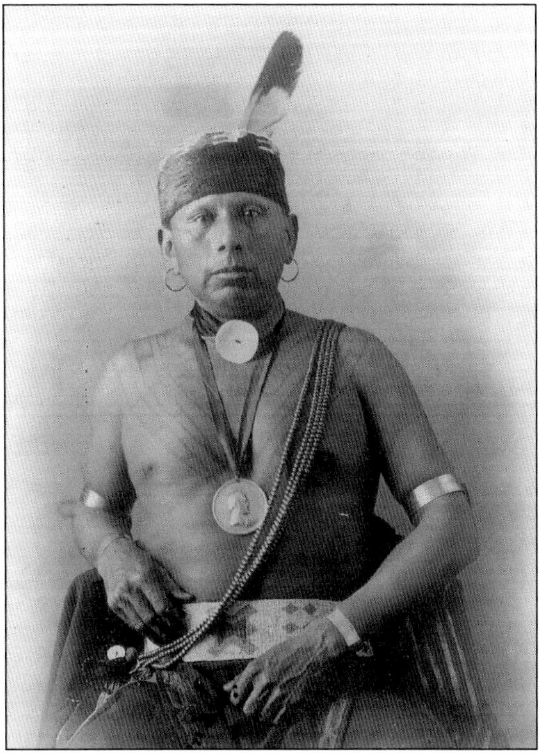

Seen here is Wa Shin Ha, a Sioux warrior. (Photograph courtesy of Fort Peck Tribal Archives.)

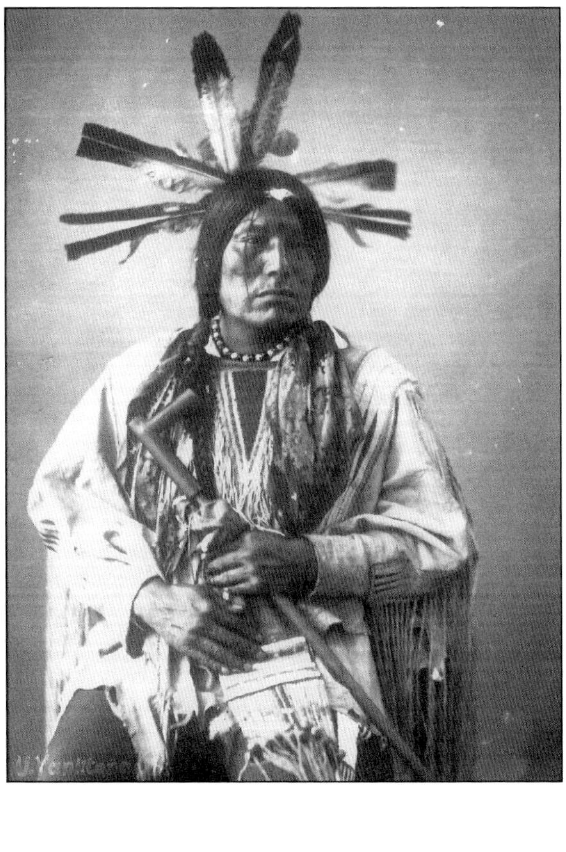

Eagle Man, Man Who Packs The Eagle, was a Yanktonai warrior. (Photograph courtesy of Fort Peck Tribal Archives.)

Heart Skin fought as a Yanktonai warrior. (Photograph courtesy of Fort Peck Tribal Archives.)

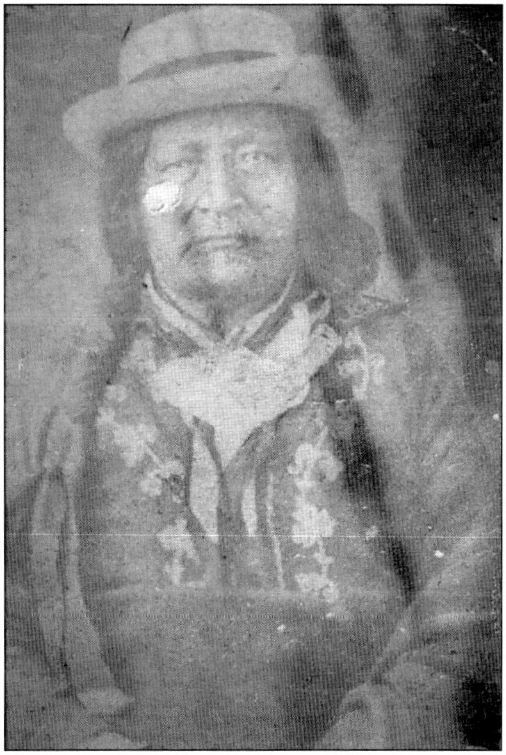

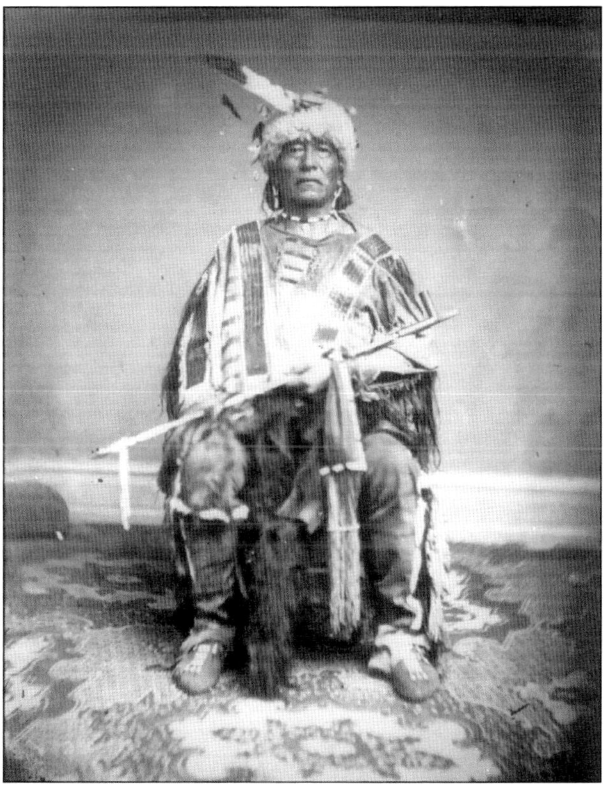

A portrait of a Yanktonai warrior is seen here. (Photograph courtesy of Fort Peck Tribal Archives.)

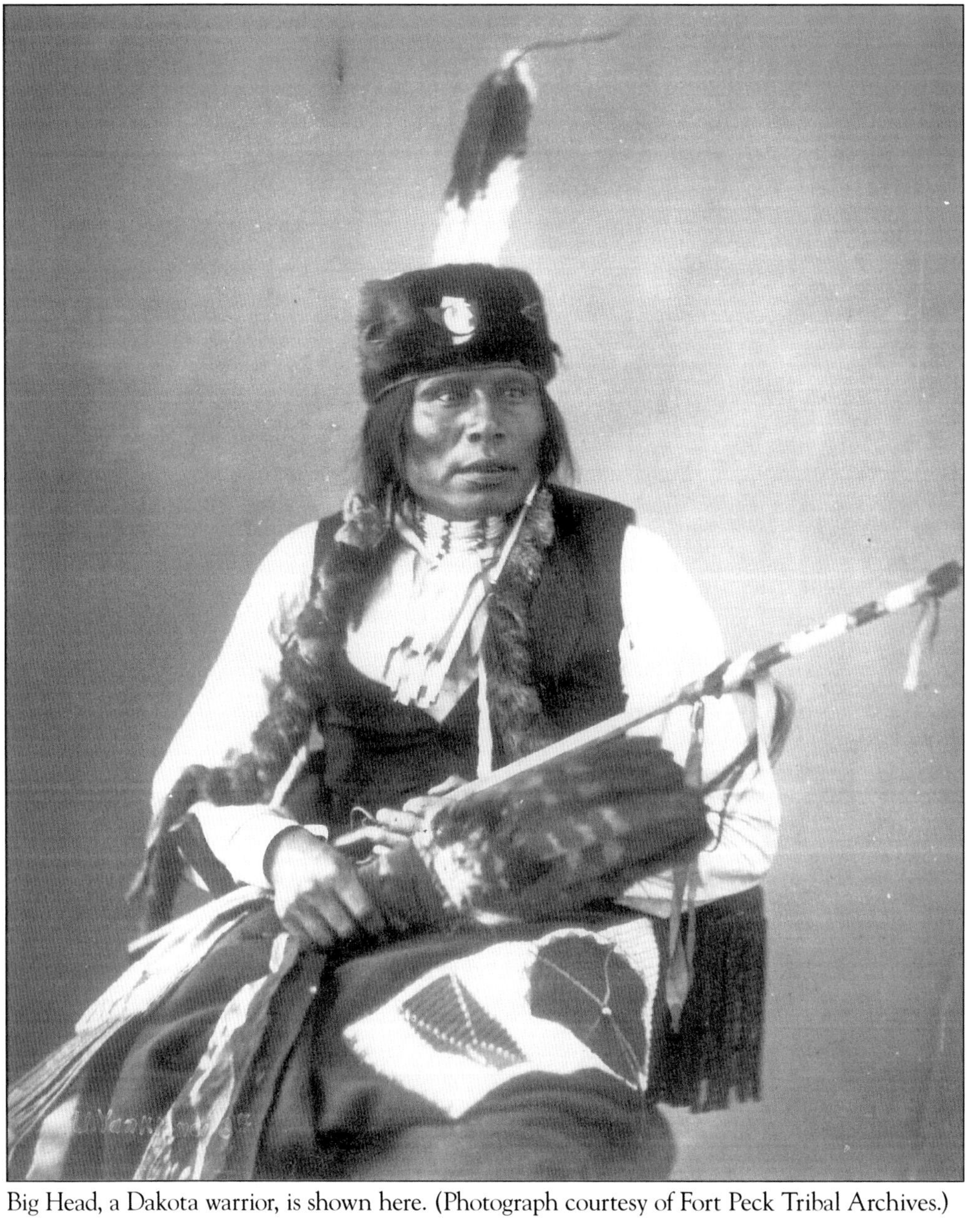

Big Head, a Dakota warrior, is shown here. (Photograph courtesy of Fort Peck Tribal Archives.)

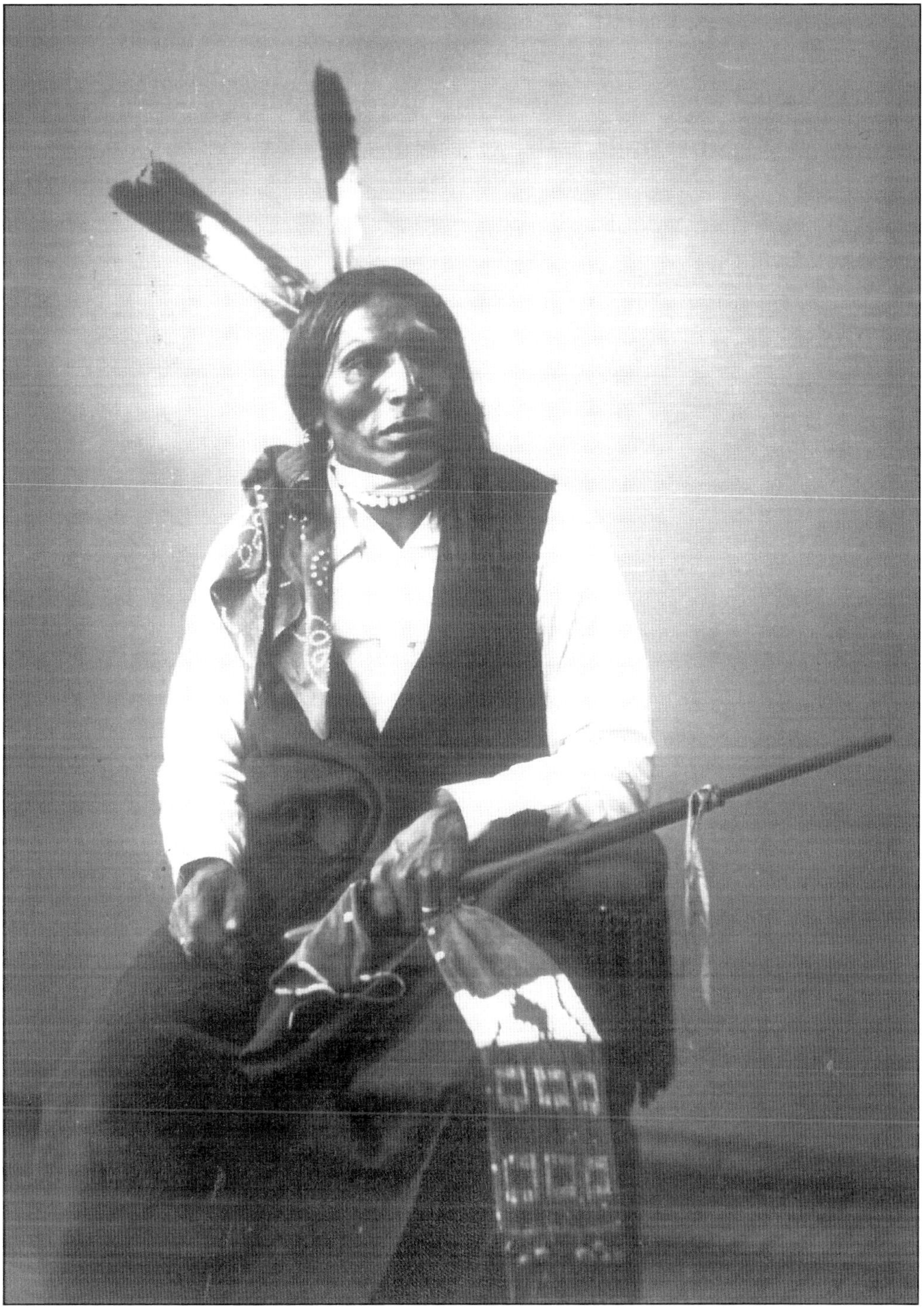

Grizzly Bears Nose was a Dakota warrior. (Photograph courtesy of Fort Peck Tribal Archives.)

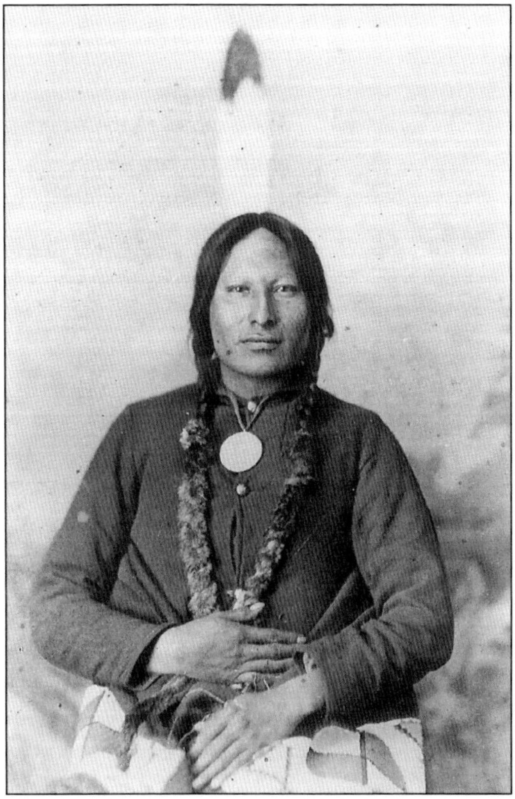

Crow King, a Hunkpapa warrior, is pictured here. (Photograph courtesy of Fort Peck Tribal Archives.)

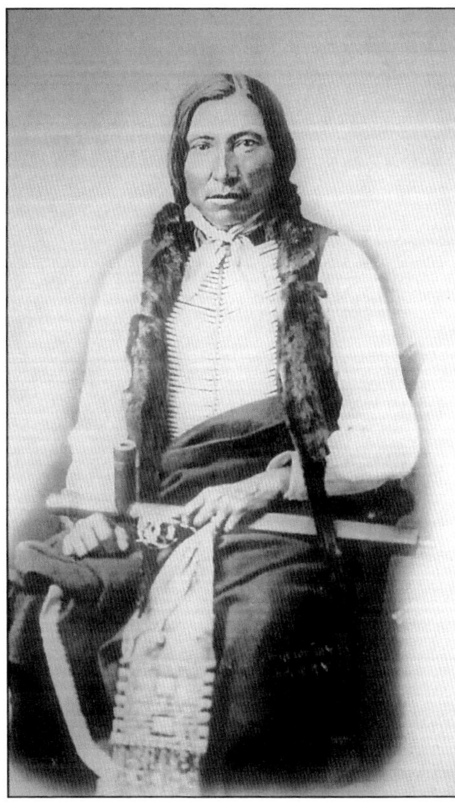

Bull Head was a brave warrior. (Photograph courtesy of the National Park Service, Little Bighorn Battlefield National Monument.)

Red Lodge, a member of the Cut Head Band of the Yanktonai, is photographed here. (Photograph courtesy of Fort Peck Tribal Archives.)

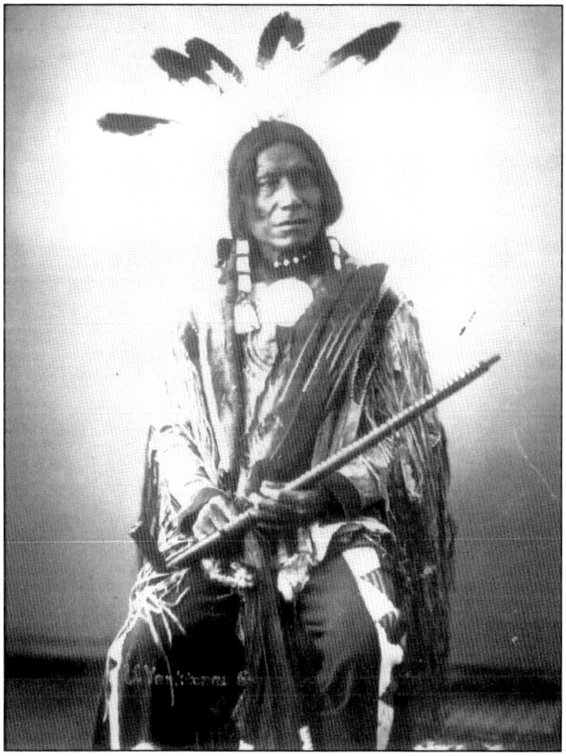

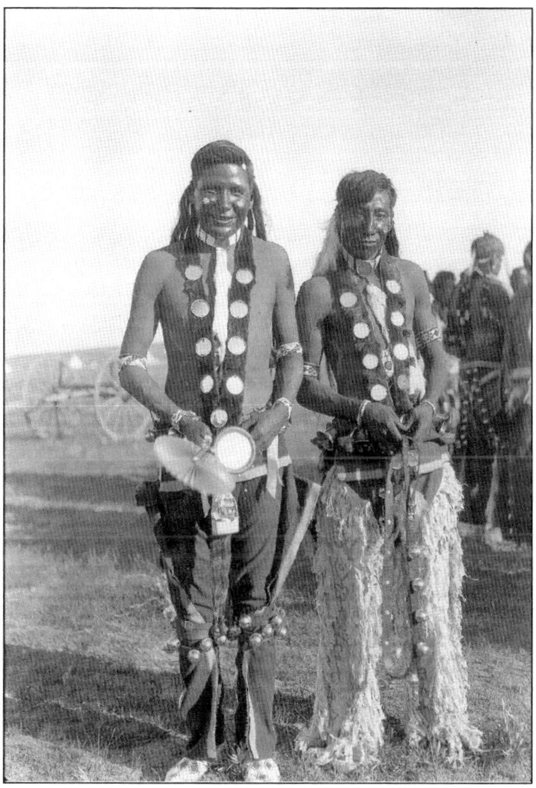

Pictured here are two young and distinguished Sioux warriors. (Photograph courtesy of Fort Peck Tribal Archives.)

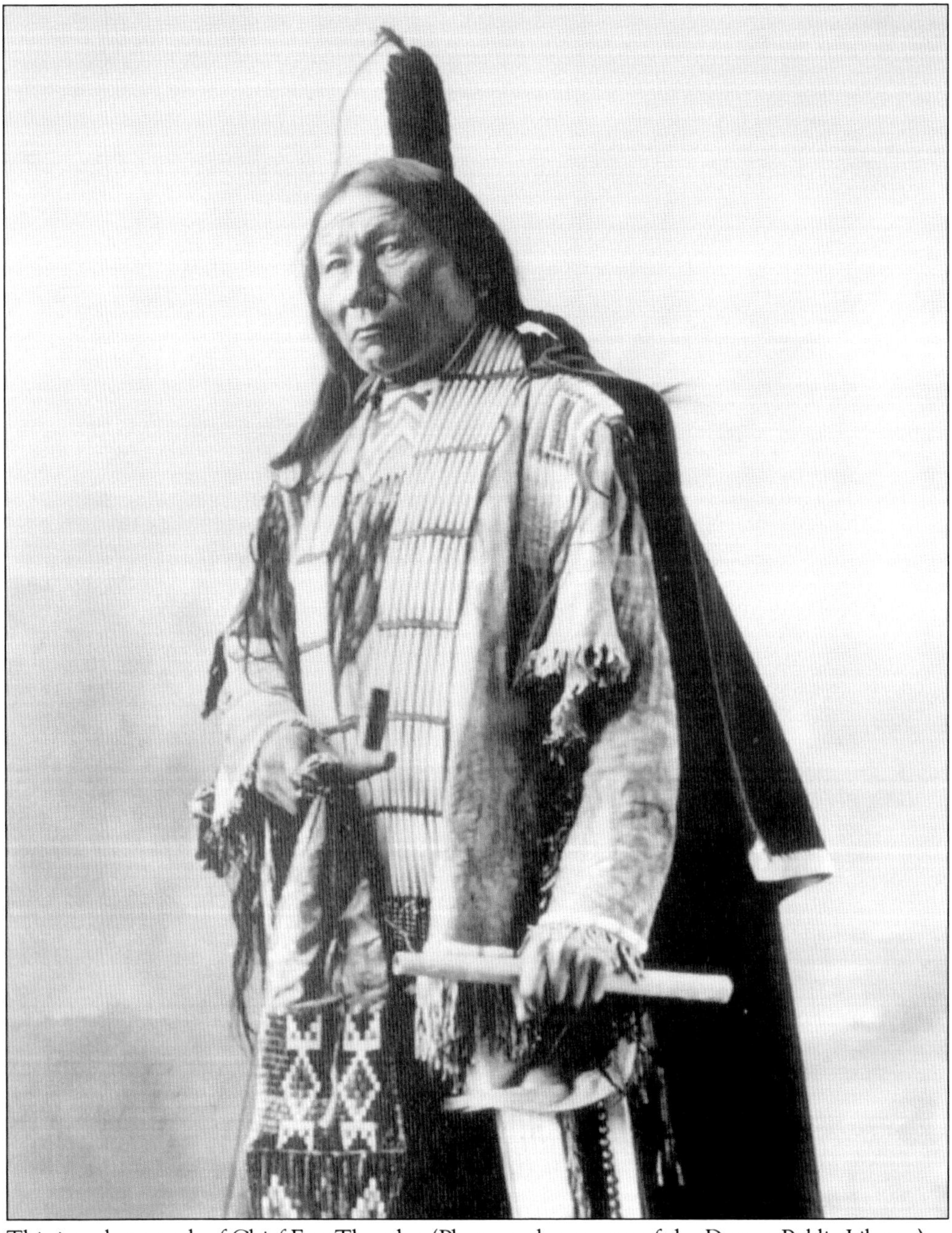

This is a photograph of Chief Fast Thunder. (Photograph courtesy of the Denver Public Library.)

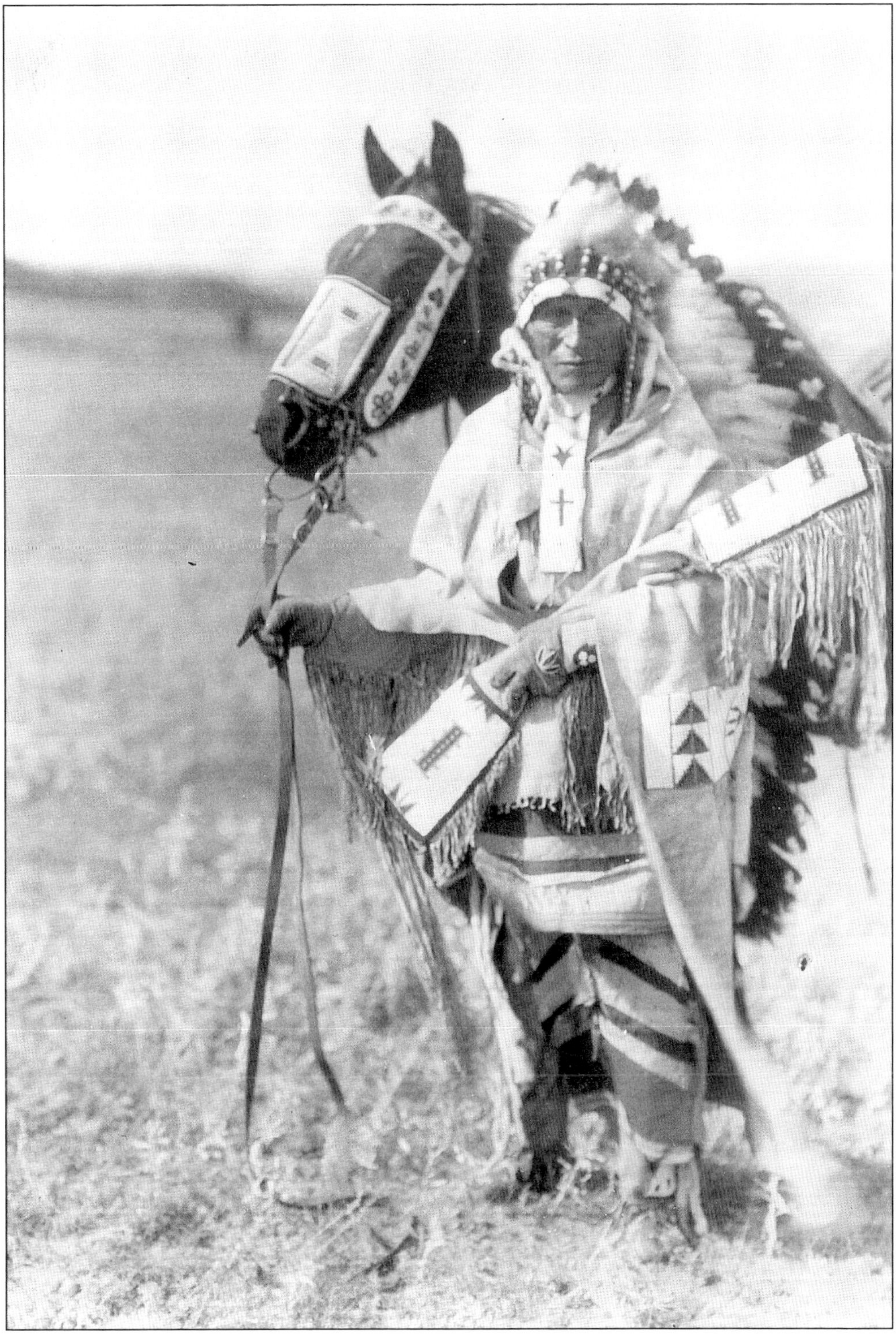

An impressive chief is ready to protect the camp. Note also extensive beadwork adorning the head of his horse. (Photograph courtesy of Fort Peck Tribal Archives.)

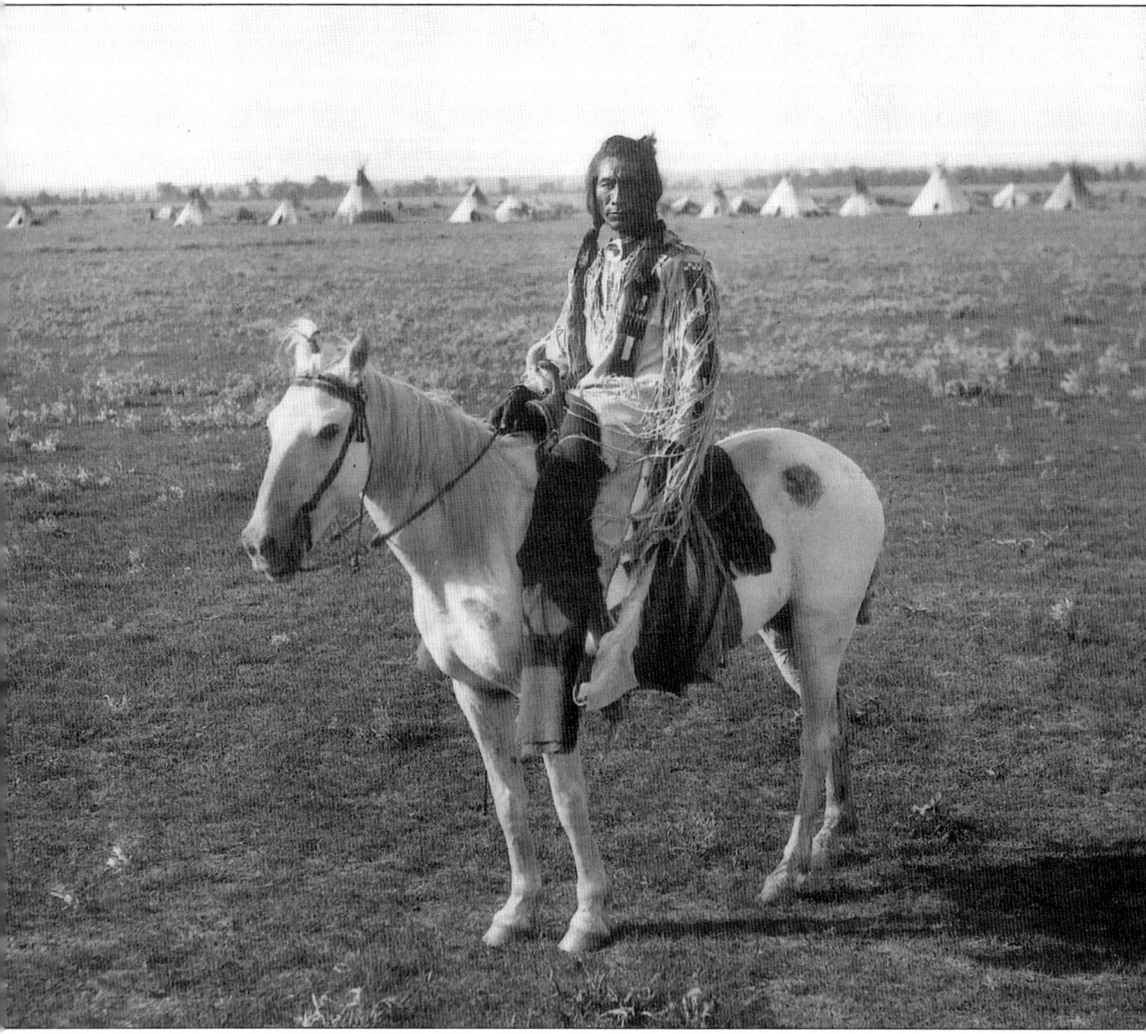

The warriors' responsibility was to protect the women and the children. They were encouraged to avoid fighting if possible. If the enemy came, they would fight to the death. Tales of their dedication and bravery are told at evening campfires and are celebrated in song and in the dance. (Photograph courtesy of Fort Peck Tribal Archives.)

Seven

Continuing The Circle

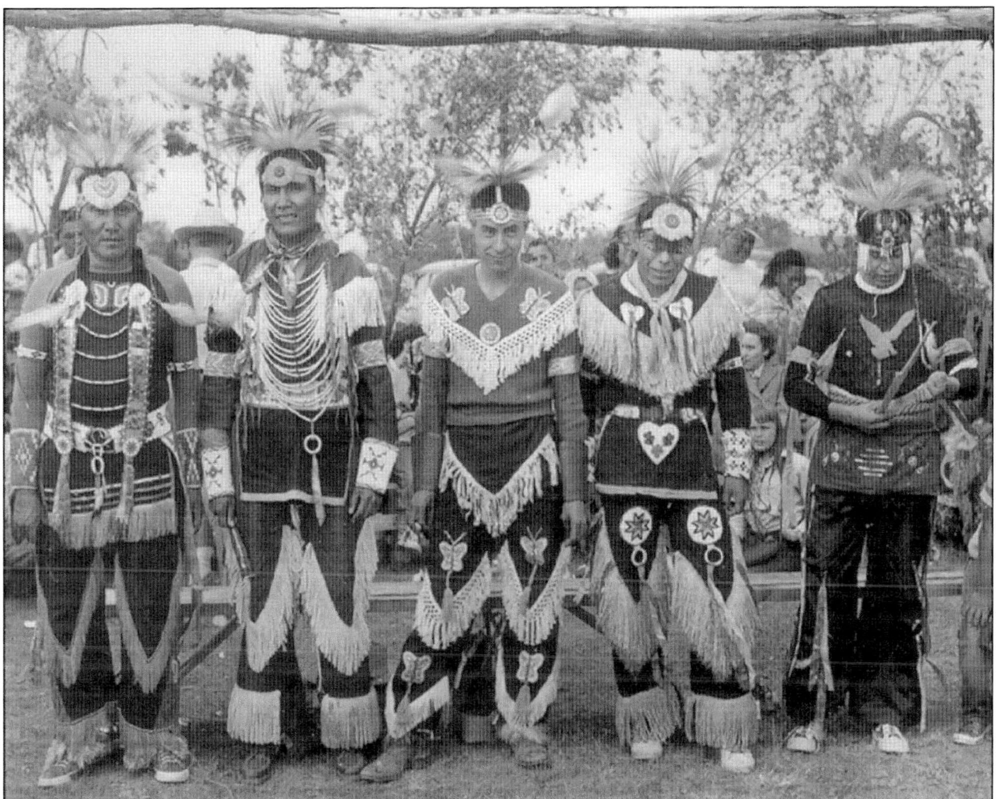

Dancers continue the circle by preserving the ancient ceremonies and dances, and teaching them to their children. This is a photograph of Grass Dancers from Poplar, Montana, included is Kenneth Shields Sr. (second from the right.), the author's father who was a singer and a Grass Dancer. (Photograph courtesy of the Author's private collection.)

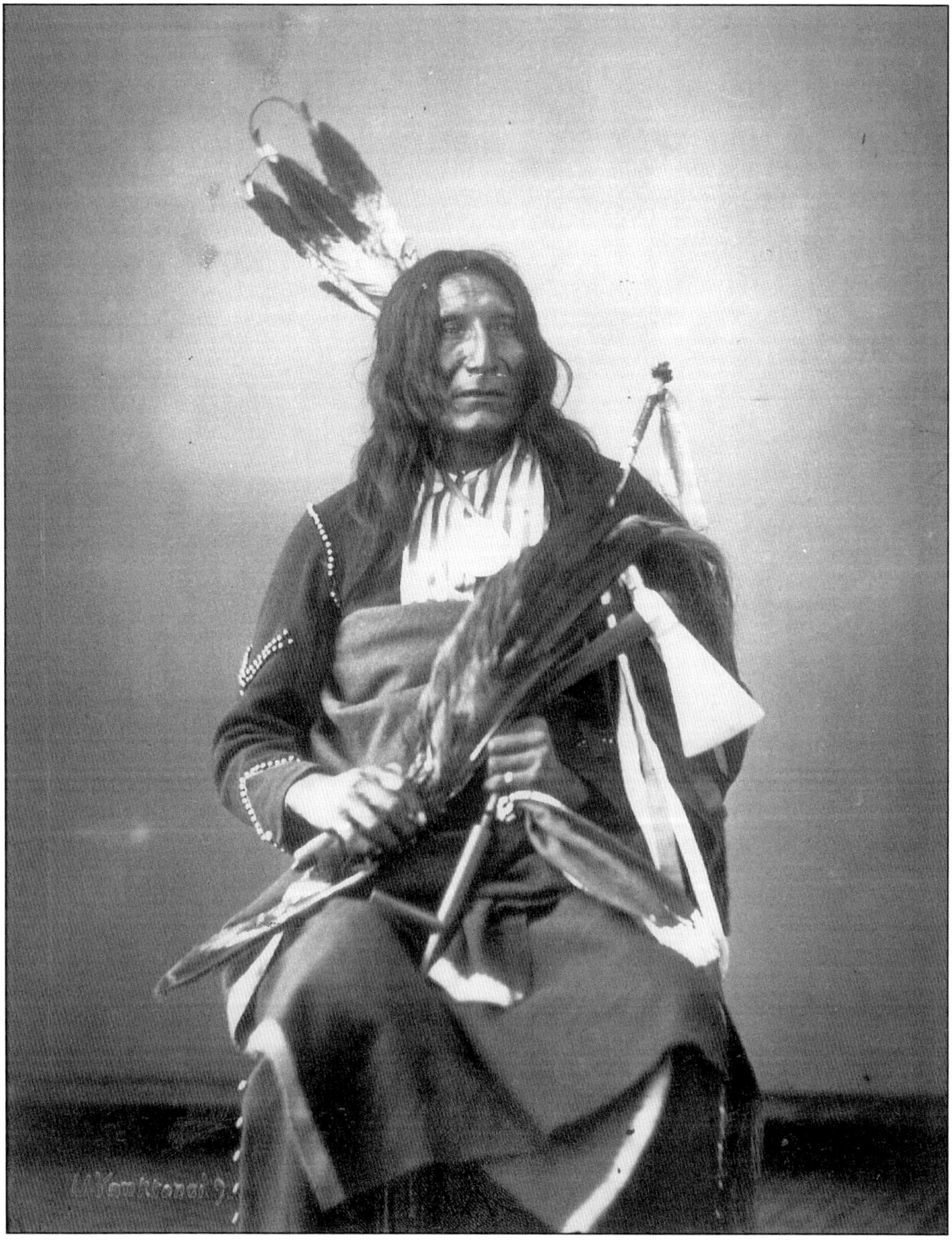

Pictured in this 1872 photo by famed photographer Alexander Gardner, Chief Big Head is wearing splendid warrior regalia replete with V-shaped piping and brass beads. (Photograph courtesy of Fort Peck Tribal Archives.)

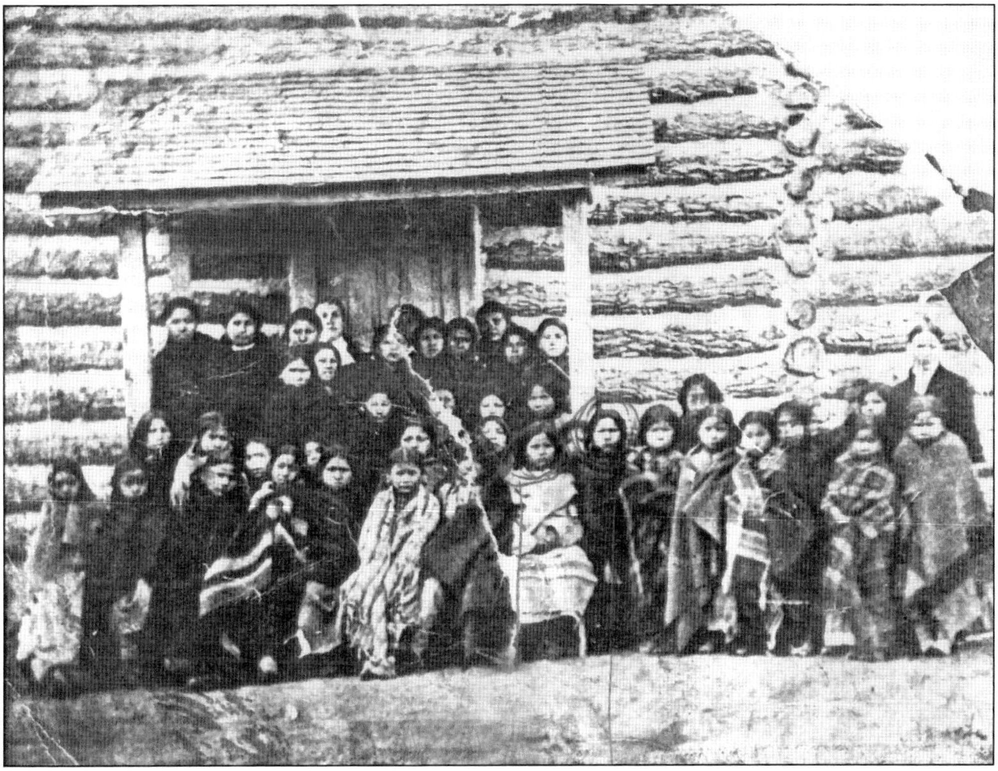

Assembled here by the entrance of a log building, adults and children stand before what appears to be an early school building. (Photograph courtesy of Fort Peck Tribal Archives.)

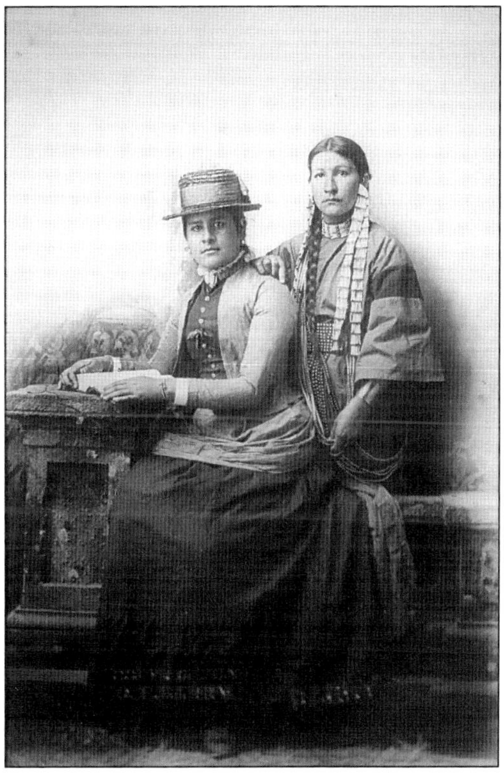

Pictured here are two daughters of Mad Bear, Alimona (left) and Sweet Clover (right). Since one had to sit perfectly still for early photographs such as these, subjects rarely smiled. (Photograph courtesy of the National Park Service, Little Bighorn Battlefield National Monument.)

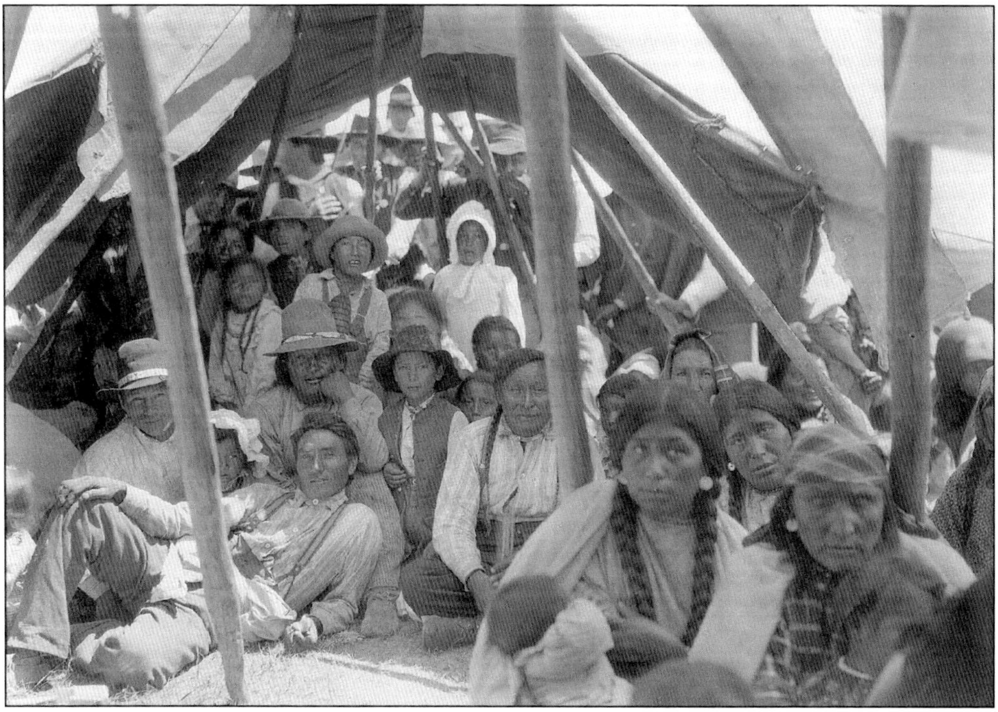

Large tents such as this one provided a wonderful setting for story telling from one generation to another. Although this tent has quite a few people in it already, there is room for still more. (Photograph courtesy of Fort Peck Tribal Archives.)

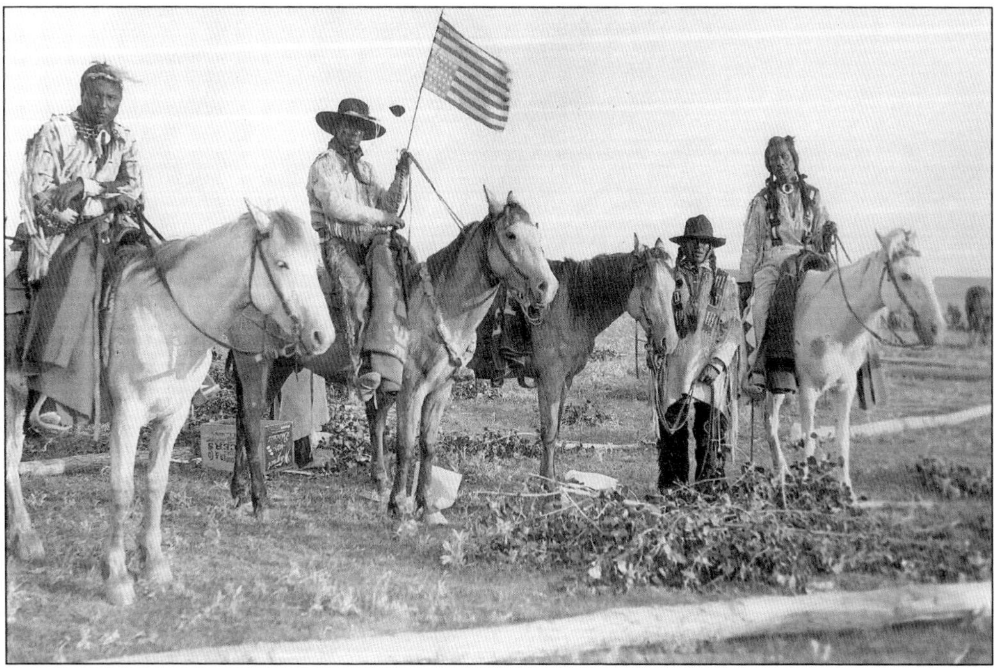

Holding the flag upside down as this rider is doing is a signal of distress. (Photograph courtesy of Fort Peck Tribal Archives.)

This Standing studio portrait is of an Oglala Sioux, identified as Painted Horse. He wears moccasins, beaded leggings, a shirt decorated with animal fur, and a full length headdress with eagle feathers and buffalo horns. In his left hand, he carries a shield upon which is painted the likeness of a buffalo and which has feathers adorning the edges. (Photograph courtesy of the Denver Public Library.)

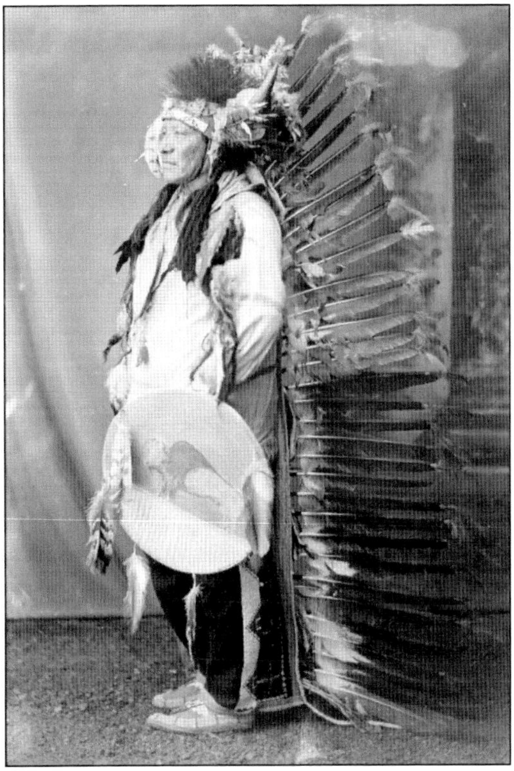

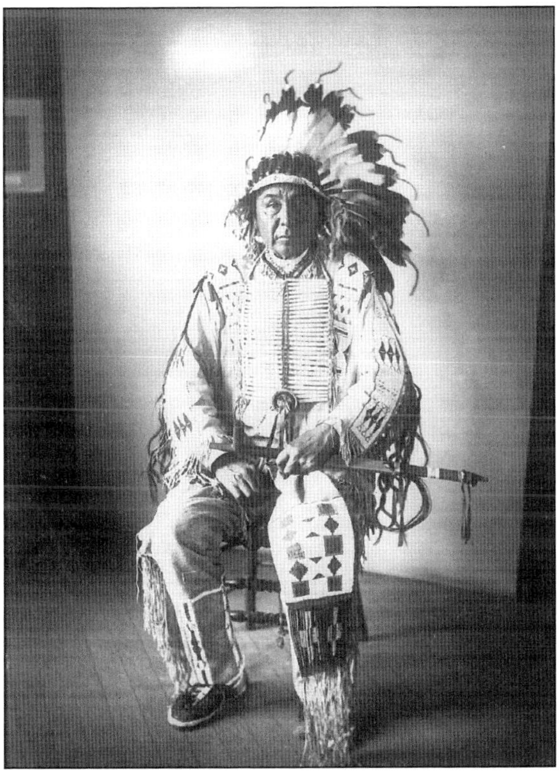

One cannot mistake the majesty and awe that this warrior commanded when he took his rightful place among the tribal leaders. Surely he was an inspiration to many an aspiring youth. (Photograph courtesy of Fort Peck Tribal Archives.)

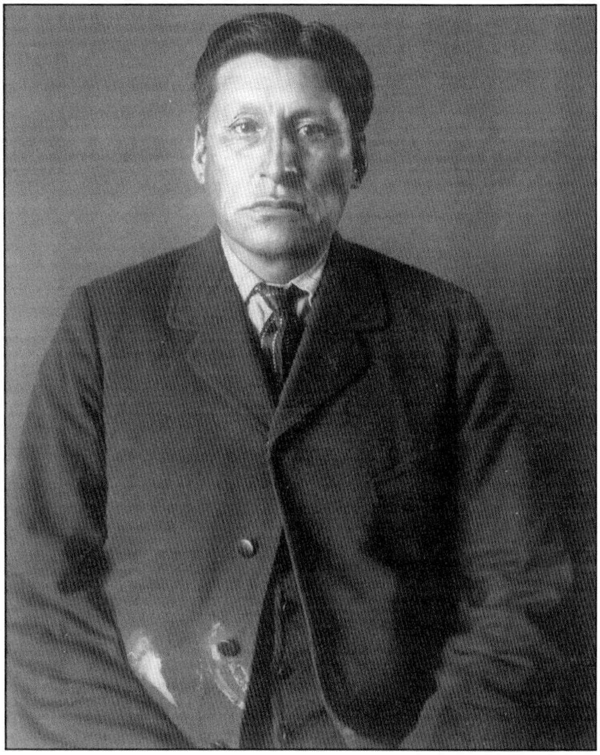

Photographed in suit, shirt, and tie, one is led to wonder what lies behind the staring eyes and determined expression on the face of Red Tomahawk taken by D.L. Gill in 1902. (Photograph courtesy of Fort Peck Tribal Archives.)

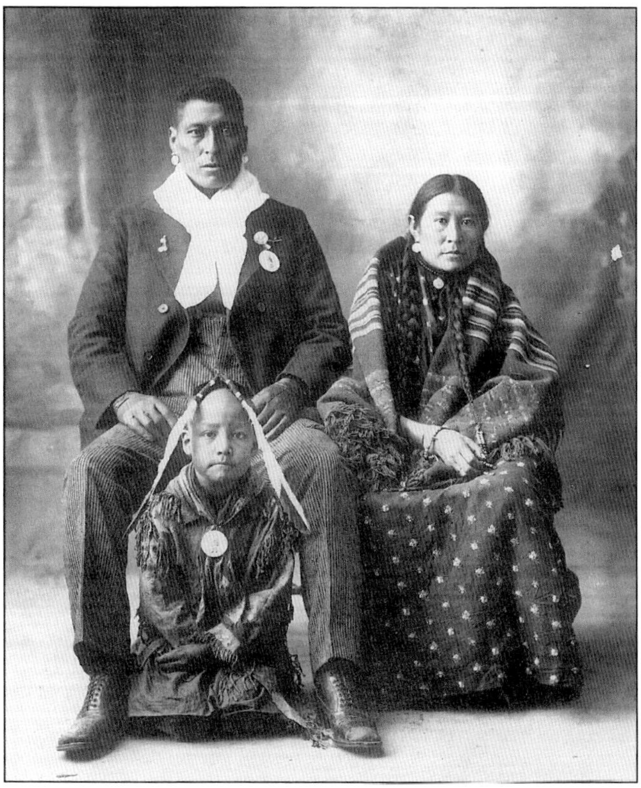

Family pride is evident in this picture of a Sioux couple and their son. (Photograph courtesy of Fort Peck Tribal Archives.)

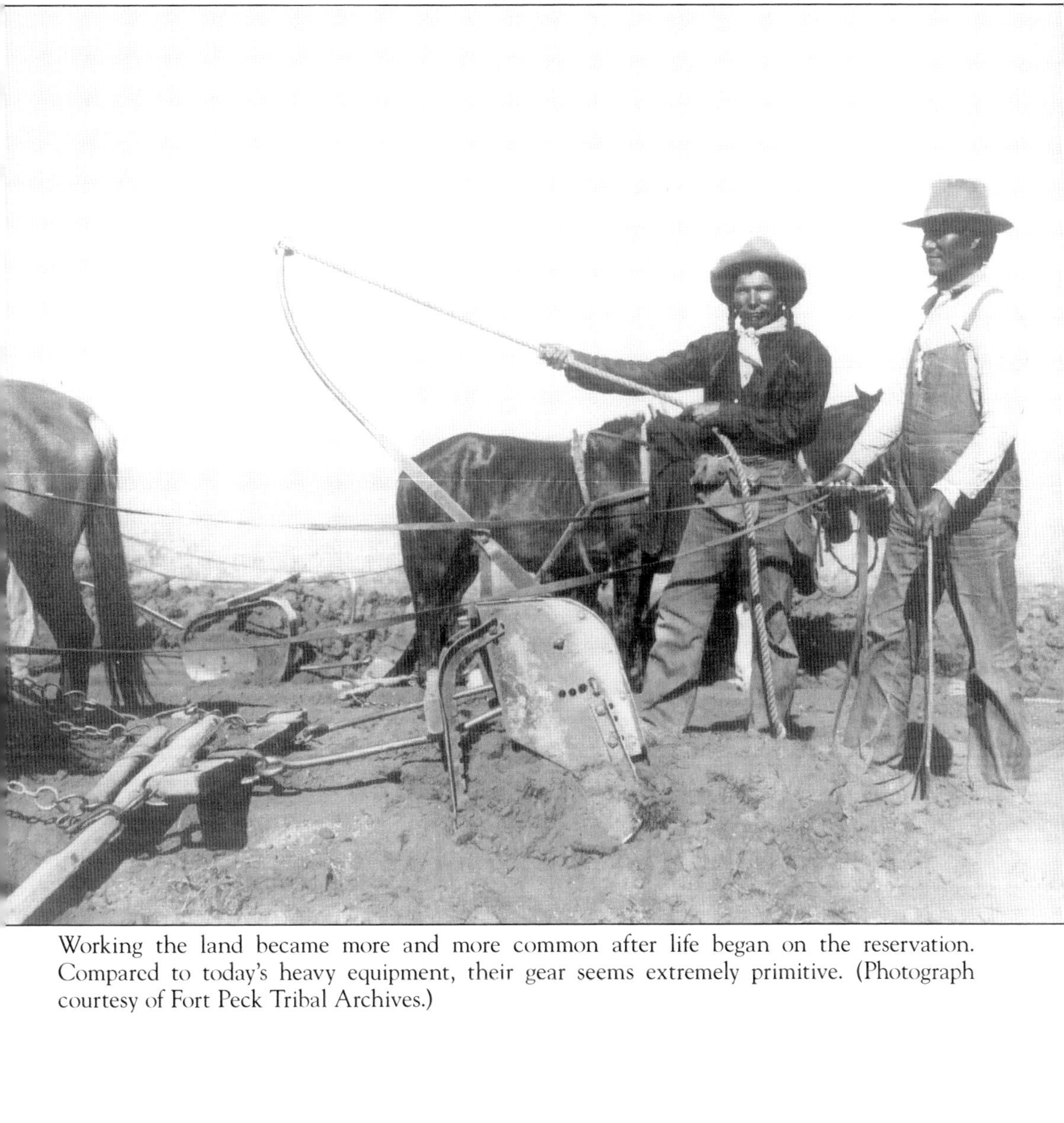

Working the land became more and more common after life began on the reservation. Compared to today's heavy equipment, their gear seems extremely primitive. (Photograph courtesy of Fort Peck Tribal Archives.)

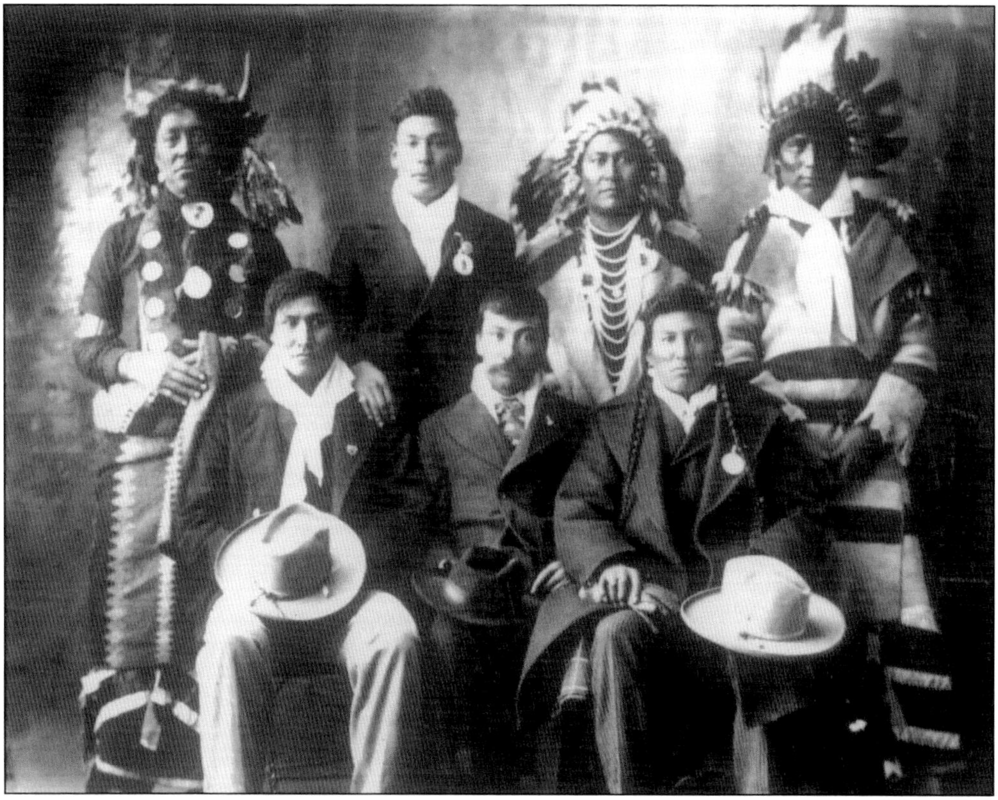

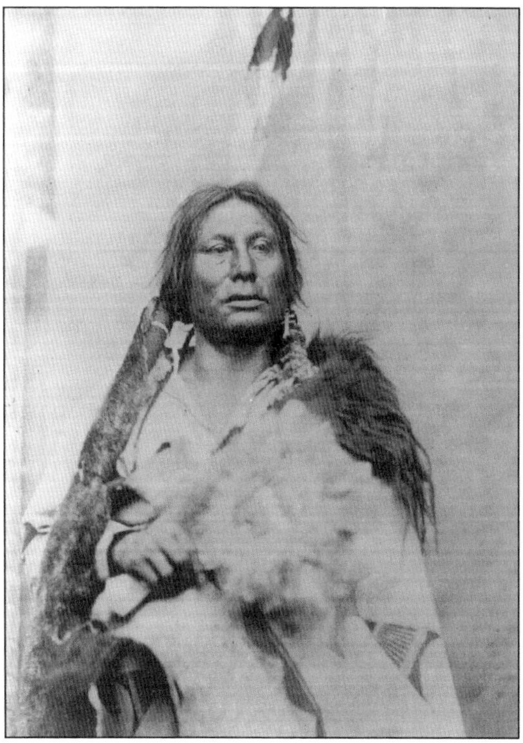

Gathered for a formal portrait, these men pose in ceremonial and stately attire. (Photograph courtesy of Fort Peck Tribal Archives.)

Gall, in an undated photograph, sits serenely in a painted skin robe. Note braids tied with fabric and fur. Gall was a member of the same tribe as Sitting Bull. Also known as "Walks in Red Clothing" and "Man Who Goes in the Middle," Gall was intelligent and a very brave leader. (Photograph courtesy of Fort Peck Tribal Archives.)

Red Cloud labored for the welfare of his people. He compromised with the old ways in an attempt to carve out a new life fitted to new conditions. Red Cloud was a true statesman. (Photograph courtesy of Fort Peck Tribal Archives.)

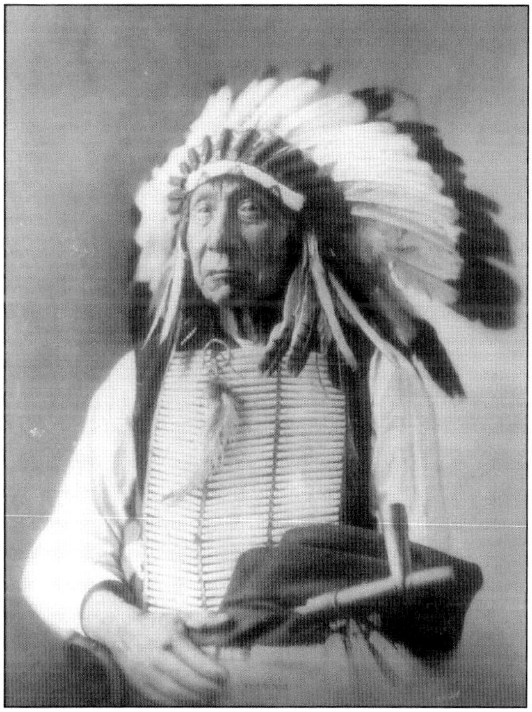

Traveling to Washington D.C., Spotted Eagle, Iron Whip, Horse's Ghost, Grow Twice, and Kill prepare to meet with members of the Taft administration, November 1911. (Photograph courtesy of Fort Peck Tribal Archives.)

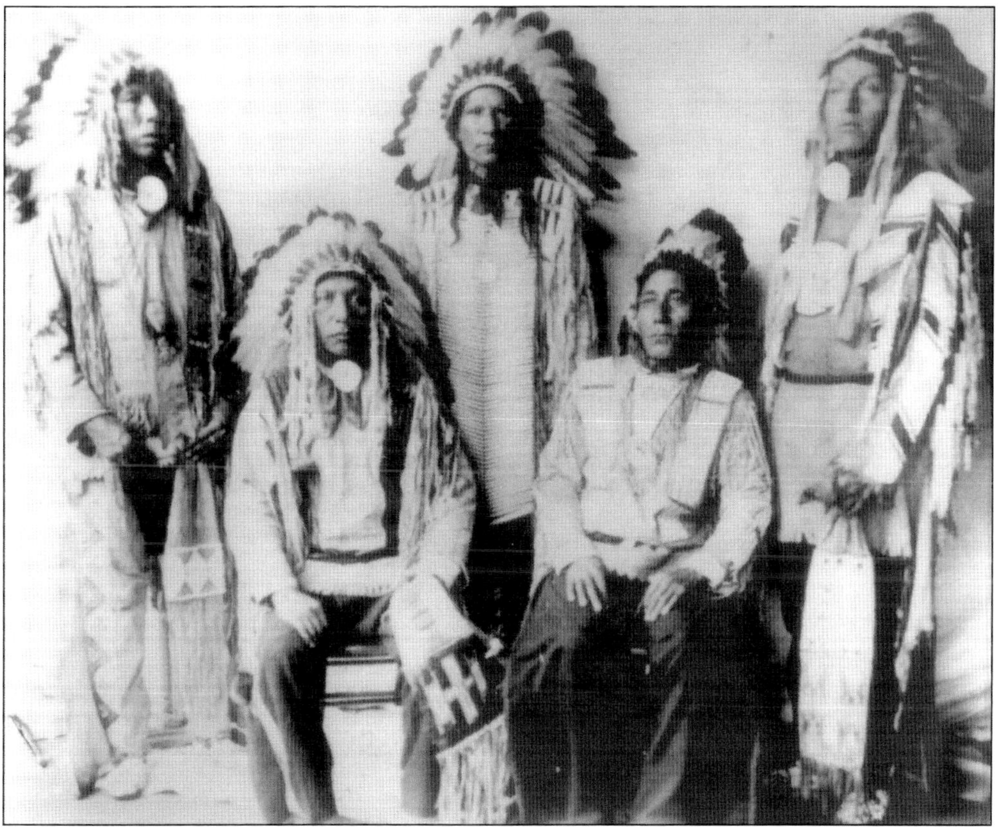

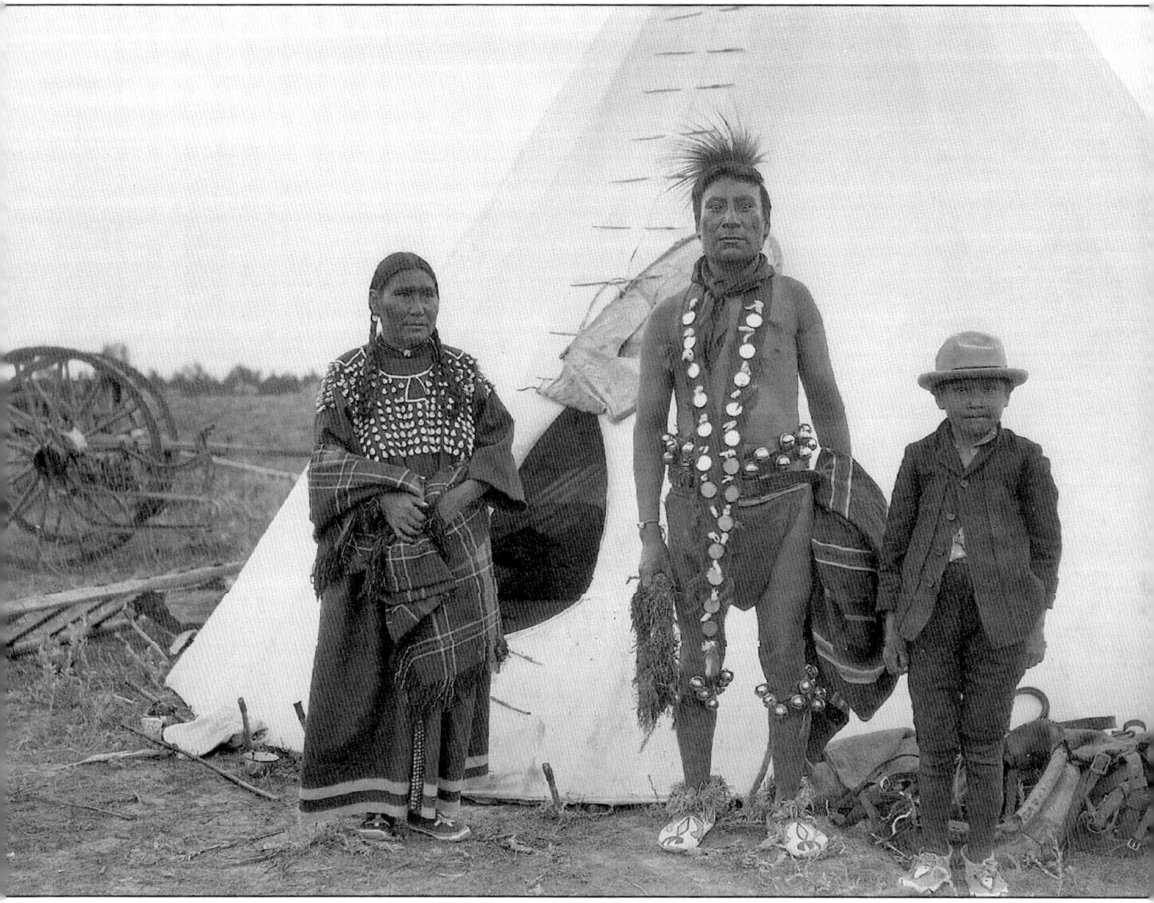

Deeply spiritual people, their reverence for the Creator and their ties to Mother Earth are reflected in both music and dance. The man at the center is about to participate in a dance for which he is appropriately dressed. The story portrayed in the dance is both a remembrance for the adults and a learning experience for the young. (Photograph courtesy of Fort Peck Tribal Archives.)

Eight

The Fires of Tiospaye
The Light of Freedom

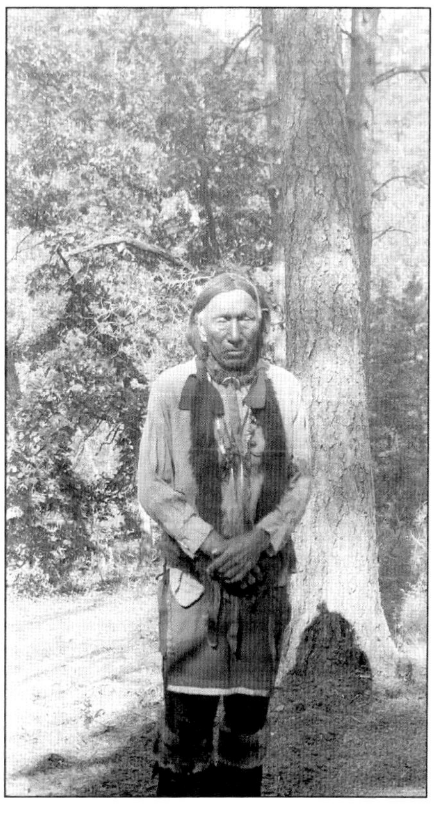

The flames that burned in the fires of Tiospaye were promises of freedom and the preservation of a way of life. We have a commitment, each to light one candle, to keep the Light of their memory from going out. This chapter presents actual photographs of the men and women who experienced the power and the mystery of Tiospaye. With each presentation, the author echoes their cry together with the collective voices of those who triumphed in that moment in time. Join us in the celebration of their spirit, don't let the Light go out.

A portrait of Black Elk, an Oglala spiritual leader. (Photograph courtesy of the Denver Public Library.)

What is the memory, that's valued so highly that we keep alive in that flame? What's the commitment to those who have died...we cry out they've not died in vain. We have come this far, always believing that justice will somehow prevail. This is the burning, this is the promise, and this is why we shall not fail.

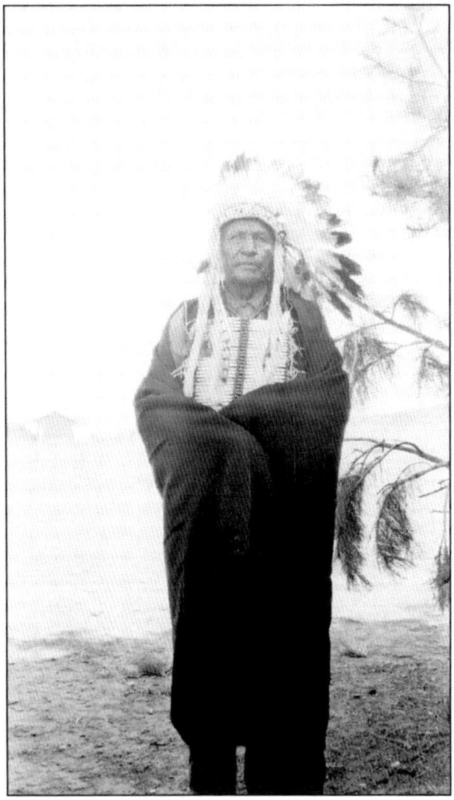

This portrait of Mark Spider, an elderly Sioux man, is dated 1936. (Photograph courtesy of the Denver Public Library.)

"Light One Candle: for the pain they endured and their right to exist was denied."

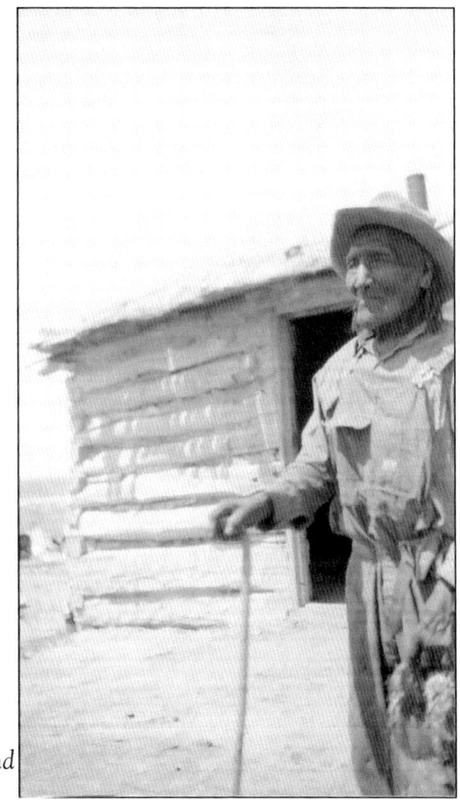

This portrait of Scabbard Knife, an elderly Sioux man, is dated 1936. (Photograph courtesy of the Denver Public Library.)

"Light One Candle: for the terrible sacrifice justice and freedom demands."

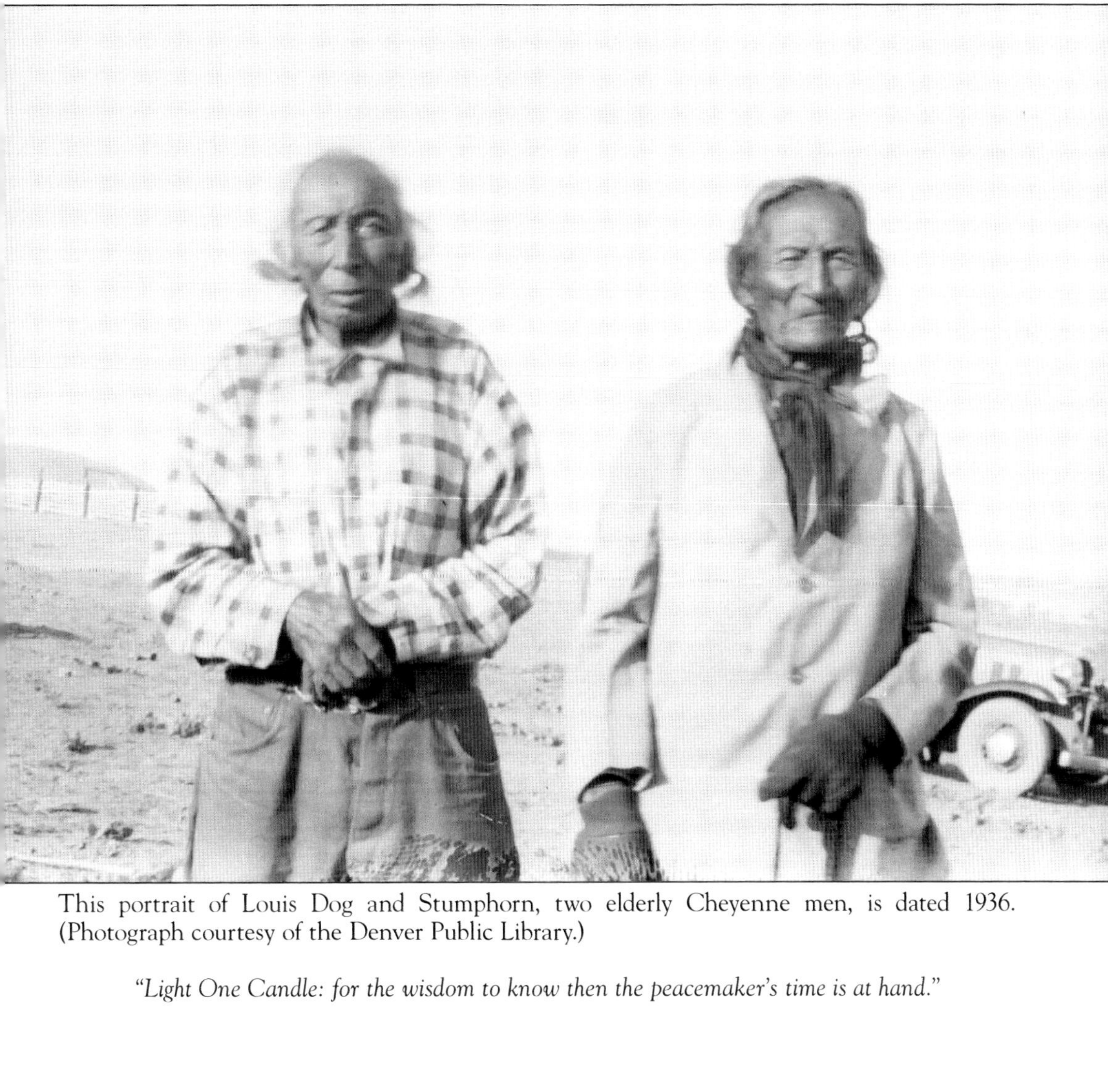

This portrait of Louis Dog and Stumphorn, two elderly Cheyenne men, is dated 1936. (Photograph courtesy of the Denver Public Library.)

"Light One Candle: for the wisdom to know then the peacemaker's time is at hand."

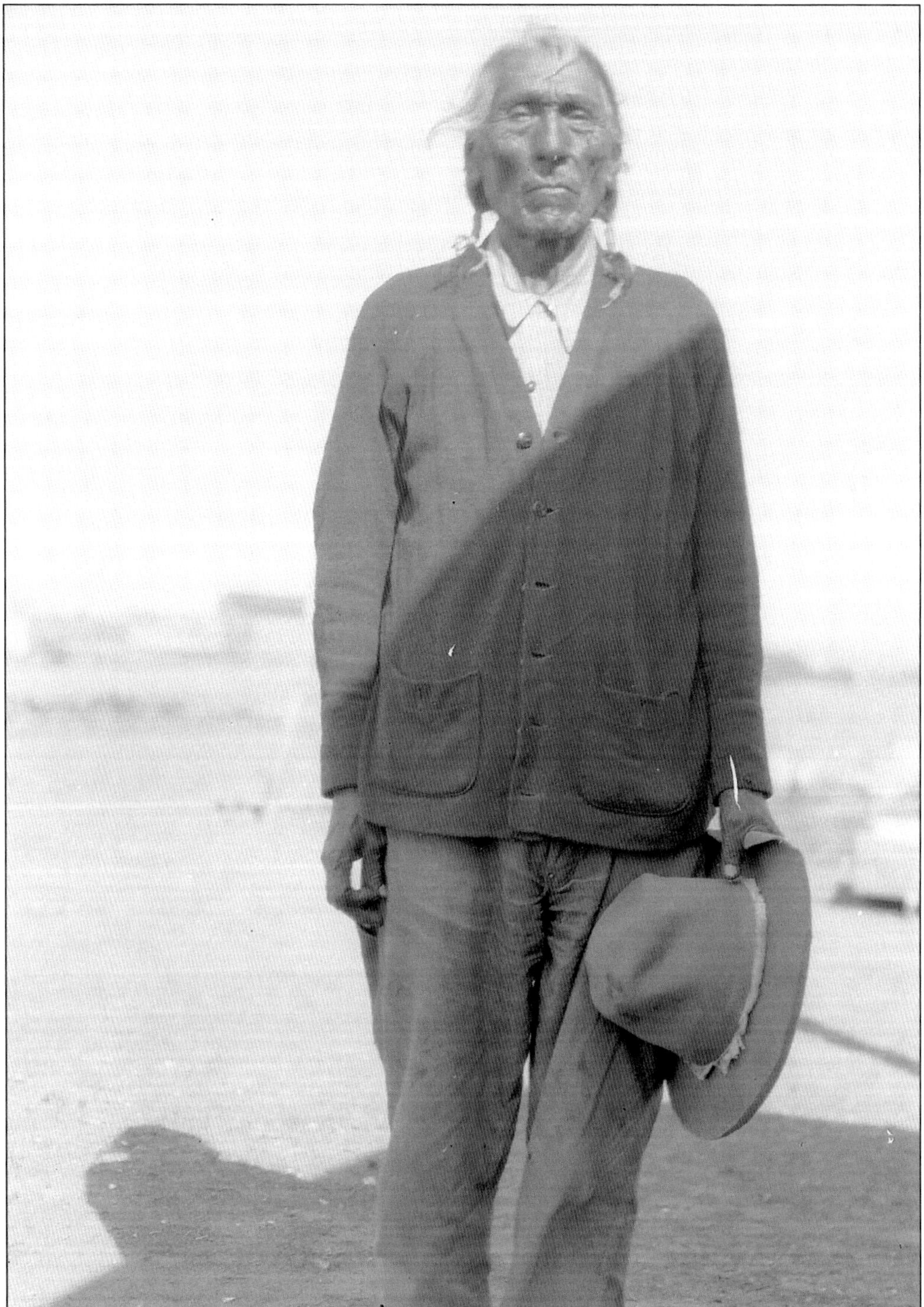

Portrait of White Bull, and elderly Cheyenne man, is dated 1936. (Photograph courtesy of the Denver Public Library.)

"Light One Candle: for the strength that we need to never become our own foe."

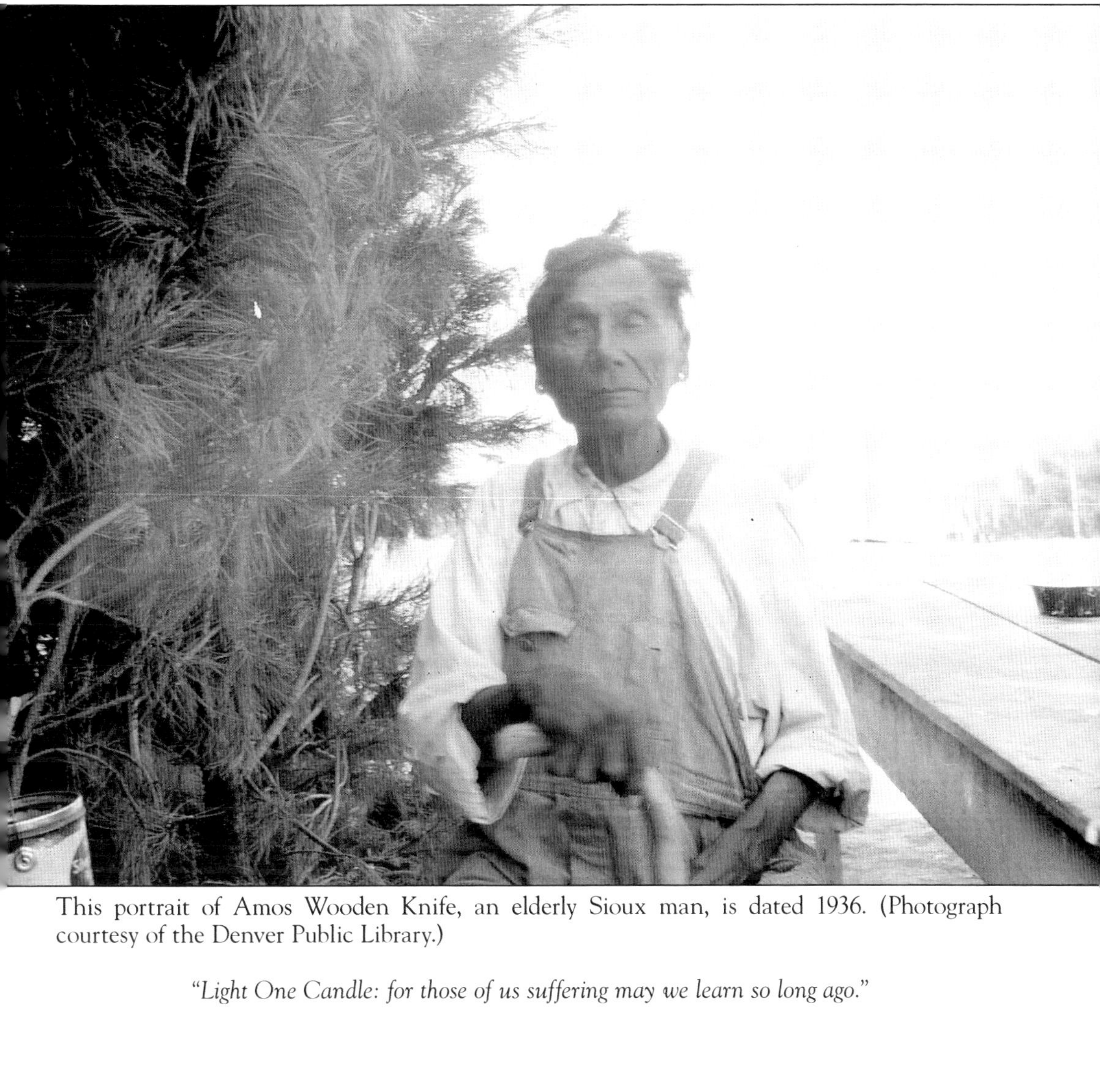

This portrait of Amos Wooden Knife, an elderly Sioux man, is dated 1936. (Photograph courtesy of the Denver Public Library.)

"Light One Candle: for those of us suffering may we learn so long ago."

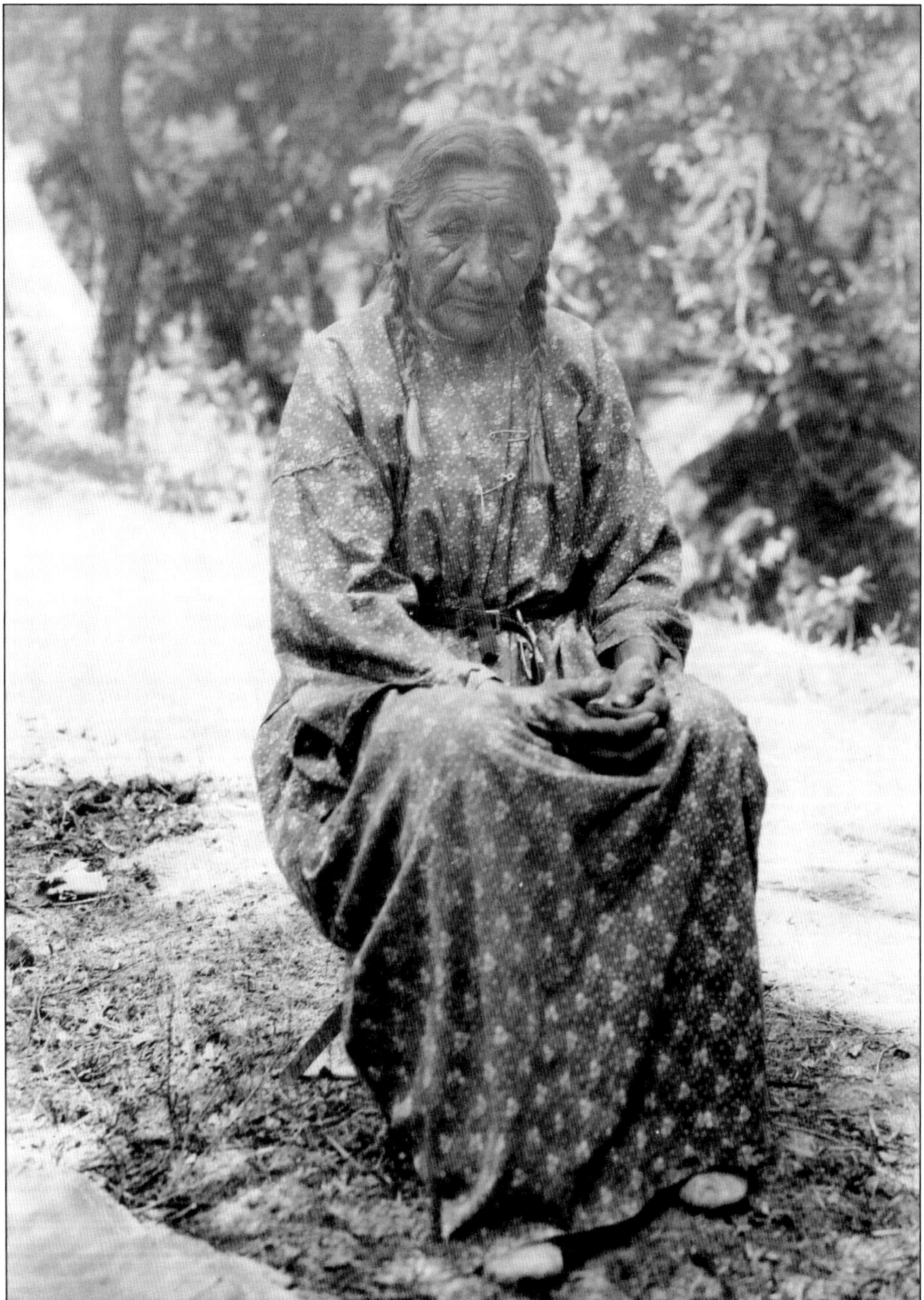

This portrait of the Wife of Wooden Leg, a Northern Cheyenne woman, is dated 1936. (Photograph courtesy of the Denver Public Library.)

"Light One Candle: for all we believe in, that anger not tear us apart."

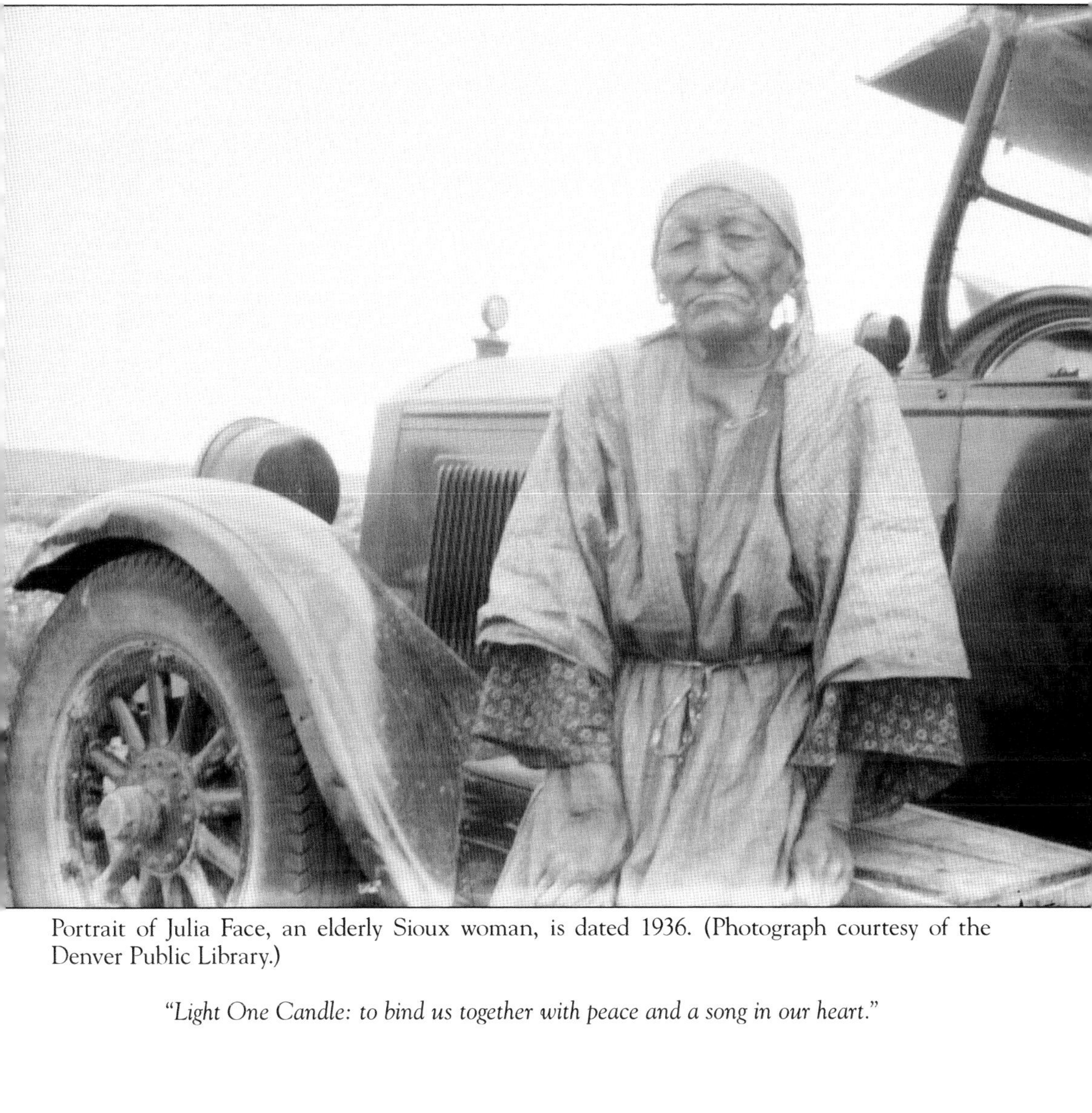

Portrait of Julia Face, an elderly Sioux woman, is dated 1936. (Photograph courtesy of the Denver Public Library.)

"Light One Candle: to bind us together with peace and a song in our heart."

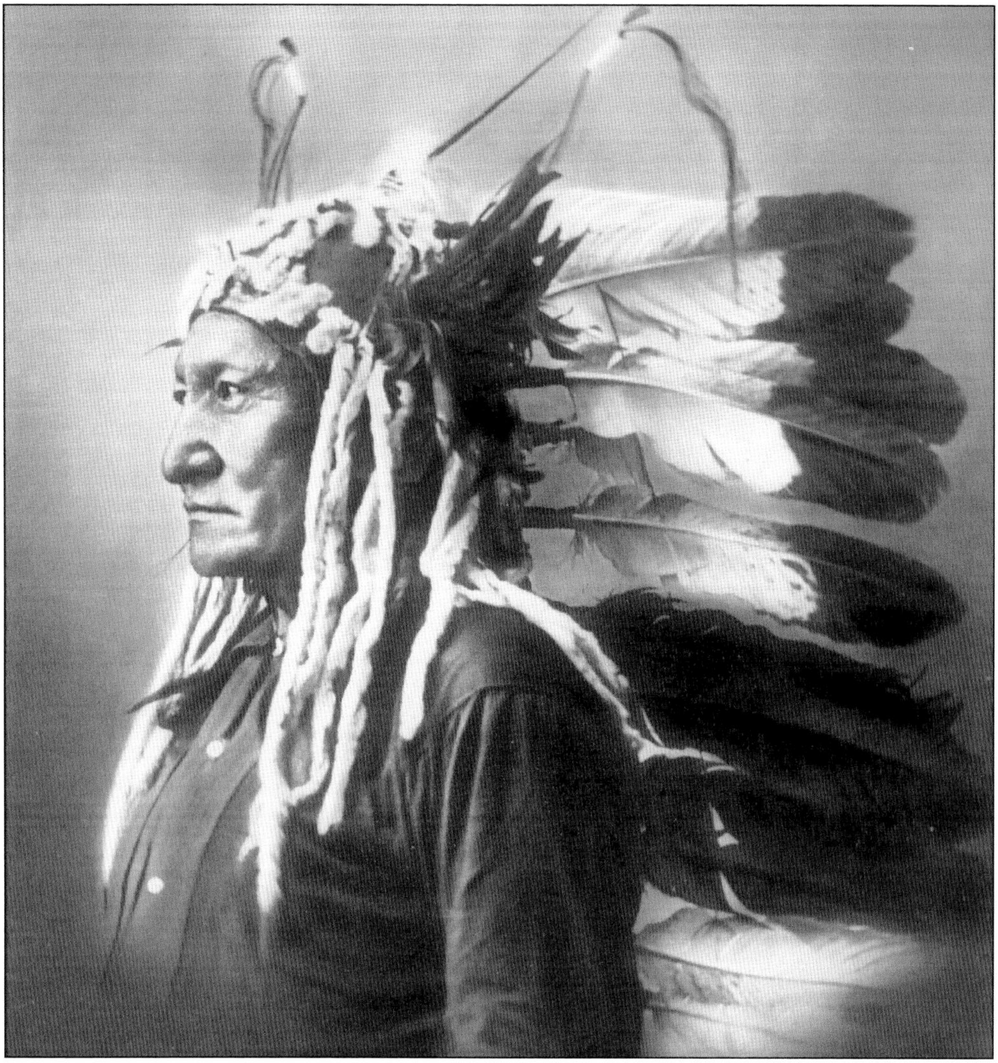

June 25, 1876

The golden sun of a new day slowly pushes its brilliance into a waiting June morning. Mists of a cool night now meeting the warmth of dawn hang as if artistically draped by the Creator between the spirit world and mother earth. Flickering eerily across the landscape are the dying embers of the campfires of Tiospaye. It is quiet. It is peaceful. It is deceiving.

Majestic, regal, strong and stoic, Sitting Bull stares ominously across the horizon on which land his people still peacefully and rhythmically slumber. One can only imagine the pain and grief and suffering within the holy man's heart as deep within he knows what others know not: it is the night not the dawn which lies ahead. It is the end, not the beginning, which the rising sun symbolizes on this June morning.

Off in the distance is the silent sound of thunder; not of the heavens but of earth; not of nature but of man. He hears not through his ears but through his spirit. Never again will his people gather and celebrate as they have just done. Never again will the freedom fires of Tiospaye burn so brightly among so many. It is dawn, but the time grows short. It is the day, but the night draws near. (Photograph courtesy of the Denver Public Library.)